The Gentle Warrior

Major General Oliver Prince Smith. *Courtesy of the Marine Corps University Research Center, Archives Branch (*MCUA*), Quantico, Va.*

The Gentle Warrior

GENERAL OLIVER PRINCE SMITH, USMC

Clifton La Bree

KENT STATE UNIVERSITY PRESS · KENT, OHIO, & LONDON

© 2001 by The Kent State University Press, Kent, Ohio 44242
All rights reserved
Library of Congress Catalog Card Number 00-062020
ISBN 0-87338-686-8
Manufactured in the United States of America

06 05 04 03 02 01   5 4 3 2 1

Library of Congress Cataloging-in-Publication Data
La Bree, Clifton, 1933–
The gentle warrior: General Oliver Prince Smith, USMC/Clifton La Bree.
p. cm.
Includes bibliographical references and index.
ISBN 0-87338-686-8 (alk. paper) ∞
1. Smith, Oliver Prince. 2. Generals—United States—Biography.
3. United States Marine Corps—Biography. I. Title.

VE25.S64 L33   2001
359.9'6'092—dc21
[B]   00-062020

British Library Cataloging-in-Publication data are available.

CONTENTS

FOREWORD

The commanding general of the First Marine Division for the historic landing at Inchon, Korea, and for the following eventful eight months, Gen. Oliver P. Smith was a prime example of the ideal man being in the right place. His calm, resolute, studious, and confident character was like a beacon as he led his division. These comments reflect those of a young Marine Corps captain serving as a general's aide-de-camp when he would have much preferred to command a rifle company.

When General Smith first interviewed me as a potential aide, he was the assistant commandant of the Marine Corps. I was a company commander of a rifle company in the Fifth Marine Regiment at Camp Pendleton, and I wished to remain with my unit. At one point during the interview I sharply stated, "I don't like to push cookies." The general looked intently at me, his blue eyes smiling, and said, "I don't either, and we will not be engaging in that kind of activity." When I walked out of his office, I was resigned to serving as his aide, but at the same time I realized that the general was a very understanding person.

Once General Smith arrived at Camp Pendleton, the pace quickened; all personnel were engaged in building the division up to strength. The general worked long hours in his office and made daily personal visits to all of the components of the division. Although there was crisis followed by crisis, he never openly lost his temper or exhibited any negative attitude. His manner was always sympathetic, reassuring, and confident, that of a leader who is assembling a winning team. He truly exemplified a teacher and a leader.

There are many examples of General Smith's leadership throughout his tour in Korea, but there are several favorites of mine. When the First Marine Division's advance command post (CP) was at Hagaru-ri, on the night of 30 November 1950, the perimeter came under such widespread attack that tracers were ripping through the roof of the native house that was occupied by the general. The chief of staff, Col. Gregon Williams, the aide, the cook, and the general's driver were at the corners of the building, as the last defense. All the while the general slept through the night on his canvas cot. In the morning he quietly remarked, "One needs sleep in order to render rational orders." No one commented as this remarkable man lighted up his pipe with his favorite Sir Walter Raleigh smoking tobacco.

Another remarkable session took place with the Tenth Corps commander and an air force general who were meeting with General Smith to discuss the withdrawal. They stated, "We will fly all of your personnel out, and you are authorized to destroy all of your weapons, vehicles, and supplies." General Smith paused, looked at each of his visitors, and stated, "We are going out as a division, with all of our equipment, and will fight our way as an organized division. We are attacking in another direction—as an organized division." The meeting came to an abrupt halt.

Another incident that I cherish is one that took place when General Smith assumed command of the Nineteenth Corps when its commanding general was killed in a helicopter accident. He was briefed by the corps staff upon his arrival at the CP, and at the conclusion of his briefing a call came from Tenth Corps G-3 (operations officer) requesting approval of a certain tactical proposal. The general considered it for a moment, then quietly stated, "Tell them no," and walked out. I remained a while and observed the smiling appreciation of the staff members who had just seen their new commander provide the reply that they had been praying for.

I could go on with many other vivid examples of the general's leadership, but I don't think that is required. There is one other thing, however, that must be mentioned—and that is that General Smith was a very devout person. He was religious, and he left no doubt in anyone's mind about his devotion to his God, his Corps, and his Marines.

Martin J. "Stormy" Sexton
Colonel, USMC (Ret.)
Fallbrook, California

Preface

Korea, land of the morning calm, has been the scene of many conflicts. Few battles can compare to the intense and brutal fighting that took place during the last weeks of 1950, when the United Nations forces were stopped on their advance to the Yalu River by an overwhelming number of Chinese Communist forces.

UN naval forces were feverishly congregating at the port of Hungnam to rescue the Tenth Corps. Many of the UN forces were inland sixty miles or more in the mountainous regions of central Korea, where the temperatures plummeted to thirty degrees below zero, with powerful winds from the bitter cold Manchurian highlands. Their only hope was to withdraw over a single supply road that led to the relative safety of the coastal plain.

The most powerful component of Tenth Corps was the First Marine Division. It was astride the single main supply road west of the Chosin reservoir and cut off from its base by large numbers of Chinese. Maj. Gen. Edward M. Almond, commanding general of Tenth Corps, had alerted Gen. Douglas MacArthur at the Far East Command Headquarters in Tokyo that it was a distinct possibility his corps would be overrun. Army units on the eastern side of the Chosin reservoir had already been decimated, and the nation prepared itself for the potential loss of the First Marine Division, with over twenty-three thousand men in its ranks. It was separated from the sea and safety by seventy miles of rugged terrain full of Chinese soldiers who outnumbered them and were intent on their destruction. It was a bleak moment for American arms.

In the midst of the pessimism, one commander took center stage. Maj. Gen. Oliver Prince Smith, commanding general of the First Marine Division, had been preparing himself for this moment since he was commissioned a second lieutenant in the Marine Corps in 1917. His performance during the Chosin reservoir campaign was the crowning achievement of a lifetime of dedicated service to his Corps and his country. He succeeded in bringing the First Marine Division and attached army units to the safety of the coast, along with all of his wounded and most of his equipment. In the process several Chinese divisions were eliminated as effective military units.

There is a direct parallel between Xenophon's heroic march with his ten thousand Greek countrymen to the Black Sea and that of the First Marine Division and elements of the army's Seventh Division to the port of Hungnam. Both formations were cut off from support and assistance, both were limited to a single passage to the sea, and both were seriously outnumbered by determined enemies. General Smith consolidated his troops into a continuous formation along the road and sent out flanking units to hold the higher elevations on both sides of the road while the main column passed through. Xenophon, a pupil of Aristotle, had used similar tactics to protect his own central body of troops. Both commanders reached the sea and safety in a condition to carry out additional missions if they had been assigned. The troops were saved to fight the enemy again.

Gen. Oliver P. Smith was an intellectual with common sense. He never forgot that his most important weapon was the individual rifleman, and he had the knack of obtaining the best his troops had to give by setting an example of confidence and faith in their ability to succeed. His style of leadership developed from his strong character and an inherent optimism that tempered everything he did. He radiated confidence and a sensitivity to the men under his command, and the troops responded in kind.

At 1400 on December 13, 1950, memorial services were held at Hungnam Cemetery, with Catholic, Jewish, and Protestant chaplains participating. Amidst the rows of white crosses and Stars of David, the plaintive notes of *Taps* echoed across the windswept plain. Smith, more than anyone else, knew how high the cost had been. Two days later he returned alone to the sanctity of the cemetery to pay a final tribute to those who had paid the supreme sacrifice and would remain forever young. Smith's sad eyes reflected the strong emotions that he kept to himself while he bid a final farewell to the best of American manhood.

He then boarded the USS *Bayfield* and left Hungnam, leaving an enduring legacy that will be studied and honored for as long as mankind admires those qualities that allow the human spirit to rise above all expectations.

The chapters that follow review O. P. Smith's varied military career. I have extensively utilized his papers in order to tell his story, and wherever possible I have used his own words to describe different situations. I have tried to portray events as he visualized them. Smith was a very private person in regard to his personal and family life, but he had a deep sense of accountability for his military actions and decisions. He worked diligently to record what he did and why he did it, so that the decisions could be evaluated by future military leaders.

In keeping with General Smith's long-standing tradition of privacy, his family has declined to provide more information about his private life. Their argument—that it is privileged information and not directly related to his performance as a marine officer—is well taken. I concur with their decision, even though I was disappointed at the time. It should be noted that the family has graciously turned over to the Marine Corps large numbers of personal documents relating to his military career. For that generous contribution to the literature of military history, we owe the general's family a resounding "well done."

Acknowledgments

I am indebted to many people who have contributed to the story of Gen. Oliver Prince Smith's military career. Col. Martin J. "Stormy" Sexton, USMC (Ret.), and Maj. Michael C. Capraro, USMC (Ret.), head the list of individuals who freely and unselfishly gave their energy, their expertise, and their friendship to me and to the General Smith project from the moment I first contacted them over ten years ago.

Stormy Sexton's respect and loyalty to Gen. O. P. Smith remained undiminished after he served as his aide-de-camp in Korea. He was in a unique position to observe General Smith on a daily basis, and he was generous with his store of information, including the 150-page transcript of his debriefing interview (at Headquarters, U.S. Marine Corps) of his experiences in Korea. The interview is a testament to his professional powers of observation and to his large reservoir of military knowledge. He reviewed all of the chapters pertaining to Korea, and his suggestions for improvement were "right on target." Stormy passed away in May 1999 from pneumonia. May he rest in peace!

Maj. Mike C. Capraro was the public information officer for the First Marine Division during its first ten months in Korea. He was a rich source of information and ideas, and he encouraged me to proceed with the project as fast as possible. He had a compelling reason for advocating a sense of urgency: I met with him for two days in Charlottesville, Virginia, in 1995 and discovered that he was fighting an advanced form of cancer. He died six months later.

At the time of our visit, Mike gave me several of his personal files. As a member of the First Marine Division on Guadalcanal in 1942, Mike had received a copy of the division's Presidential Unit Citation. He had forwarded it to his mother with a handwritten note at the bottom of the document: "To a First Marine's mother whose heart was with us, and whose visions guided us through the dark hours, from her son."

I valued Mike Capraro's counsel and suggestions. I am sorry that he could not share in the completion of the story, for he respected General Smith as much as he did his own father, and he was instrumental in guiding my research.

I have also interviewed or corresponded with as many men as possible who served with General Smith. I made it a priority to contact as many veterans as I could, because Smith's generation was rapidly declining in numbers. I'd like to say "thank you" to the following individuals who have substantially contributed to General Smith's story:

Lt. Gen. Alpha L. Bowser, USMC (Ret.), who served as the G-3 section head of the First Marine Division during General Smith's tour of duty in Korea. General Bowser has been most generous with information and helpful suggestions. He graciously agreed to review the chapters on Korea, and his comments were helpful in making the text as accurate as possible. It was a privilege to work with such a sterling character and powerful intellect as General Bowser. His legacy of professionalism, integrity, and character parallels that of General Smith.

Brig. Gen. Gordon D. Gayle, USMC (Ret.), was helpful with information and encouragement to continue this project. I hope that he approves of my treatment of General Smith.

Col. Henry "Hank" Aplington, USMC (Ret.), and his wife graciously invited me into their home at Warner, New Hampshire, for hours of invigorating "Marine Corps and military talk." Hank, a three-war marine, filled in many blank spaces of my knowledge of military affairs. I received encouragement for this project and gained a friend in the process. Thank you, Hank!

Brig. Gen. Edwin H. Simmons, USMC (Ret.), made perceptive comments on several situations that I queried him about. He was just leaving the directorship of the Marine Corps Historical Center at Washington, D.C., when I last had contact with him.

Brig. Gen. Roger Willock, USMCR (Ret.), an accomplished author of Marine Corps and maritime history, added appreciably to my knowledge of Marine Corps personalities.

Maj. Gerald J. Clinton, USA (Ret.), an army "mustang" (ex-enlisted man) with extensive combat experience, was most helpful in presenting an army officer's perspective on the Chosin reservoir campaign. His son, Lt. Gerald Clinton, Jr., an army reserve officer, provided me a copy of a thesis that he had done on the combat engineering problems encountered in the Chosin reservoir campaign. It was a pleasure to visit such a dedicated military family.

Lt. Gen. Edward A. Craig, USMC (Ret.), responded to my inquiry with a wealth of information about General Smith. General Craig was ninety-two at the time. I did not have a chance to interview him, but his warmth and sincerity were evident in his lengthy letters and notes. General Craig was truly one of the Marine Corps greats and is worthy of a biography of his own.

I am indebted to Dr. James Kim, M.D., who provided me with important information about Maj. Gen. Frank E. Lowe, USAR (Ret.). Dr. Kim was Lowe's guide in Korea; he was later adopted by the general and his wife. He gave me several photos taken in Korea and provided information that I could not have obtained from any other source. I was impressed with his dedication to, and affection for, General Lowe.

Col. George A. Rasula, USA (Ret.), has been the main driving force behind the efforts of veterans of the army's Thirty-first Regimental Combat Team to obtain recognition for its actions east of the Chosin reservoir. I have relied heavily upon George for information about the travails of the Thirty-first RCT. Thanks to him, more information is now available, and we can finally make restitution for years of neglect and indifference.

Col. Harold R. Roise, USMC (Ret.), patiently told me what it was like at the battalion level during the Chosin campaign.

Col. Robert D. Taplett, USMC (Ret.), was one of the finest battalion commanders in the Korean War. He responded to numerous inquiries for information with dispatch and well-thought-out answers.

My visit with Col. Edward Blewett, USAR (Ret.), was a pleasant experience. He was dean of the College of Liberal Arts at the University of New Hampshire when I was there in the early fifties. He filled in some blank spaces on Gen. Frank E. Lowe's personal life and provided some interesting background regarding Lowe's relationship with MacArthur.

Col. Robert A. Cleaves, USA (Ret.), served with General Lowe and helped me a lot with general military affairs.

For all of the above and all of those individuals who responded to inquiries, too numerous to list individually, a hearty thanks and "well done" are in order.

The Marine Corps Historical Center (MCHC) was helpful in providing answers to numerous questions. The oral histories at the MCHC have been invaluable sources of information. Gen. Oliver P. Smith's family removed his personal paper collection from the MCHC and deposited it at the Archives Branch of the Research Center at the Marine Corps University at Quantico, Virginia—a part of the Marine Corps Research and Development Command. I spent the better part of two weeks at the Archives Branch. A. Kerry Strong, archivist, was unfailing in her support of my quest for information. She and her staff made my visits rewarding experiences.

The Gen. Douglas MacArthur Memorial at Norfolk, Virginia, provided me with most of the material that I used about Gen. Frank E. Lowe. The memorial has copies of every letter and note General Lowe sent to Pres. Harry Truman from Korea. James W. Zobel, archivist for the memorial, handled every request for information in a timely manner. I appreciate his professionalism.

The Texas Parks and Wildlife Department administers the battleship USS *Texas*. Its staff has been helpful with information pertaining to the period when General Smith was stationed on board the ship.

The U.S. Army Military History Institute at Carlisle Barracks, Pennsylvania, has been most helpful with requests for documents in the General Almond collection.

There is a movement within the Marine Corps that was approved by now-retired commandant Gen. Charles C. Krulak, to emphasize the fact that the original name of the Chosin reservoir was Changjin. The army units in Korea used the original place-names on their maps. The Marine Corps used maps drawn by the Japanese occupation forces. Whereas the name "Chosin" has been enshrined in our national heritage for the past fifty years, and Gen. Oliver P. Smith is so intimately associated with the Chosin reservoir designation, I have elected to use it in this work. I mean no disrespect to the Korean people by such usage.

This work could not have been completed without the unwavering support and encouragement of my family over the several years that the manuscript has been a part of our lives. My wife, Pauline, heads the list of people to whom I am indebted. She has worked tirelessly to create an atmosphere of tranquility and privacy for my work on General Smith's story. I want her to know that I appreciate her countless acts of unselfishness. She must share as a partner in the celebration of the completion of the book.

In conclusion, I want to thank John T. Hubbell, director of The Kent State University Press. He took a raw, rambling manuscript and gave it a new life with his skillful editing. His patience, his professionalism, and his support are appreciated.

Finally, I wish to state that even though several people have contributed to this book, I am solely responsible for errors that might remain.

MAPS

Abbreviations

AKA	attack cargo ship
APA	attack transport
APD	high-speed transport
BAR	Browning automatic rifle
BLT	battalion landing team
CCF	Chinese Communist forces
CG	Commanding General
CincFE	Commander in Chief, Far East
COMNAFE	Commander, Naval Forces Far East
CP	command post
DD	destroyer
DSC	Distinguished Service Cross
DSO	Distinguished Service Order
DUKW	amphibious truck, troop
F4U	Corsair fighter aircraft
FMF	Fleet Marine Force (Pacific or Atlantic)
GHQ	general headquarters
G-1	division staff personnel section head
G-2	division staff intelligence section head
G-3	division staff operations section head
G-4	division staff logistics section head
HQMC	Headquarters Marine Corps
JCS	Joint Chiefs of Staff
KIA	killed in action

LCI	landing craft, infantry
LCM	landing craft, mechanized
LCP	landing craft, personnel
LCVP	landing craft, vehicle and personnel
LSD	landing ship dock
LST	landing ship tank
LVT	amphibian tractor
MAG	Marine Aircraft Group
MAW	Marine Aircraft Wing
MB	Marine Barracks
MCHC	Marine Corps Historical Center
MCRDC	Marine Corps Research and Development Command
MCUA	Marine Corps University Research Center, Archives Branch, Quantico, Va.
MIA	missing in action
MSR	main supply route
OP	observation post
OSS	Office of Strategic Services
POW	prisoner of war
RCT	regimental combat team
TAC	Tactical Air Force
UDT	underwater demolitions team (navy)
UN	United Nations
USA	U.S. Army
USAR	U.S. Army Reserve
USMC	U.S. Marine Corps
USN	U.S. Navy
VMF	Marine fighter squadron
VMO	Marine observation squadron
VMS	Marine scouting squadron

1

BUILDING THE FOUNDATION

Oliver Prince Smith was born on 26 October 1893 on a cattle ranch near Menard, Texas, a small town one hundred miles northwest of San Antonio. His father, who died when Oliver was only six years old, was a lawyer who taught school for several years. After his father's death, Oliver's mother, an independent and resourceful woman, moved her three children and their modest belongings to Santa Cruz, California, where she found enough work as a seamstress to maintain her family.

Oliver did his share by delivering papers and working in the local orchards during the summers. By the time he entered high school, he was working at higher-paying jobs as a janitor while school was in session and in the Santa Cruz Mountains logging camps during summer vacations. Values that are instilled in young people have a tendency to remain with them. That certainly was true of Oliver Smith, who learned at a young age the value of a dollar and what it represented in sweat from his own brow. He approached any task given to him with singular intensity.[1]

Oliver had a strong desire to go to college and was encouraged to do so by the rest of the family. When he entered the University of California at Berkeley, he had exactly five dollars in his pocket. He worked diligently to maintain his scholastic record and to support himself, continuing to work in the logging camps during the summer months and as a gardener when school was in session. He never lost his passion for growing things, especially roses. The personal narratives of his military campaigns later in life would frequently refer to the vegetation and flowers in some of the exotic places in which he would find himself.

Oliver P. Smith and friends in their senior year at University of California, Berkeley, 1916. *From left,* Ryerson, Smith, Waltz, Dobbs, and Biggs. *Courtesy of* MCUA.

Oliver's mother gave him another precious gift that sustained him for the rest of his life, a strong religious faith. She was a devout Christian Scientist and passed her religious beliefs on to her children.[2]

Oliver did well in his academic studies at Berkeley. At the end of his junior year (1914), he was placed on the honor roll. He took nine and a half credits of military science (at the Reserve Officer Training Corps, or ROTC, unit there) in addition to the course requirements for a degree in economics. The college yearbook for 1916 lists him as having been a member of Alpha Kappa Lambda fraternity, a member of the Commerce Club, a member of the Senior Men's Banquet Committee, the Military Ball Arrangements Committee, and a cadet first lieutenant in his senior year. He graduated on 15 May 1916 and went to work with the Standard Oil Company.[3]

When the United States entered World War I, Smith applied for one of the ten commissions offered by the Marine Corps to graduates from Berkeley with ROTC training. He was successful and was sworn in at San Francisco on 17 April 1917. He reported for duty at Mare Island one month later with thirty other college graduates from the West Coast area.

Lt. Oliver P. Smith entered a Marine Corps quite unlike the one he was to retire from. "The command at Mare Island did not know quite what to do with us. The officer training command at Quantico, Virginia, had not yet been established. Mare Island was well qualified to train enlisted recruits, but fell far short of having an adequate program for training officers. Our training consisted of close-order drill and classroom work where we were required to stand at 'Parade Rest!' and recite paragraphs of Infantry Drill Regulations. This was interspersed with periods of grenade practice, which consisted of lofting round rocks representing grenades at a white line not over thirty yards distant" (OH, 2–3).

Smith and five other new officers were ordered to Guam to relieve more seasoned officers for duty in France. On the trip to Guam, aboard the army transport *Sheridan,* an interesting incident took place, as related by Smith: "On the *Sheridan,* traveling as a casual [alone], was Captain Benjamin O. Davis, a negro Army officer, who had been commissioned by President Theodore Roosevelt. The embarkation officer asked Captain Davis if he'd mind eating in his stateroom. Well, Davis said he preferred to eat in the wardroom. So the quartermaster came around to us young lieutenants and said, 'Would you mind having Captain Davis at your table?' . . . We said, 'Certainly not, we'd be glad to have him.' And he sat at the head of our table. He was a fine gentleman and he gave us a lot of information. He had been in the service for a long time" (OH, 45).

Smith served two years on Guam. The island was poorly developed except for the airfields and supply warehouses at Orote Point. Perhaps the most exciting thing to happen was the scuttling of the German raider *Cormorant* in Apra Harbor. The crew was subsequently taken into custody, and Smith's company kept it under guard at Piti.[4]

In August, Lieutenant Smith sent a request to the quartermaster of the Marine Corps that his fiancée, Esther L. King of Haywood, California, be granted passage on an army transport to Guam. The request was approved, and upon her arrival, they were married.[5] It proved to be a good marriage, one that weathered all of the hardships that were and are imposed upon a military family—constant moves, inadequate facilities at many duty stations, and the harsh financial reality of the Depression years.

Smith was posted to Agana, where two companies of marines were stationed. He served as the mess officer, adjutant, and company commander after temporary promotion to the rank of captain. He was also editor of the Guam newsletter. Smith always felt "left out" because he did not experience combat in France; however, he advanced as rapidly as those who had been at the front lines.

The next tour of duty, after the war in Europe ended, was at the Marine Barracks at Mare Island, where Smith was given command of the Machine Gun

School and named assistant to the adjutant. "I was given good quarters at Mare Island. I had a nice little bungalow on the base and we were very happy there. Then Col. Karmany took a three months' leave and went to China. . . . They then brought Col. Gamborg-Andersen down as his temporary relief. Col. Gamborg-Andersen couldn't move into Col. Karmany's quarters, so he came around to me and said, 'After all Captain, I draw more commutation [pay in lieu of quarters] than you do, I have to rate you out of quarters in order to save money for the government.' So he rated me out of quarters and moved into my bungalow" (OH, 14). Obviously, Captain Smith was not pleased.

Smith's third assignment was as the commanding officer of the marine detachment on the battleship USS *Texas,* a sister ship of the USS *Maine.* The *Texas* was based at San Pedro, California, where Smith rented an apartment. Lt. Cdr. Chester W. Nimitz, who would be commander in chief of the Pacific Fleet in World War II, was a neighbor. "I didn't get to know him very well until World War II. He was a very fine gentleman; I admired him greatly" (OH, 18).

The *Texas* was the junior ship in Battleship Division Three, with *New York* and *Oklahoma.* The normal routine frequently involved daily trips to sea for gunnery, torpedo, and navigational exercises, and a return to home port by 4:30 in the afternoon. It was like working at a civilian job. Once a year the ship went to Bremerton, Washington, for its annual overhaul, which lasted for about six weeks. During that time Smith was able to take his detachment ashore for rifle practice and infantry maneuvers. In 1924 the *Texas* was ordered to Norfolk, Virginia, via the Panama Canal, to remove the cage-style masts and replace them with tripod masts, as well as other improvements. Smith was detached for duty as a detailing officer at Headquarters, Marine Corps, at Washington, D.C.[6]

The Personnel Department of the Marine Corps was a busy place in the mid-1920s. The Marine Corps was composed of 1,092 officers and eighteen thousand enlisted men. Over thirteen thousand men were assigned to sea duty, foreign duty, or expeditionary duty, which left about five thousand men for all other purposes. "I remember when we assembled the first battalion to go to Nicaragua; it was done according to the old Marine Corps style: we simply pulled the officers and men from all of the posts and stations up and down the east coast and they assembled at Norfolk, went aboard ship, and the battalion commander organized his battalion after he got aboard ship" (OH, 22).

Smith had financial difficulty because of the costs of living in Washington. Rent for a very small apartment in the Petworth district of the city was ninety dollars a month. "My goodness[,] I had an awful time making ends meet" (OH, 22).

He also wrote articles for the *Marine Corps Gazette* and other professional publications during his tour of duty at Washington, mainly because it was a source of extra money. The *Gazette* paid five dollars per article, and the U.S.

Naval Institute *Proceedings* paid an unbelievable eighty-five dollars per article. The tour of duty at the detailing office was, Smith acknowledged, the least enjoyable of his career (OH, 22–26).

Detachment for duty in Haiti in June 1928 was a welcome change. It got Smith and his family out of Washington, and he was paid an extra $150 per month by the Haitian government for his services as a gendarmerie officer. He sailed to Port-au-Prince, where he was assigned as assistant chief of staff to the commandant of the Garde d'Haiti, a paramilitary police force established with American assistance. Most of the officers were marines, while the enlisted men were Haitian.[7]

Smith sums up his Haiti experience:

The Occupation down there did a tremendous amount of good. They sent a Financial Advisor, an American, with a couple of assistants, and they demanded vouchers for all expenditures, which was something new in Haiti. The Haitian Gourde was just as sound as the dollar by the time I was there. The Gendarmerie provided law and order; we had roads all over the place; we had an excellent hospital and medical service; we had an operating telephone network. Today [1975], it's all gone; you can't make a telephone call in the city of Port-au-Prince. And of those 2,000 miles of roads, probably there's a couple of hundred miles left. And they are head over heels in debt. They are back where they were when the Marines came . . . in 1916. (OH, 40)

In June 1931, after three years in Haiti, Captain Smith was assigned to the army's Field Officer's Course at the Infantry School at Fort Benning, Georgia. This formal instruction in practical military matters constituted the first of its kind that Smith had received in the Marine Corps. The ten-month course was considered a prime assignment for any officer with a future. There were two other marines attending the junior course at the same time that Smith attended the senior course—Capt. Lewis Puller and Capt. Gerald Thomas.

Smith was fortunate to be a student under a proficient faculty of professionals:

The Assistant Commandant of the Infantry School who ran the school, was Lt. Col. [George C.] Marshall, who became Commander in Chief of the U.S. Army. Lt. Col. [Joseph W.] Stilwell was an instructor in tactics; he became a four star. Major [Omar N.] Bradley was an instructor in machine guns, and he became a five star. Maj. [Harold R.] Bull was an instructor in logistics and he became a four star. Capt. Bedell Smith[,] . . . a classmate of mine, became Chief of Staff to Eisenhower. Capt. Porter, another classmate of mine, became G-3 [chief of operations] in the Army. Maj. Terry Allen, a student and classmate, [became] commanding general of the First Infantry Division in North

Africa and Sicily. This was 1931, and the Army, like the Marine Corps, stagnated in the grade of Captain, and most of these students in this senior course, the Field Officer's Course, were Captains except for Terry Allen. (OH, 42)[8]

The training sessions were similar to those used in World War I: "On the tactical problems, I would have liked to have been the opposing commanding general, because I could know exactly what a Fort Benning graduate would do in a given tactical situation. . . . But we did learn so that you could look at a given bit of terrain and you could see a battalion in defense or you could see a place where you could attack. . . . You got a feel of the terrain, and that's where it was very valuable. Although in France [at the École de Guerre] I got a better feel for the terrain" (OH, 43).

Most of the terrain exercises were carried out on horseback. One day, Smith recalled, the students were making a rapid reconnaissance, at a trot. He had drawn a horse that liked to kick other horses in the column. Smith had all he could do to keep the unruly horse's head up so that he couldn't kick. When the column halted, the instructor called upon Smith to give an estimate of the terrain they had just passed through. "I said. 'Look, frankly, I've been trying to handle a kicking horse all the way, and I haven't the least idea of what the terrain looked like.' He laughed and let me off the hook" (OH, 43).

The inevitable price that Smith had to pay for attending Benning was assignment in June 1932 to the Marine Corps Schools at Quantico, Virginia, as an instructor in the Company Officer's Course. In 1932, Quantico had not reached the level of excellence it would attain later. Most of the manuals and books were the same as the ones used by the army schools until the early 1930s, when an exhaustive review of the complete curriculum of the Marine Corps Schools was initiated. As a result, changes were made in the curriculum to reflect better the Marine Corps's needs and doctrine, especially in regard to amphibious warfare. The establishment in 1933 of the Fleet Marine Force—an organized "striking force, well equipped, well armed, and highly trained," kept continually "in a state of readiness for operations with the Fleet"—had a strong influence on the curriculum.[9]

Gen. James C. Breckinridge was commandant of the Marine Corps Schools and was instrumental in the development of a more amphibious flavor in the instructional material. Members of the faculty and students of the Field Officer's Course devoted themselves full-time to preparing the *Tentative Landing Manuals* in 1934. A revised edition of the manual became the major guideline for all of the amphibious landings of World War II, in the European and the Pacific theaters. The Marine Corps had been "on track," and when the reality of war arrived, it had a doctrine that worked.[10]

In the summer of 1933, Smith was delivering a lecture on the use of the bayonet when he was interrupted by the school adjutant, who handed him a list of officers who were to report immediately to B Barracks for duty with the Seventh Marine Regiment, then being formed. Smith released the officers and continued with his bayonet lecture for another ten minutes, after which he was interrupted again with a new list of names, including his own. He finished the lecture and reported to B Barracks, where he was assigned to the Seventh Regiment as assistant operations officer under Maj. Julian C. Smith. The Seventh Marines was being hastily organized in case it was needed in Cuba, where Ramon Batista was overrunning the country.[11]

In 1934 the commandant of the Marine Corps, Gen. John H. Russell, wrote a personal letter to Smith informing him that he would be sent to the French École Supérieure de Guerre, or war college, unless Smith had some reason for not accepting the assignment. Smith was reluctant to leave his regiment, because there was reason to believe that it would soon be sent on expeditionary duty; he was still anxious to gain experience with troops. The activation never materialized, so Smith accepted the chance to attend one of the most prestigious military schools in the world. He was given several months to learn to speak and write French. He had taken four years of French in college, but he had not spoken it except on some occasions in Haiti.

Smith was posted to the American embassy as an assistant naval attaché in January 1934 and was immediately sent to a school that specialized in teaching French to foreigners. When he completed the language course, in November 1934, he was enrolled at the École de Guerre. The material covered in the course was demanding, and it could not have been completed by anyone not having a thorough knowledge and understanding of the language: "I went to every lecture that I could find just to get my ear trained. And it is quite a thrill when you finally get to the point where you listen to the speaker, you understand what he is saying, and you don't realize he is talking in French. Then you know that you have arrived" (OH, 64).

The first year was devoted primarily to the division and its supporting arms. The second year encompassed handling army corps and armies with their supporting arms and attached service units. Smith was favorably impressed with the faculty: "The instructors were highly qualified. They knew their subjects, were sincere and were thoroughly interested in their work. The students, as a group, were quick, intelligent, ambitious and hard working."[12]

In the American army, a field order was typically composed of five brief paragraphs that answered the questions of who, what, when, where, and how in as succinct a form as possible. French orders were much more detailed; they not only answered the same questions as American orders but also went into how to do it. Smith thought the French seemed to envy the initiative granted to subordinates in the American system (OH, 54–77).

At the end of the course at the École de Guerre, Smith returned to Quantico, where he could share his new perspective on French military matters. The Marine Corps Schools had changed since Smith's last tour of duty there. The schools were now oriented to preparing officers for a military campaign across the Pacific Ocean. Specific campaigns had already been prepared for such islands and island groups as Truk, Guam, Saipan, and the Palaus. It was during these years that Smith's reputation as an intellectual spread throughout the Marine Corps. His contemporaries started calling him "the professor" or the "student general." One of his students in the senior course in 1937 was Lt. Edward A. Craig, who later remembered Smith: "He was an infantry tactics instructor and highly regarded by his students. I remember one of the problems he gave us. It involved a critical command decision, and we had to solve it in fifteen minutes. This included reading the problem and writing and turning in the answer. Gen. Smith was never one to give an order and then tell you how to do it."[13]

Maj. Oliver P. Smith was promoted to lieutenant colonel on 1 May 1938. Times were changing—he had been a captain for fourteen years![14] At long last, a wish came true—he was assigned to San Diego with the Fleet Marine Force Pacific as an F-3 (later G-3, or staff operations officer) for his next tour of duty. While he was at San Diego, the Marine Corps leased a nineteen-thousand-acre tract of land that had been a part of the Santa Margarita Ranch and called it Camp Pendleton.

Even though Smith was pleased to be with the FMF staff, he still preferred to command troops. His chance came when he mentioned to Lt. Col. Bill Ashurst, who commanded the First Battalion of the Sixth Marines, the "beauty" of staff work and that he would like to trade jobs: "I talked him into it. We went to General Vogel who commanded the Brigade and he approved, and Bill came up and took over F-3. Shortly after that he was ordered to Peking and was locked up as a prisoner of war in 1941. . . . My conscience hurt a little bit on that" (OH, 84).

The Marine Corps was actively creating new battalions by robbing cadre (that is, experienced personnel in key leadership positions) from established battalions. The way the Sixth Marines was hastily brought up to strength for duty in Iceland was typical.

The Sixth Marines sailed for Iceland on 1 May 1941. For twenty-four years Smith had been preparing himself, by honing the skills he would need for the ultimate test—leading troops in combat.

2

ICELAND

Great Britain declared war on Germany in 1939, when the latter invaded Poland. By the spring of 1940, Germany had occupied Norway and Denmark. France, Belgium, and Holland would shortly experience the blitzkrieg tactics of the powerful German war machine, which forced British and French troops from the European mainland to the temporary safety of the British Isles. Great Britain now faced the German threat alone.[1]

One of the important strategic moves made by Great Britain was to secure the Arctic regions necessary to predict weather, which had an important influence on operations on the European mainland. In May 1940, Royal Marines landed at Reykjavik, the capital of Iceland, to arrest the German consul general and to destroy the German weather station on the island.[2] Iceland was one of the most isolated and vulnerable outposts that came into prominence at the start of World War II. Its strategic location was important for weather forecasting, as well as for air and naval bases needed to secure the sea-lanes from the United States and Canada to Europe.

By early 1941, the United States and Great Britain had agreed upon contingency plans for the safety of Iceland and the Azores, and for the possibility that the United States might become involved in the war with Germany. In May 1941, Prime Minister Winston S. Churchill asked Pres. Franklin D. Roosevelt to send troops to Iceland to relieve the British troops for duty elsewhere. The president agreed, if the government of Iceland would accept the plan. This a reluctant Icelandic government did on 1 July 1941.[3]

The army was unable to send draftees overseas in time of peace; thus the task was given to the Marine Corps, which as a volunteer force was not subject to such restrictions.

Deployment of 1st Marine Brigade in Iceland. *Courtesy* MCHC.

The Marine Corps was already assembling garrisons for the Lend-Lease bases acquired from the British in exchange for fifty World War I–vintage destroyers. Initially, Smith's battalion was to be used for the formation of six special rifle companies to help garrison those bases. Smith was upset over the news, because he had brought his battalion to a high state of readiness and he thought it ill advised to fragment it. The order was eventually canceled, to the relief of all concerned.

By May 1941, several commercial passenger ships from the Grace Line and from the Baltimore Mail Line were assembled at San Diego to transport the marines for training exercises at San Clemente Island. Several battalions had participated over the past few months, and the First was expecting to take its turn when orders came for it to be brought up to full peacetime strength. The Sixth Marines had inadvertently prepared itself for the distinction of being the first American force to serve on foreign soil in World War II.

Replacements for the expanded battalion came from other units at Camp Elliott, California. Reinforcements included a battalion from the Tenth Marines (artillery), a tank company, and a parachute company. Only men who had been in the Corps for at least a year and had good records were selected. Smith recommended that the men take as much clothing as possible, especially overcoats. It was difficult to know what to take, because the marines did not know where they were going.

The day of departure from San Diego was a festive occasion. The three battalions were distributed, one each, on three APAS (amphibious assault ships, converted from passenger liners). The *Fuller,* carrying the First Battalion, had been a Baltimore Mail Line ship. (The skipper was Capt. P. S. Theiss, later chief of staff for Adm. Richmond Kelly Turner at the battle for Okinawa.) There had been much speculation about their destination. Captain Theiss had been given orders to traverse to specific check points, with no knowledge of the final destination.

Smith was the senior marine aboard the *Fuller* and was assigned a cabin on the port side on the same level as the forward weather deck. He did not know where they were going either. The Navy Department was anxious to keep the transit of the ship as much a secret as possible, and Smith put his men below decks for the passage through the Panama Canal on 10 June 1941. There was no contact with shore. Shortly after traversing the canal, the convoy picked up additional destroyer escorts and proceeded to Charleston, South Carolina, where it arrived on 15 June.

Liberty for about half of the men was granted, and the remainder held a landing exercise at nearby Fort Moultrie. Security precautions were relaxed, compared to the restrictions that would soon take effect for all military movements.

Consequently, everybody was calling home, including Smith. The call to his wife, Esther, in Los Angeles cost him $8.10. She knew where he was calling from, but he did not tell her where he was going, because he still did not know himself.

On 20 June, while the troops were at Charleston, Maj. Gen. John Marston informed them that he had been designated commanding officer of the First Brigade and that they were going to Iceland. The Marine Corps was unprepared to supply its troops for cold weather from its own quartermaster stocks, so it purchased vast amounts of winter wear from stores in Charleston. It virtually cleaned out Sears and Montgomery Ward's! Smith later wrote, "It is hard for us to realize now what a pitiful state of preparedness existed just prior to the war" (ID, 18).

While the Sixth Marine Regiment was at Charleston, Capt. Victor H. Krulak (who would retire a lieutenant general), on the staff of Gen. Holland M. Smith, commanding general of Amphibious Corps, Atlantic Fleet and other officers were selected to go on a fact-finding mission, which he describes in the following letter:

In June 1941, three Marine officers, Lieutenant Colonel R. O. Bare, Capt. Dean C. Roberts, and I were sent by Gen. H. M. Smith, on brief notice, to Floyd Bennett Field in New York.

We were to fly from there to Reykjavik, Iceland, to make preliminary arrangements for the arrival of a Brigade of Marines. Particularly, we were to ascertain the condition and adequacy of billeting, the availability of food, fuel, and other supplies the British could turn over to us, the enemy situation, the nature and extent of defensive dispositions, the capacity of the port and anchorages, plus many other specific questions. . . .

We landed in the fjord just south of Reykjavik. . . . What we saw was bleak in the extreme. The British Brigadier was hospitable, indeed more than glad to see us. He gave us lunch in his mess—canned Argentine beef, gray bread, canned butter, coffee. I knew right then that they had little food our Marines would care for.

We inspected their billeting areas—Nissen huts with oil or charcoal stoves, no cots for the men. . . . The roads were poor, largely narrow, gravel tracks. The British defensive positions were rudimentary and the port of Reykjavik [had been] built for fishing boats, not military transports.

All told, it was an unattractive picture, except for one thing, the British were cheerful, willing to give us anything we could use, but, above all, anxious to know when U.S. forces were coming. They had had their fill of Iceland. . . .

We spent our frigid 24-hour flight home composing the disappointing report we would be making to Gen. [Holland] Smith. He took the bad news in stride, said it was about what he expected.[4]

The convoy was prepared to sail from Charleston by 0800 on 22 June. Any man not aboard ship by midnight of the night before would be declared a deserter. At the last moment before the gangplank was unhooked from the dockside, a lone marine was seen running hard to make the ship in time. He collapsed at the foot of the gangplank and was hauled aboard. He had had too much to drink the night before and had fallen asleep. "Naturally," said Smith. "I was not very hard on him at office hours [commanding officer's nonjudicial punishment]. It was months before his status was straightened out" (ID, 26). The brigade had a total of only seven absentees.

The heavily escorted convoy arrived at Placentia Bay, Newfoundland, on the night of 27 June. Argentia, a small base on the bay received from the British in return for Lend-Lease material, was being expanded, with construction under way as the marines went ashore for exercise. The stopover is described by Smith: "Our delay at Argentia must have been occasioned by some last minute qualms on the part of President Roosevelt. He was taking a long chance in sending a troop convoy to Iceland. Had the convoy been attacked with resultant loss of life, he would have had a difficult time explaining the matter to Congress and the American people. No information whatsoever was given out as to the destination of the convoy. This explains our uncertainty as to our eventual destination" (ID, 28).

The convoy left Newfoundland the evening of 1 July 1941 and headed east and north in extremely heavy seas, which lasted for several days. On 6 July the *Fuller* anchored near Reykjavik. The next day, Smith and a small group from the battalion went ashore to inspect the camps that were waiting for them.

Captain Theiss was anxious to start unloading, which, according to Smith, was typical of prewar naval officers, who did not concern themselves with procedure or the sequence of unloading supplies. The prevailing attitude was to place the material on shore as soon as possible and let the marines sort it out later. Smith informed Thiess that "unloading operations were a convoy problem, and not just a single ship affair" (ID, 30). Consequently, Smith made up a schedule for the billeting of the troops, designating the areas to be used as brigade supply dumps and those for the individual units. The three ships were to utilize the rocky beach sections where trucks could back up to the water's edge and be loaded directly from the ships' small boats. The unloading of troops and material was complete by 12 July.

The brigade was scattered along the western coastline to the north and south of Reykjavik. The First Battalion was split between two camps, Victoria Park Camp and Camp MacArthur, which had been previously occupied by a battalion of the Duke of Wellington Regiment. Some of the British remained behind to welcome the marines and show them the setup of the camps and the routines to be used during their stay at Iceland. The First Marine Brigade now came under the command of the British army.

The quarters that the marines inherited were British Nissen huts, which were slightly less sturdy than the steel Quonset huts that the American military would later use in World War II. The original Nissen hut, however, as set up in Iceland, was an effective cold-weather shelter. The walls were banked on the outside with earth and lava topsoil or sod. The huts had to be anchored securely to the ground to prevent them from being blown away in the severe winds that constantly swept the area. Heat was from coal or coke stoves at each end of the structures. The heaters were used continuously during the nine months the marines were there. There was no fuel on the island except for low-grade peat, which meant that the coal and coke had to be shipped in and stored in dry storage dumps. It was a commodity that was diligently stockpiled and jealously guarded by each squad.

Victoria Park Camp, near Alafoss, on the west slope of the Varmi River about ten miles from Reykjavik, housed the Second Battalion, commanded by Lt. Col. William A. Worton. One of the first problems encountered by the newcomers was the possessiveness of the Icelanders in regard to their swift-flowing rivers, which were full of large salmon. The marines found that a hand grenade dropped in the waters would produce several choice fish to supplement the bland diet. The native Icelanders paid for fishing rights, so violations of their exclusive access were viewed with displeasure. The marines soon found that the British and Americans were outsiders to be grudgingly tolerated, never welcomed.

By 14 July no orders had been received by the brigade, so it went about preparing for its own defense in conjunction with the British plans for the island. Smith wrote:

> The British were extremely air and parachute conscious. The troops on Iceland had come out of Dunkirk. They had considerable experience with German air and knew what it was capable of doing. The landing of airborne troops on Iceland from bases in Norway was not beyond the realm of possibility. Parachutists could land in a great many places and in southwest Iceland there were extensive flat gravel beds where glider troops could have been landed. Drew Middleton, author of the recent book on war entitled 'Our Share of the Night,' in looking back could not see why the Germans did not attempt to capture Iceland by this method in the winter of 1941–42. With Iceland in their possession the Germans would have gone a long way toward winning the Battle of the Atlantic. Our defense preparations reflected the British concern over the possibility of air attack and air landings. (1D, 37–38)[5]

A large naval base was under construction at the deep water fjord of Hval-fjordur, north of Reykjavik and surrounded by bleak rugged mountains. This would soon become a major anchorage for the Allied forces involved in the battle of the North Atlantic.

The marines soon became integrated into the British system of defense. Smith's battalion was assigned the same responsibility as the Duke of Wellington Regiment had had in the Alafoss area. It was to maintain a roadblock, man three coastal lookouts, and operate a refugee-control post. Besides those duties, it had to be prepared to supply a mobile reserve force, on an "as needed" basis.

On 29 July 1941, Smith received orders to draw up an estimate of the situation for the defense of Iceland to be sent to the commandant of the Marine Corps on the 6 August mail ship. Lt. Col. Charles N. Muldrow, executive officer of the Fifth Defense Battalion, and Maj. Edwin C. Ferguson, operations officer at brigade headquarters, were to assist. Smith's detailed description of the project follows:

> There was no time for more than a map reconnaissance. The other two members of the board were not particularly qualified professionally for the task. I, therefore, started to write my own. No one had ever officially told us that we had been sent to Iceland to assist in its defense. Therefore, the first task was to prove that we should assist in the defense of Iceland. Mr. Roosevelt had told the Icelandic government that he would protect it against any eventuality. It was therefore necessary to look at the black side of the picture: that Russia might fold up, that German air might be able to neutralize British air forces and cause sufficient losses to the British Fleet to warrant the German Fleet taking to the sea. The estimate was worked out on this basis. It was determined that it would require about five divisions with appropriate air and naval forces to defend Iceland.
>
> I found later that the estimate had been turned over to the Army and that Gen. Charles E. Bonesteel's staff had read it before they came to Iceland. [On 22 September 1941, President Roosevelt would place the brigade under Bonesteel, the designated commanding general of the Iceland Base Command.] The reaction of some of our officers at headquarters was peculiar. A marine brigade was sent to Iceland, therefore it was assumed by these officers that the estimate should show how one brigade would defend Iceland. Tactically, to assume one brigade could defend Iceland, 200 miles by 200 miles in area, was simply not in the realm of realism. (1D, 47)

When General Bonesteel arrived in Iceland, he concluded that only twenty thousand men could be supplied through the existing port facilities. He appointed

Lieutenant Colonel Smith in Iceland, 1941. He wrote to his wife on the back of the photo: "Yours truly snapped in front of my quarters. Notice the long shadows. The picture was taken in the middle of the day. Victoria Camp." *Courtesy of MCUA.*

three committees to draw up new estimates of the situation. One was from the Marine Corps, another from the headquarters of the Iceland Base Command, and a third from the army units. Smith was placed on the Marine Corps committee. When the estimates were completed, the three groups were close to agreement on the number of men needed to defend Iceland in the event of a major attack. Their figures varied between sixty and eighty-four thousand men, but with the eventual failure of Germany's invasion of Russia, no attempt was made to increase the garrison already on the island. Army troops began to arrive by 8 August 1941. The first units were aviation and advance elements of the ground troops to come later. The army troops did not perform as efficiently as the marines in unloading their ships, so the marines gave them a helping hand. This arrangement was acceptable until the army started to let its men go into town, leaving the marines behind to unload the ships alone. Strong objections could soon be heard from the sea soldiers!

Duty in Iceland was not easy for the Americans. Social activities had to be of their own making. The nearest city was Reykjavik, which had a hotel, where some of the officers would occasionally eat a meal, but the rest of the city was

Prime Minister Winston Churchill (center) with Adm. Louis Mountbatten and Lieutenant Colonel Smith, May 1941. *From right:* Lieutenant Colonel Smith, Adm. Louis Mountbatten, and Prime Minister Churchill. *Courtesy of* MCUA.

uninviting. A few Americans made friends with individual Icelanders, but it was not a widespread phenomenon. The British had a long-standing custom of turning their evening mess into an enjoyable occasion, and the marines were quick to adapt to the custom.

One night in August 1941, Smith and several marine officers went to an evening party at a British airfield. The British had been assigned to the relatively quiet sector of Iceland to recuperate from the extreme stress of combat flying in the Battle of Britain. It had been a custom of this squadron to buy a beer mug for each member who had died in the war. They were proudly displayed in the officer's mess. Smith thought the large number of mugs on display was a powerful statement (ID, 49). The marines agreed that their new allies could teach them something about war, and they also found that the British were as aggressive in play as they were in battle.

The British officers do a lot of drinking and singing. A favorite of the aviators was hot rum. The singing was not for mixed company. I noticed that the chaplain did not remain long after dinner. As the evening wears on the

Britishers begin to get rough. . . . They were avid for souvenirs, such as buttons and insignias. For Marine officers, these items were scarce in Iceland. Worton and I decided to get out early. . . . To protect my ornaments I wore my raincoat during the latter part of my stay. Those who stayed to the end lost all of their buttons and insignias. 'Dutch' [Colonel Leo D. Hermle, CO. Sixth Marines] traded his uniform for that of a British colonel. As a parting shot the Britishers put water in the gasoline [tank] of one of the reconnaissance cars. [Capt. John H.] Cook drove the party home and he was not in too good shape. (ID, 50)

The British sang ribald versions of many popular songs. Smith thought that the songs he had learned in Paris while studying at the École Supérieure de Guerre were more lurid and descriptive, and consequently unfit for mixed company. He was pleased to hear that the versions used at the marine messes were fit for any occasion. The practice of singing in the mess halls and officers' lounges was unique to the marine brigade in Iceland. Smith later said he had never seen it before or after in any of the marine camps of the Pacific or in Korea.

Duty in Iceland may have been restful to the war-weary British, but to the Americans one condition stands out from all the others—boredom. The occasional threats from German planes and U-boats were almost welcome. They helped dispel some of the boredom and took the marines' minds off the incessant winds and damp, cool weather.

One thing that made duty in Iceland more tolerable was that the men knew that it needed to be done. A day that stands out as special was 16 August 1941, when Prime Minister Churchill visited Iceland after his meeting with President Roosevelt at Argentia. The most important product of that meeting was the Atlantic Charter, which was designed to be the rallying document for the war effort. Smith allowed his command to spend a day to get ready for the visit. He described it as follows:

Entrucked for the parade at 0830 . . . to our place on the road near Ripon [in the outskirts of Reykjavik]. Fell in on the line at 1100. Mr. Churchill and party arrived at the Battalion at about 1200. We were formed up on the line facing south, organized as five rifle companies of three platoons each. The reviewing party approached from the direction of Reykjavic [*sic*]. I took post in front of the right flank man of the Battalion. My staff was at the left of the line because we had to move out in that direction. When Mr. Churchill approached I called the Battalion to attention and faced front. I saluted Mr. Churchill, shook his hand and took position on his right. He looked the men over very carefully. About midway he removed his overcoat. It was a very balmy day.... When I got to the left flank of the Battalion, I saluted and shook hands again. We then adjusted slings, slung arms, did a left face, and passed in review. (ID, 53)

Lt. Col. Worton remembers the Churchill visit:

Churchill . . . won the hearts of all the men because as he came along our lines, the colors were there, and he noticed that our regimental colors were dipped as he came by. He turned to me and said, "Colonel Worton, I notice that you never dip the national colors." I said, "No, Mr. Prime Minister, the national colors of our country are dipped for no man on earth, not even the President of our country. We dip our regimental colors, but the national colors belong to the people." He said, "I'm half an American, and I understand that.". . . As he came along the line, it just happened that he came to Muller [a marine of German descent who had voiced criticisms of Churchill]. Muller wore World War One ribbons and so forth. He [Churchill] said, "You're an old soldier aren't you?" Muller said, "I'm an old Marine," like that. He said, "Well, an old sea soldier. Is that a good term?" Muller said, "Yes, sir. We like to regard ourselves as sea soldiers." He said, "Would you like to shake hands with another old soldier?" And he put his hand out. Of course he won Muller over, and he won all the rest of them over that minute.[6]

The day after Churchill's visit, General Marston, who was inclined to be rank conscious, announced that he was going to be in command of all the forces in Iceland. Worton had this to say: "Marston was just an old-fashioned, lovable character who was promoted in line because he was in the line to be promoted. . . . He was a post exchange officer. . . . That's all he worried about—the post exchange and his cadillac. . . . We did have three fine battalion commanders if I do say so myself in Maurice Holmes, Oliver Smith, and myself. . . . We worked very closely together. [Smith] was very much a scholar, but a good field soldier. Oliver was a good soldier all the way through. I've always been very proud of my friendship with Oliver. I thought he was a very good man. He had a lot to him."[7]

Most everybody who came in contact with Smith remembered him as a gentleman. It was his quiet way of doing things that impressed subordinates and superiors alike. He had a quiet demeanor that sprang from a slight shyness. There was no question that his strength as a military commander originated from his character. He was a man who was at ease with himself and who imposed upon himself a demanding set of standards of performance. His intellect allowed him to assess the work before him and seek alternative answers. He was rarely surprised with the "unknown." The men in his command had his respect, and it was reciprocated from the bottom to the top.

Smith was a nondrinker, but he never made an issue out of it, and he appeared to tolerate those who did drink, as long as it did not get out of hand. After an especially drunken party in August, Marston called a meeting at brigade headquarters and announced there would be no more open bars for officers. Smith summarized the conference as follows:

> General Marston was perfectly right about the drinking. We were in the combat zone. Whatever we may have thought regarding the matter, the British were considerably concerned over the possibility of an attack against Iceland. They seldom had any big parties. They tried to spread their drinking over the week. They did not want any day of the week to be considered as a day for relaxation. By the time Holmes' party was over about two-thirds of the officers were unfit for duty. The General at his conference told us he was going to take off his stars and talk to us man to man. He started out by saying, "My chief of staff was 'blotto'; Maurice (Colonel Holmes), you were 'blotto'; Arthur (Colonel Worton), you were 'blotto.'" Worton protested that he was not "blotto," that he had taken a drink but was in full possession of his faculties. Dutch (Colonel Hermle) tried to patch things up by stating that with the exception of myself (a nondrinker) all the senior officers had been at fault. This did not make me very popular with Maurice or Arthur. (ID, 54)

Worton had made preparations before leaving the United States with the prestigious Massachusetts grocery firm, S. S. Pierce, to ship ten thousand dollars' worth of whiskey to his battalion. He personally paid for it and used it during his stay in Iceland as bartering material for his troops and himself. Worton managed the select distribution of the liquor to the bulk of the marine officers in Iceland. He also supplied the drinks for the party held in honor of Churchill's visit. Later, when General Bonesteel became commander of all forces in Iceland, Worton regularly supplied the general and his staff with whiskey, having the general sign receipts for it as it was delivered.[8]

General Marston wrote to the commandant of the Marine Corps in late August that he was going to relieve his chief of staff, Col. "Charlie" I. Murray, who was drinking too heavily. His replacement was to be selected from the officers already in Iceland. As Smith remembered it, "General Marston told me he was contemplating detailing me as his chief of staff. I told him he had put me on the spot; that, of course I would like to serve with him in any capacity but I felt that the job I then had of battalion commander was the best one I ever had and I would like to continue on. He then told me that it would be between Colonel Hermle and myself. Colonel Hermle was the regimental commander. Colonel Hermle stepped into the breach and volunteered for the job" (ID, 56).

Marston warned Smith that he might have to become his chief of staff if he, Marston, could not complete the transfer of officers he was currently working with. In mid-October Smith wrote, "He [Marston] also told me my fitness report was outstanding and that I was considered the best battalion commander in the Marine Corps. That is quite a bit to live up to" (ID, 75).

One feature of service in Iceland that was heavily protested by the marine brigade was the decision by Gen. George C. Marshall, chairman of the Joint Chiefs of Staff, to place the marines under army control. Smith tells what happened:

> The basic law provides that Marines may, by order of the President, be detached for service with the Army. When this occurs Marine organizations so detached become administratively a part of the Army. In other words, they are subject to the Articles of War and no longer are subject to the Articles for the Government of the Navy. That threw our Courts and Boards out of the window. The order affected us in many ways which we did not like. We, of course, retained our uniforms. We all felt that the Marine Corps had let us down. It would have been possible to attach us to the Army tactically under the principle of unity of command. This . . . was done later in the Pacific.
>
> We were particularly annoyed by the disciplinary restrictions imposed. Under naval law a battalion commander can convene summary courts martial and deck courts and can also give out commanding officer punishments. Under the Army system the battalion commander is by-passed. The company commander could give out company punishments. For serious offenses the company commander made recommendation to the regimental commander via the battalion commander. I was in a detached camp and was responsible for discipline in that camp, yet had no disciplinary authority. I got my company commanders together and told them that although we were under the Articles of War, I expected them to come to me regarding disciplinary matters and we would in each case decide what action would take place. (ID, 66–67)

By mid-October the marines had realized that they would remain in Iceland for the winter, and they prepared themselves for the cold months ahead. Smith had set up a school of instruction for his officers, doing the bulk of the teaching himself. He had taught for four years at the Marine Corps Schools and felt an obligation to help others benefit from his experience. Other qualified officers offered to instruct the men in their own areas of expertise, which resulted in high-quality, if informal, instruction. Courses in French and other languages, mathematics, history, and literature were set up for the enlisted men. Several men who were teachers in civilian life could be found within the enlisted ranks, and the classes were well attended. Efforts were increased to obtain musical instruments for the men's recreation, and the United Services Organization was most helpful in assuring an ample supply.

One of the most qualified speakers in the battalion school was the new executive officer, Maj. J. F. Hankins, who was a demolition expert. He came from the Second Battalion, where it was an asset to be able to balance a teacup. Hankins had a few rough edges as to the social graces, so Colonel Worton was anxious to replace him. Smith wrote,

> Gerard [Worton's replacement] had the necessary social graces, but to my mind was not much of an officer, an opinion which was later confirmed by numerous selections boards and a final "plucking" board. When Hankins came to me he had an inferiority complex. He felt that nobody wanted him and he had an idea this was because he was a reserve officer. Hankins and I lived together in the same room for several months and I believe I was able to dispel some of his gloom. . . . He was slow of speech and his reactions were slow but he had plenty of character. He also did some good work for me. (ID, 74)

Colonel Hankins was later killed in action on Peleliu.

The attack on Pearl Harbor came as a surprise to the marines at Iceland, as it did to the rest of the nation. It did not change their military routine, because they were already functioning in a war zone and had conducted their operations accordingly. Smith helped the men in his command understand the ramifications of the attack with a discussion of the problems in the Pacific and the war ahead of them all. He reviews the situation:

> The officers in the battalion had not had the advantage of professional schooling other than troop schools. They were ignorant of the problem of an amphibious campaign in the Pacific. I had spent several years in the Marine Corps Schools studying this very problem. I told them that Pearl Harbor could not be a main effort but was a raid; also that the Japanese main effort in the Far East was probably the Malaya Peninsula rather than the Philippines. I

pointed out to them that we could not hold Guam, and that in pre-war planning no one considered that Corregidor could hold out more than six months.
I explained to them our shortage in auxiliary ships which meant that we
would have to launch a building program before we could undertake offensive
war in the Pacific, an undertaking which would probably require two years.
The information I gave them was considerably different than they heard over
the radio. Our Marine Schools paid dividends during the war. There resulted
a body of officers who had attended the schools and could make a realistic
approach to the problem in the Pacific. (1D, 96–97)

We can get some insights about Smith's thoughts on leadership from the
following statement:

I had had many arguments with Col. Hermle regarding the question of leadership. He belonged to the school of thought which expected an officer to
impress himself on the men by his size, looks and personality. Intelligence
was secondary. "Dutch" had a horror of the brilliant officer. I maintained
there was such a thing as intelligent leadership; that if it were humanly possible a leader should know everything his officers and men should know;
that you simply cannot pass everything as a detail with which the commander
should not concern himself. "Dutch," with his legal training, loved argument and they were interminable. Of course, there is no such thing as a
standard type of leader. Successful leaders have used a variety of methods to
make their leadership effective. (1D, 98)

Marston informed Smith on 7 January 1942 that his promotion to full colonel had been approved. The general awarded the promotion at a ceremony in
which the other officers in the battalion presented him with new collar insig-
nia, a colonel's eagles. The joy of being promoted must have been overshadowed by the sad duty of burying two days later the first member of the American forces to die in Iceland, in a cemetery overlooking a seaplane anchorage. A
Sergeant Pickins had been stabbed during a party for sergeants, and it was Smith's
duty to write the parents. "The cemetery might have been beautiful in the summer with green grass and the blue water beyond, but the aspect certainly was
bleak when we buried Pickins. When I wrote the mother I did not have the
heart to describe the weather in connection with the funeral. I told her what
the cemetery would look like in summer" (1D, 106).
    The end of February brought news that the marines were to be relieved by
the army's Second Infantry and that some advance elements were already en

route to Iceland. Smith's battalion was being replaced by the First Battalion of the Second Infantry. When Smith showed the army commanding officer, a Major Gill, the ground the army troops would be defending, the major was amazed at its size. The marine battalion had about twenty-four machine guns to cover its sector, whereas the army battalion had only eight machine guns to cover the same area. Smith left some of his reserve machine guns for the army when he left Iceland.

The anxious marines helped the army unload the ships so that they in turn could put their own equipment aboard and leave the frozen world of Iceland behind. With a Herculean effort the First Battalion loaded its gear on the USS *Munargo*. The ship cast off at 0800 on 9 March 1942, carrying the last element of the brigade to be loaded and to sail from Reykjavik—destination, New York City.

The long ocean voyage across the most dangerous stretches of the North Atlantic was a time to reflect on what the marines had accomplished. By sending armed forces to aid the British in the defense of Iceland, Roosevelt had made it possible for Britain to deploy troops elsewhere. The marines had fit into the British scheme of doing things, and the British had learned to respect the marines' standards of efficiency and competence.

An interesting footnote to marine operations in Iceland was the phenomenal success of the post exchange, or "PX." As Smith described it: "General Marston's hobby was the Post Exchange. He directed a good many of the purchases, and watched the prices very carefully. The Post Exchange at San Diego had loaned us $5,000.00 in cash. In order to get on our feet, the General decreed that prices should be kept high in order to accumulate working capital. This procedure eventuated in a net profit of $60,000.00 by the time we were ready to leave Iceland. None of this money was distributed to the units when they left Iceland; the Marine Corps Fund appropriated it all" (ID, 93).

Maj. Walter A. Churchill, the post exchange officer, later wrote, "Brigadier General Marston, who wrote the book on PX operations, gave me this responsibility because of my food retailing experience and called me 'John Wannamaker' [*sic*, for the founder of a famous chain of stores] because of how successful our operation was. . . . Lt. Col. Smith was senior member of a nine member PX audit committee which found our operations commendable."[9]

Smith gained valuable command experience in Iceland. He was somewhat of a "mother hen," and his desire to seek what was best for the men was apparent to all. He was approachable at any time and could be depended upon to give commonsense advice.

The voyage to the port of New York took place with no disciplinary trouble, which may be explained by the fact that the men were going to get leave as soon as they returned to the United States. Men who lived east of the Mississippi would be granted leave for fifteen days when they got to New York. The men who lived west of the Mississippi were to be granted leave after the subsequent train trip to San Diego. The *Munargo* docked at Brooklyn on 25 March 1942 at 2030. The leave parties were released first, then the balance of the brigade was offloaded and entrained at Pennsylvania Station. The men ate the stewards out of house and home, and they drank all of the milk that was on the train; the conductor had to wire ahead for replenishment.

The men did not set foot on solid ground until they got to San Diego, where they ate at the depot. The restaurant would not take any money from the men or officers for the food and drink they consumed. A band had turned out at Linda Vista to meet the train. The balance of the men went on furlough; they would be transferred to units that were forming when they returned. Smith was met by his wife, Esther, at the U.S. Grant Hotel in San Diego on the evening of 30 March 1942.

When Smith had shipped out for Iceland, the United States had been at peace with the rest of the world. He returned to a country at war with two powerful nations. His rest period was richly deserved, but the daunting task ahead of the nation and its military forces had to have been on his mind.

3

THE NEW BRITAIN CAMPAIGN

After a few days with his family, Smith drove across the country by automobile and reported on 2 May 1942 at Headquarters Marine Corps, where he was assigned as the M-4 logistics and the executive officer, Division of Plans and Policies, commonly known as "Pots and Pans." Among Smith's duties was the oversight of the studies by various boards that evaluated new types of equipment developed for the army and other services (at that time the Marine Corps was still dependent upon the army for most of its infantry equipment and other supplies). The Division of Plans and Policies then made recommendations about whether or not such equipment should be adopted by the Marine Corps. Most of Smith's time was spent in building up and equipping the Fleet Marine Force, or FMF, for the war against Japan.[1]

When Gen. Alexander A. Vandegrift became commandant of the Marine Corps in December 1943, it was expected that many changes would be made. The Marine Corps was still in an accelerated growth period, and Vandegrift wanted to have trusted subordinates around him. The most influential officer from that group was Col. Gerald C. Thomas, Vandegrift's chief of staff during the Guadalcanal campaign and also in the First Marine Amphibious Corps, which had been formed after Guadalcanal. Thomas was scheduled to take over as director of the Division of Plans and Policies, with a promotion to brigadier general. Thomas used his association with Vandegrift to help him carry out the enlargement and improvement of the Marine Corps as he personally visualized it. (The Division of Plans and Policies was abolished in 1952, when the Marine Corps went to a general-staff type of organization.)[2]

Volupai and Talasea, New Britain. *Courtesy* MCHC.

At the end of Smith's tour in "Pots and Pans," Vandegrift told him that he would be named chief of staff of the First Marine Division as of January 1944. Smith wrote, "He [Vandegrift] stated that he realized that all the colonels wanted to command regiments but that I was getting along in years and that duty as Chief of Staff was a more suitable assignment. He also stated that 'Lem' Shepherd [Brig. Gen. Lemuel C. Shepherd,] who was then Assistant Division Commander of the First Marine Division, should be given his chance for more responsible command and that when this occurred, if I had proven myself, I would be considered to relieve Shepherd" (NB, 1).

On 17 January 1944 Smith began the long, circuitous journey to the southwest Pacific. He had landed and changed flights six times by the time he arrived at Third Amphibious Corps headquarters on Guadalcanal eleven days later. The Third Amphibious Corps was commanded by one of the legends of the Marine Corps, Gen. Roy S. Geiger. In 1944 Geiger was a fifty-nine-year-old professional who had started his career as an aviator. He had been the director of the Division of Aviation in 1943 and had then succeeded Vandegrift as commanding officer of the First Marine Amphibious Corps on Bougainville (later redesignated the Third Amphibious Corps), where he demonstrated an extraordinary ability to handle ground troops and work harmoniously with the army. He was a stocky, no-nonsense commander who handled both marine and army troops with equal competence. He possessed a deadly stare that was famous in the Corps, especially if you were the subject being scrutinized. Time after time Geiger demonstrated his sharp grasp of tactics and leadership, earning the respect and admiration of those who knew him. Smith greatly admired Geiger and rated him as one of the best the Marine Corps ever had.

Smith was lucky enough to hitch a ride with Geiger in his own plane, a PBY, which the general frequently piloted himself. They arrived at Finschhafen, New Guinea, which was the headquarters of the Sixth Army, commanded by Lt. Gen. Walter Krueger, under whom the First Marine Division was operating for the New Britain campaign. Krueger was a soldier's soldier who had risen from the ranks, avoided the public eye, and earned the respect of most who served under him. The Sixth Army was a superb instrument; it would see action on New Guinea, New Britain, the Admiralties, and Biak before it participated in the reconquest of the Philippines (NB, 3–4).

Geiger and Smith discovered that there was no Allied airfield in the Cape Gloucester area that could handle the larger planes used for the earlier part of the trip. Consequently, they took a patrol torpedo (PT) boat from Finschhafen to Cape Gloucester, on the northwest tip of the island of New Britain. It was a wild ride across ninety miles of the Dampier Strait, and it turned a lunch of coffee and sandwiches into a messy affair. Smith recalled that as they approached New Britain, in the vicinity of Borgen Bay,

> the PT boat skipper began using his blinker gun [signal light] to announce our arrival. About this time we saw a couple of splashes about one-half mile off our bow. We thought for a minute the Japanese might be on a bombing raid, but then we heard the boom of the 155mm guns of the 12th Defense Battalion which had a battery placed near Yellow Beach. Two more salvoes followed the first but all splashed well off our bow. The PT boat did considerable blinking and the firing ceased. . . . Willie Harrison [Col. W. H. Harrison], who commanded the 12th Defense Battalion, told me afterwards that he was shooting at what he thought was a submarine. . . . He came in for a good bit of kidding for firing three two-gun salvoes at his Corps Commander, General Geiger. (NB, 4)

The First Marine Division was staffed with many old friends and acquaintances. Lem Shepherd was the assistant division commander, and his old roommate and battalion executive officer, Joe Hankins, was commanding the Third Battalion of the Fifth Marines. Col. Johnny Selden commanded the Fifth Marines.

Smith reported to Maj. Gen. William H. Rupertus, commanding general of the First Marine Division, without telling him that Vandegrift had sent him to the division to be the chief of staff. He knew that Rupertus preferred to select his own staff members, and Smith also remembered Vandegrift's desire to have Shepherd assume a more responsible command.

The constant juggling of officers in the war zone is demonstrated by Smith's comment that

> General Rupertus was expecting to be ordered home in the near future. Unfortunately, Headquarters Marine Corps in issuing dispatch orders for [Col. Amos L.] Sims, who was then Chief of Staff of the First Marine Division, stated that Sims would be detached upon my reporting as his relief. General Rupertus made up his mind that he would not let Headquarters Marine Corps dictate to him . . . and he ordered me to report to "Lem" Shepherd for duty as the Assistant Division Commander's Chief of Staff, relieving Hanneken. . . . [Later] it occurred to General Rupertus that if he were relieved by Shepherd, Shepherd might want me as his Chief of Staff of the Division. He therefore called up "Lem" and asked him for his views. "Lem" said he would be very glad to have me if he took over the Division. My orders were therefore rescinded and I came back as the Division Chief of Staff. (NB, 4)

The assault on the northwest coast of Cape Gloucester had taken place on 26 December 1943, against heavy resistance. The Seventh Marine Regiment had suffered the heaviest losses; it was positioned on the southern end of the airdrome on the Cape. The First and Fifth Marines formed a continuous line to the left of the Seventh as far as Borgen Bay. Smith took over as chief of staff on 28 January 1944, when the first phase of the New Britain campaign had ended. The Japanese were withdrawing easterly, and for the next month the division conducted aggressive patrols along the northern coast toward Iboki Plantation, which was halfway between the Willaumez Peninsula and the initial landing beaches at Cape Gloucester. The patrols would cut off large numbers of retreating Japanese troops as they tried to escape through the jungle toward their major naval base at Rabaul, some 250 miles away at the eastern end of the island. Smith believed that the best defense was to keep the enemy off balance with aggressive patrolling in sufficient strength to maintain momentum. Iboki Plantation had been a main staging area for the Japanese and was the terminus of the trail that led to the south shore at Arawe, where there was a small airfield under the control of U.S. Army forces. The headquarters of the Fifth Marines was established at Iboki, with most of its units nearby.

The Joint Chiefs of Staff had ordered the bypass of Rabaul, but Gen. Douglas MacArthur, commanding the Southwest Pacific Area, wanted the western portion of New Britain neutralized so that he could conduct operations along the New Guinea coast without interference.[3] In mid-February, Sixth Army, under MacArthur's orders, proposed that the First Marine Division and an army combat team assault and capture Rabaul. Rupertus delegated Smith to assess the feasibility of the operation; Smith concluded that an attack by inadequate force against the hundred thousand Japanese defenders would end in disaster. Rupertus took Smith's proposal to Sixth Army and heard nothing more about an attack against Rabaul.

Smith's short stint as chief of staff ended in late February 1944, when he was ordered to command the Fifth Marine Regiment. He did not say in his diaries how he felt, but no doubt he was pleased to be back in command of troops. As soon as Rupertus knew that Shepherd was not going to replace him immediately as division commander, he decided to choose his own division chief of staff; he had Smith swap positions with Colonel Selden. Rupertus may have been uncomfortable with a subordinate, such as Smith, who possessed a very high intellect, had a tendency to do things "by the book," and was able to defend his decisions and orders effectively.[4]

"When I was given the Fifth Marines I was informed that it was the intention to use the Fifth Marines to land on the Willaumez Peninsula and capture the Talasea area. A verbal directive was received by General Rupertus from the Sixth Army" (NB, 12). In accordance with the directive, Smith started planning the operation, which was scheduled to take place on 6 March as a shore-to-shore operation with boats from an army engineer brigade. The supporting force would be six PT boats and planes from the Fifth Air Force. Smith drew up the orders for the operation as division chief of staff and carried them out as a regimental commander. Very little was known about the Talasea area, but intelligence estimates predicted the Japanese had built up defenses to prevent such an attack as Smith was now planning. It is significant that Smith recorded the following in his diary: "Under the circumstances, it was not politic to show other than enthusiasm for the operation" (NB, 12).

Smith began to plan the operation with information that was skimpy at best. This was a good example of Smith being the "good soldier" without personal reservations. The narrowest part of the Willaumez Peninsula was due west from Talasea, at Volupai Plantation. No current photo coverage was available, but an earlier map indicated that there was a channel through the reefs to the beach at the plantation and a trail leading overland to Talasea on the eastern shore of the peninsula. Intelligence information as of 20 January 1944 showed that two commanders within the Japanese Seventeenth Division had been ordered to prepare for the defense of Talasea. The estimate of enemy strength, at that time, was about five thousand men in the Talasea–Cape Hoskins vicinity (Hoskins was about forty miles southeast of Talasea), with an airfield and other installations. There were perhaps an additional six thousand enemy soldiers that could be used in support of those at Talasea. It was apparent to Smith that a single regiment would not be sufficient if all available Japanese troops were deployed against it.

The reinforced Fifth Marines (4,131 men) was being assembled at Iboki Plantation, forty miles west of Volupai along the northern coastline. Smith decided to use amphibian tractors, and tracked LVT-2s for the initial assault through the unknown channel to the beach. The boats were provided by the army's 533d Engineers, under the command of Lt. Col. Robert Amory, Jr., a very competent and resourceful officer. Landing craft (LCTs) to follow the amphibian tractors ashore would be provided by seventeen vehicle and personnel landing craft (LCVPs), and forty medium landing craft (LCMs).

There was no naval gunfire support available, so five medium Sherman tanks were positioned in the LCMs and maintained afloat for supporting fire during the initial assault. The six PT boats were supposed to provide escort for the trip from Iboki to Volupai and for the return trip with wounded aboard. Air support, as noted, was promised by the Fifth Air Force, which was supposed to have made softening-up strikes prior to D day. Fifth Air Force was also responsible for raids on the major base at Rabaul at the extreme eastern end of the island, prior to and during the assault phase. Air cover had been promised for D day and for D plus one.

On 1 March 1944, Operation Order 7-44 was issued. Essentially, the plan was to land and occupy a beachhead near Volupai, then attack easterly to seize and occupy the Talasea area. The First Battalion of the First Marines was to be held in reserve at Iboki. The operation looked like an invitation to disaster, and the unknown component of any plan, no matter how well prepared, must have weighed heavily on Smith's mind. He wrote,

> Having done the best I could in assisting to draw up the orders, they were promulgated. To keep the record straight I was shown as Commanding Officer, Fifth Marines, and Colonel Selden as Chief of Staff. On March 1, 1944 I secured a Cub plane and taking my essential equipment and the copy of the operation order proceeded to Iboki to relieve Selden. . . . It is about a 60 mile trip from Cape Gloucester to Iboki. . . . The plane is so small and so open that you have a feeling of insecurity. We ran into storm clouds and the pilot had to dodge around them. I spent my time picking likely spots to make a forced landing, on the reef or in a kunai patch. . . . After considerable dodging we reached Iboki and landed . . . on a 300 yard strip of sand which had been dragged by a bulldozer. (NB, 16)

Selden met Smith at the field with a jeep and drove him to his new head-quarters, where he met Private First Class Tenney, an orderly who had been assigned to Smith. Smith was thankful but had some misgivings: "I became attached to Tenney but as time went on he began to wear on me. He was a self-assured youngster who had served on the USS *New York* at the time it was con-voying us to Iceland. He had all the instincts of a butler. . . . He would go through my things and rearrange them and I would have difficulty finding items when I wanted them in a hurry. However, his heart was in the right place" (NB, 16).

Selden took Smith around the lines and, after a short visit with his officers, said his good-byes. Smith would recall Selden was quite broken up about leav-ing the regiment; he could well understand and appreciate such sentiment.

The units were disposed around the Iboki Plantation, with the exception of the Third Battalion, which was still several miles to the west and still sending out patrols in that area. Several other components of the assault force were not in place and had to be moved to the staging area at Iboki. Embarkation for the assault troops was set for 5 March; a lot of the troops had to be concentrated at the Iboki assembly area before that date.

When Smith went over the plans with the staff, he had a huge sales job on his hands:

> The idea of embarking in small boats, proceeding over water for 57 miles, then landing on a beach about which we knew little, against an enemy about whom we knew even less, did not appeal to the staff. The staff was also not sure of the feasibility of launching amphibian tractors from LCTs. Of course, we had the promise of photographs of the beaches and the expectation of valuable information regarding the enemy when the planned amphibious reconnaissance could be conducted. We also had been assured that G-3 [op-erations officer] of the Division would test the launching of amphibian trac-tors from LCTs and report to us by dispatch. It is true that it was rather late in the game to be obscure on these points. However, we had an order to carry out; therefore, we got to work. (NB, 17)

The initial landing force had to be self-sustaining for the first day. It was to go ashore in the amphibian tractors (LVTs) which would be seriously overloaded in the assault phase. The half-tracks and medium tanks had to be secured in the severely overloaded LCMs to deliver the important gunfire support for the first troops ashore. There was a real danger that the overloaded craft would be swamped if the vehicles shifted when they fired their guns.

On 3 March, Shepherd moved his headquarters to Iboki. Smith elaborated on his terms of reference: "General Shepherd's status was peculiar. He was informed that the chain of command went direct from the Division to the Fifth Marines and that he was to operate merely in a liaison capacity. As 'Lem' Shepherd and I were old friends I knew we could work together closely and I certainly intended to keep him fully advised of everything I intended to do" (NB, 19).

On the day Shepherd arrived, Smith drew up a memorandum that listed items that needed attention, such as the test of disembarking LVTS from LCTS (nobody knew at that time if it could be done with any degree of safety), the photos of the beach that had not been received, the total lack of information on air support, and the desperate need for added supplies of ammunition, water, and food. Attached to the memorandum was a short request that "it would be highly desirable to have these items assured by 4 March, 1944 in order to meet D-day on 6 March, 1944" (NB, 19).

The memorandum was typical of Smith's attention to detail. He had a knack for documenting any situation that would be construed as controversial; it would appear that sometimes he did it to assist himself in analyzing a situation. He discussed this memo with Shepherd, who "felt that he [Shepherd] should send the memorandum to the Division concurring in it and requesting prompt action. The memorandum was forwarded to Cape Gloucester by plane. It was not well received by Division and General Shepherd was informed that both of us were apparently trying to prove why we should not conduct the operation. I believe, however, the memorandum did have some effect in getting information and supplies" (NB, 20).

The general plan for the assault on Volupai Plantation was adhered to, and the requested information slowly filtered in, making the planners feel more confident about its outcome. The air support problem had been taken care of, and an air liaison officer was to accompany Smith to the beach. The Fifth Air Force had promised to provide for bombing runs on the landing beaches until the assault troops were five hundred feet offshore. Intelligence was received from native scouts, accurate except for the number of Japanese in the landing area. The native scouts estimated about 150 enemy soldiers in the area, but captured documents later confirmed that there were 575.

The convoy left Iboki at 2300 on 6 March in order to arrive at the landing area by 0800 on D day. The lead boat was commanded by the intrepid Lieutenant Colonel Amory, an army reserve officer, who had been most energetic and helpful in developing a satisfactory scheme of maneuver for the boats. The lead boat had the most sophisticated navigational equipment on board, so the other vessels followed the leader. Smith's boat followed the main convoy and picked up several stragglers along the way. The shore-to-shore dash was completed without mishap, except for a few boats that got lost or broke down. The plan called for landing on the beach west of the Volupai Plantation and driving easterly across the

Fifth Marine staff pose in front of Bitikara Mission, Talasea, March 1944. *From left:* Major Adams, Lieutenant Colonel Buse, Colonel Smith, Captain Williams, Captain Dill, and an unidentified staff member. *Courtesy of MCUA.*

Willaumez Peninsula to Talasea in order to occupy that position, which would become the main assembly area of the Fifth Marines. It was also expected that the regiment would occupy several small islands off the coast of Talasea, in particular Garua, so that ships could supply it directly from the east coast of the peninsula.

The moment of truth had arrived. The first foul-up was the failure of the air support element to arrive on time for the initial assault. By 0720 no planes could be seen. Amory, with the advance units, signaled Smith: "Shall we proceed despite air failure?" Smith answered, "Carry on."[5] It was too late to turn the boats around.

Amory lowered the ramp of his lead LCM and launched the first amphibian tractor at 0825. Within ten minutes, over five hundred men were on the beach and advancing inland. There was no air support, but a lone Marine Corps Piper Cub showed up over the beach with a General Ogden, commanding officer of the army boat brigade that was furnishing the amphibious boats for the operation. The pilot, a Captain Petras, flew over the landing area just before the assault took place and dropped five hand grenades on the enemy.

The First Battalion secured the beachhead with light casualties and sporadic opposition. The natives had reported a large pillbox on the northeast slope of a small hill, called Little Mount Worri, southeast of the landing beaches. A single platoon eliminated that threat. So far, the assault had gone well. Most of First Battalion had landed, and Maj. Gordon Gayle's Second Battalion was to follow shortly. Gayle, however, was stranded at sea for some time when his boat developed engine trouble. When he did land, he was towing a second boat, which had also been knocked out of commission. It was carrying the Army Air Corps radio jeep, which proved valuable in later stages of the operation. The beach area that was secured was small and was limited by swampy ground to the south along the track leading to Talasea. The Japanese had assembled 90 mm mortars inland from the landing beach, and they found the range of the area just as the Second Battalion was landing. Smith ordered the advance to accelerate so that the marines might overrun the mortars or cause them to be withdrawn out of range.

Offshore, the artillery was beginning to move into position for landing. The tortuous channel through the coral reef was being feverishly marked by Amory to facilitate the routing of landing craft to the small usable section of beach. The narrow channel was the only way to the beachhead, and it was imperative that it be well marked as soon as possible so that resupply efforts could be speeded up.

A valuable map found on a dead Japanese soldier at Volupai Plantation showed the dispositions of enemy forces located at Talasea. By midafternoon of D day, copies of the map had been distributed to all of the marine forces, thanks to a superb job of translation and compilation by the intelligence section (known as R-2).

The Second Battalion, with the assistance of a two-gun section of 37 mm guns and some Sherman tanks, forced their way through the lush jungle growth toward the coconut groves at the Volupai Plantation, where it set up a perimeter defense and dug in for the first night. The medical section (A Company, First Medical Battalion) had been located, at Smith's direction, near the beach, to where the wounded could be evacuated with relative ease. However, this location also made it vulnerable to an attack from the south; consequently, Smith ordered an additional platoon from the First Battalion to cover that flank so that the medical teams could perform their life-saving work with as little threat as possible. Smith felt deeply about his casualties, and he worked diligently to see that they had everything they needed. His concern was genuine, and everyone who knew him remembered his capacity to appreciate their sacrifice.

On the first day over fifty badly wounded men required more sophisticated facilities than were available under the tent at the beach. Smith tried to get PBYs from the division to evacuate the men, but none were available, so he sent them back to Iboki by boat, clearing the reefs offshore before darkness.

By nightfall, the Second Battalion was holding a perimeter at the northern end of the coconut grove about two thousand yards from the beach. The First Battalion was still holding in place, about five hundred yards from the shore. A battery of artillery was set up on the southern side of the coconut grove; it was registered—that is, it was aimed properly at fixed map references, from which fire could be adjusted to actual targets—by dark, when it began to deliver harassing fire against the Japanese. An estimate of thirty to thirty-five enemy had been killed on the first day. Marine losses were seventy-one wounded and thirteen killed. The tabulation of casualties was an obsession with Smith. It was frequently the last thing he entered in his diary at the end of the day. Later, in Korea, Smith continued the same practice and went to great lengths to make sure of the numbers' accuracy.

Plans for the second day were reviewed on the first evening. The First Battalion was to drive toward the main enemy stronghold in the vicinity of the Waru villages after it had been relieved by the Third Battalion, which was to be transported from Iboki on the same boats that had taken the seriously wounded there on the evening tide. Second Battalion was to continue toward the Waru villages from the north. The ultimate objective was Talasea and the airfield nearby.

The second day, 7 March, started with a change of plans when the Third Battalion failed to relieve the First completely. In the meantime, the Second was advancing, with artillery support, toward the northeast slopes of Mount Schleuther when it ran into a major force of Japanese. Major Gayle handled his battalion with great skill when the Japanese tried to turn his right flank. He called in another company, which reached the high ground first and countered the Japanese attack. An estimated twenty-five to thirty enemy were killed and many more wounded. The Japanese dug in for the evening on the northern slopes of Mount Schleuchter; throughout the night the Second Battalion kept them off balance with mortar fire.

Close air support was still nonexistent, and Smith was dissatisfied with the performance of the air component, which he had been led to believe would be available to him "on demand." For example, a call went out for strafing and bombing runs as soon as intelligence confirmed the presence of large numbers of Japanese at the Waru villages. Smith was told by air controllers that it would take at least six hours to deliver a strike. He told them that if the strike could not be made by 1500 on 7 March, it would not be needed. Nothing happened until the next morning, when the strike was delivered without his having requested it. No friendly troops were in the area, but a major disaster could have taken place.

On the third day a mistake occurred that is described by Smith: "The First Battalion, less its patrol already in the vicinity of Liapo, started in the direction of Liapo, which was reached by noon. Just before reaching Liapo occurred one of those accidents which occur too frequently in war. The patrol of the First Battalion already near Liapo, in the thick jungle, mistook the leading company of the remainder of the First Battalion for Japanese and opened fire. One man was killed and a couple wounded. One of Marsland's [Flight Lt. G. H. Rodney Marsland, Royal Australian Air Force] scouts was also wounded" (NB, 31).

The First Battalion pushed on through deserted Liapo toward Waru and dug in for the night just short of the Waru villages. The Second Battalion drove toward the enemy positions on the northwest side of Mount Schleuther, to find them destroyed by artillery fire. An artillery barrage was "walked" down the coastal plain to Bitokara, followed by a strong patrol, which secured the area. Other patrols were sent along the foot trail to the Waru villages, to Talasea Point, and to the airstrip nearby. The only appreciable opposition was against the Waru villages patrol; that action was the focal point for concentrated artillery fire all evening. The next morning, the area was secured by the First Battalion.

The next day (9 March), Smith moved his command post. Originally, it had been planned to establish the permanent command post at Talasea Point, which had a golf course and was the site of an abandoned Australian agricultural experiment station. The tactical situation dictated locating at Bitokara Mission, which was halfway between Talasea and the Waru villages. Bombers had flattened the buildings at Talasea.

Smith felt that the main mission for the regiment would be to defend the airstrip and Garua Harbor against any enemy force that might attempt to go north to Cape Hoskins and eventually to Rabaul. He therefore decided to disperse his force as follows: First Battalion would turn the Waru villages into a defensible stronghold; the Second Battalion would assume the responsibility for the defense of Talasea Point and the airstrip; the Third Battalion was directed to send a company to the original landing beaches until the men and material left there could be evacuated and moved to Bitokara, where the battalion became the regimental reserve. Patrols sent out to the south toward the Santa Monica Plantation found the jungle more of an obstacle than the small number of Japanese stragglers. A company-sized outpost garrison was established at Kilu.

Piper Cubs were used for patrolling the northern end of the Willaumez Peninsula, where several gasoline dumps were found abandoned. The airstrip had been used by the Australians before the war and was maintained in grass cover; if the strip had been bulldozed, it would have been turned into a huge sea of mud up to four feet deep. The first Cub to land on the airstrip was piloted by the doughty Captain Petras and Maj. Gen. E. C. Long, chief of the Supply Service. Smith walked to the airstrip to meet General Long, because the trails were impassable even for the jeep. Smith had to walk for a couple of miles to the plateau where the airstrip was located; and he developed a painful "charley horse" that took a long time to work out.

Smith described the flag raising in his own words: "General Rupertus had entrusted to me the flag which had been raised at Cape Gloucester. He wanted the same flag raised at Talasea. As soon as we were settled at Bitokara we made a flagpole out of a slender royal palm and had an official flag raising. [Lt. Col. Henry W.] Buse and I hoisted the colors" (NB, 34).

A congratulatory message from division was dropped by a Piper Cub: "Time filed 0730. Message Center #289 SCR 299 Routine 8Mar44 To CO [commanding officer], Fifth Marines. You and your regiment have accomplished a magnificent job. Please inform your command that the Division and the Marine Corps is proud of them. The Fifth Marines have dood it again. We like your guts. Stand by for Cub plane over field tomorrow at 1000. [Signed] Rupertus, Division CO, 1946" (NB, 35).

Also received was a copy of a message from General Krueger: "From CG [commanding general], Alamo [Sixth Army] To CG, Backhander [First Marine Division]. From Gloucester to Talasea the Marines and their supporting Army and Navy units have again demonstrated the highest degree of skill, courage, and resourcefulness. My heartiest congratulations and personal appreciation to you and all ranks for your part in the destruction of the enemy in western New Britain" (NB, 35).

By pushing a patrol to the south along the coast of Cape Hoskins, Smith felt he had complied with the original division order. He did not want to have his command scattered over too large a territory, in case the Japanese, who had a considerable force at Cape Hoskins, decided to move north against it. As soon as the enemy had been eliminated from the targeted area, the Fifth Marines settled down to a more routine defense, with daily patrols intended to eliminate the chance of surprise.

Smith was impressed with the mission at Bitokara, where he shared a three-room house with a large porch with other members of the headquarters staff. The religious who had run the mission were at Rabaul, under "protective custody" of the Japanese army. Left behind was a complete theological library, most of the books in German. Smith ordered that the priest's vestments and the church equipment be turned over to the Australians, including a beautifully bound German bible. Smith described the mission's setting: "In the yard were royal palms, bougainvillea, flame trees, croton bushes, hibiscus, and lime and orange trees. The view from the front porch of the Mission House out over Garua Harbor was suitable material for a travel poster" (NB, 38).

Most of the men at headquarters slept in jungle hammocks, which had attached mosquito nets with zipper openings. Once, General Shepherd, visiting the Fifth Marines, decided to sleep in a hammock. He somehow got turned over in the middle of the night and could not get back upright or get out of the hammock. He struggled in silence for a half-hour before he righted himself again. He had not wanted anybody to know of his situation!

Shortly after settling into the Mission House, Smith was informed that the navy was sending two PT boat squadrons to be based at Garua Harbor. Their main base was at Finschhafen, but since the Fifth Marines had secured the northern coast up to San Remo Plantation, Garua Harbor would be better for locating Japanese shipping for destruction. Smith was elated: "We were glad to learn that the PT boats were coming. It gave us a tangible reason for capturing Talasea. Marines are willing to fight hard if they feel that what they are fighting for is essential for the war effort. Many of the officers and men had a feeling that the Talasea campaign had been conducted for the purpose of making a communiqué. The arrival of the PT boat squadrons helped dispel this idea" (NB, 43).

PT boats were attacked by friendly aircraft on at least two occasions. One occurred off Cape Hoskins, where two Australian Beaufort bombers mistook them for Japanese. The two PT boats suffered over eight dead, and all twenty-six surviving members of the crews were wounded. The lieutenant in command of the PT squadron, a man named Thompson from Smith's alma mater, expressed to Smith his bitterness and frustration. Smith was senior officer present but had nothing to do with the sailors, who were directly under the control of the Seventh Fleet. An Australian major arrived at Smith's headquarters to conduct an investigation of the tragic accident at the same time as Thompson arrived. Smith was afraid they would have a fight, but the Australian was most apologetic, and the two men went their ways apparently satisfied. The second occasion, and sequel to this story, is that Thompson was later fired upon by two Marine Corsairs; he fought back, bringing down one of the planes. The surviving Corsair called for help and sank both PT boats, wounding several men, including Thompson. Smith thought that PT boats should be used only at night unless specific fail-safe signals had been arranged to prevent such incidents.

General Rupertus had not visited the Fifth Marines since it had been ordered to the Willaumez Peninsula, so he scheduled a tour, arriving when the Second Battalion was at the San Remo Plantation. He mentioned a desire to see the battalion, in its remote outpost location. When he was told there was no way to get there except by boat, he was less anxious to take the time for a visit. That prompted him to suggest that an airfield be built at San Remo. Smith dutifully sent a captain there to make recommendations. The captain estimated the number of coconut trees that would have to be removed and the amount of earth to be moved by bulldozer. Added construction equipment was requested from the First Marine Division; it did not arrive, and no field was ever built.

General Rupertus was not finished with the Fifth Marines yet! He also suggested that it build a road from the original landing beach across the peninsula to Bitokara. The advantage of the road would be to eliminate about forty miles from the supply runs from Cape Gloucester. However, as Smith pointed out, supplies would still have to be distributed to Talasea, the Waru villages, and San Remo Plantation, thus nullifying any gain from the project. The division engineer, Col. Frank E. Fenton, was sent to assess the situation and ultimately recommended against the proposal. Smith would recall, "Fenton . . . told me later, however, that the Division, in spite of his adverse report, had directed him to send the entire engineer battalion to Talasea to undertake this project. Notice of impending relief from the Army caused the matter to be dropped" (NB, 44).

With the capture of western New Britain, a well-trained amphibious division was less crucial to MacArthur's operations. Admiral Chester Nimitz, commander in chief of the Pacific Fleet, wrote to MacArthur that he needed the First Marine Division to begin preparations for the Palau operation prior to 1 June 1944.[6]

The Fifth Marines was getting ready to leave its jungle outposts for some other island, but it was likely to be the last tropical jungle terrain its men would have to fight and die for. Relief by the army was coming.

In early April I had received advance information that the 40th Infantry Division was going to relieve the First Marine Division and that the Division would go to the south Pacific for rehabilitation. On April 11th, I was notified that advance representatives of the Army Regiment which was to relieve us would arrive the following day, and that I personally was to return to Cape Gloucester on that date and assume the duties of Assistant Division Commander as the relief of General Shepherd who had been detached to the First Brigade. I turned over the regiment to Buse on April 12th and returned to Cape Gloucester by the same plane that brought up the Army officers of the 40th Division. I found that the regiment which was relieving us was commanded by Colonel John U. Calkins, of the class of 1911 from the University of California. (NB, 46)

Operations on the island of New Britain have been criticized as unnecessary to the subsequent movements in the Pacific. However, MacArthur wanted to operate along the New Guinea coastline without being threatened by Japanese forces that were known to be operating from Rabaul. MacArthur also wanted to control the air and waters of the Dampier Strait, between New Guinea and New Britain. The Joint Chiefs of Staff agreed with him; consequently the Allies eliminated the threat by occupying the western portion of New Britain.

Rupertus wrote to Vandegrift, his friend of many years, about the conclusion of the Cape Gloucester campaign, "We have learned much, [from] our errors from Guadalcanal, and I feel that we have profited by them in this operation. It has been one of the smoothest, most coordinated operations that it has been my experience to participate in, even including our peacetime exercises."[7]

Smith contributed to the success, with his professionalism and ability to adapt to a fluid situation, such as the Fifth Marines found itself in at the Willaumez Peninsula. He sums up the affair:

> In retrospect, the Talasea operation was a small affair, but it was not a simple operation. It was the longest small boat shore-to-shore operation conducted by Marines in World War II. Also, it was conducted against opposition without the benefit of air support or Naval gunfire support. Certainly no regiment ever had a longer or a more tenuous supply line. Our casualties during the first two days were greater than those of the entire Division at Cape Gloucester for the first two days. Our daily casualties were as follows:

DATE	WIA	KIA
6 March 1944	71	13
7 March	10	1
8 March	31	3
9 March	2	0
12 March	1	0
15 March	3	1
16 March	4	0
	122	18

> We killed about 200 Japanese and captured 150. During the course of one month the regiment had cleared the Japanese out of an area equal to that of Guam. (NB, 46)

Total American marine and naval losses for the New Britain campaign were 450 killed and 845 wounded in action.[8]

4

The Russell Islands (R&R)

At the end of the New Britain campaign, O. P. Smith hoped to retain command of the Fifth Marines, but instead he was appointed assistant division commander to replace General Shepherd. Vandegrift had promised Shepherd a command of greater responsibility, and the opportunity came when the First Marine Provisional Brigade was formed from the newly reconstituted Fourth Marines and the Twenty-second Marines, along with supporting arms and services. The brigade performed well in the capture of Guam. Later it was expanded to become the Sixth Marine Division, which took part in the Okinawa campaign. Shepherd performed extremely well as a large-formation battlefield commander.

Smith left Talasea on 12 April 1944 for Cape Gloucester, where he found that Shepherd had left the previous day. He was also informed that two officers had recently been dispatched to the Russell Islands, in the Solomons group, to lay out a camp before the First Marine Division arrived there for a period of rest. The division was to be relieved by the Fortieth Infantry Division, a California National Guard division that had been at Guadalcanal. To Smith's delight, several of the officers of the army division were classmates from the University of California, and he enjoyed their company. It also made the exchange of command much easier to negotiate.

When Smith became assistant division commander, news arrived that the marines would soon be under the command of the navy and would return to the South Pacific after their well-earned period of replenishment, of "R&R"—rest and recreation. MacArthur had only reluctantly released his best division, but most of the fighting anticipated in his drive to the Philippines would be land battles, so there was less need for the amphibious expertise of the marines.

The First Marine Division was almost as battle-worn as it had been when it came out of the Guadalcanal campaign; tropical diseases had debilitated the division as much as the enemy. Malaria was widespread throughout the ranks, and the physical equipment of the division was in poor condition. An agreement was reached with the Fortieth Division to exchange some items, such as telephone wire, signal equipment, and vehicles, but very little was actually turned over, because the marine equipment was battered from the arduous jungle campaign.

Two important visitors to Cape Gloucester were Brig. Gen. William J. Donovan, head of the Office of Strategic Services, and General MacArthur. Donovan was returning from a tour of the southwest Pacific, searching for areas where his type of work could be of benefit to the war effort. He told Smith, with whom he stayed during his visit, that MacArthur was opposed to such tactics and that consequently he generally avoided the Philippine area.

MacArthur had not visited Cape Gloucester since the marines captured it, and nobody at division headquarters knew that he was coming. He was en route to observe the landings at Hollandia and decided, on the spur of the moment, to visit "his marines." On 17 April, at about dusk, the call came to headquarters that MacArthur had just landed and was on his way to the division command post. Smith relates what happened: "The General had with him a couple of photographers, a couple of newspapermen, and a member or two of his staff. They came up on the porch of the General's quarters and General MacArthur posed with General Rupertus for a picture. Then the General shook hands all around. He was very affable and gave you the impression that he was very glad to see you again (although he had never seen you before). The handshaking and pictures did not take two minutes. The party then departed for the beach to re-embark" (RI, 48).

On the day after MacArthur's visit, the first echelon of ships arrived to transport the division out of the war zone. The navy was prepared to take on the marines and their supplies, but according to the navy, it had to be on a tactical-move basis. That meant that items needed first would be loaded last. Smith argued that they were making an administrative move, not a tactical move, and that they needed every inch of space the ship's holds could give them. The question was eventually settled in Smith's favor after a sharp radio message was received from Southwest Pacific Area command instructing the naval officer to load in accordance to the marines' needs.

On 28 April, Maj. Gen. Rapp Brush, commander of the Fortieth Division, arrived with the second echelon of ships, which was bringing in his division and was to embark the marines for the Russells. As soon as Brush arrived, Rupertus left for the Russells by air; Smith was left to bring out the second and third echelons of troops.

Also on 28 April, Smith received a dispatch telling him of his promotion to brigadier general. All that was required was a physical and an eye examination. His aide was surprised to learn that Smith could not read all of the optical test without glasses. However, if one's vision could be corrected with glasses to twenty-twenty, it was considered acceptable. Smith was getting to that age when many people need glasses to read small print.

One final problem remained—the division could not move all of its men and material in the vessels assigned to it. Rupertus had been aware of this situation before he left Cape Gloucester; he stopped at Guadalcanal, where he was able to obtain the use of twelve more LSTs. The added tonnage enabled Smith to load and transport all of the division from Cape Gloucester and to pick up scattered units and detachments at Finschhafen, Goodenough Island, and other locations. The last of the transports sailed for the Russells on 4 May 1944. Smith reflected, "We saw New Britain Island disappear over the horizon with few regrets" (RI, 50).

Naval ships have one thing that marines envy—food that can be prepared properly and served in reasonable comfort. Smith enjoyed several good meals, baths, and movies en route to the Russell Islands. He had intended to stay aboard for a steak dinner, but as soon as the ship arrived at Macquitti Bay, on Pavuvu Island, Rupertus sent word for him to report immediately. Rupertus and Selden were leaving for Washington the following day for business and to take leave. The main item of business to be discussed in Washington was the question of rotation. The division had several thousand men who had been out of the country for more than twenty-four months, and it needed replacements before attempting another island assault. When Rupertus and Selden left on 9 May, Smith was left temporarily in command.

Smith's arrival at Pavuvu was made especially joyful by a dispatch advising him that he had a new granddaughter—Gail Benedict, born on 23 April. His older daughter, Virginia, had married Charles C. Benedict, Jr., who had graduated from West Point in January 1943. He had carried on a family tradition by selecting the Air Corps; his father, Charles Calvert Benedict, Sr., who had graduated from the academy in 1915, had been killed in an air crash at Langley Field in 1925.[1] It is significant that this piece of information is included in General Smith's notes, because he avoided writing about family affairs.

Pavuvu is a part of the Russell Island group of the Solomons. Located about seventy-five miles northwest of Guadalcanal, the Russells had been viewed as a threat to future operations in the Solomons, so Adm. William F. Halsey had ordered their capture in February 1943 (Operation Cleanslate). The Japanese had used the Russells as a staging area to reinforce Guadalcanal and for the successful evacuation of their troops from that island, in spite of the powerful U.S. naval presence.[2] The Third Marine Raider Battalion, under the command of Col. Harry B. "Harry the Horse" Liversedge, had assaulted Pavuvu on 21 February 1943, with the army's 159th Infantry following it ashore.

The landing had been unopposed, but the conditions ashore had been a harbinger of things to come. The Raiders had stayed on the island for four weeks and had been severely debilitated. A third of the men had developed tropical skin rashes, while every man had lost weight because of the heat and scanty field rations. The severe physical conditions on the island had blunted the finely honed cutting edge of these elite troops.[3]

The two principal islands of the Russells, Pavuvu and Banika, are separated by Sunlight Channel. Pavuvu was mostly unoccupied when the First Marine Division came, except for a small army radar detachment. Banika, however, was a busy naval and army supply base, and a large number of aircraft were using its two airfields. The camp for the First Marine Division was located in a six-hundred-acre coconut grove on a finger of land that was surrounded by Macquitti and Hooper Bays. The site was covered with rotting coconuts and palm fronds, which had to be removed. The smell was powerful, and it permeated clothing, tents, and food in equal measure. Even after the disposal of the coconuts on the ground, the ones in the trees caused several severe injuries to unsuspecting men below.

Foot traffic under the trees soon turned the ground into a sea of mud, because the drainage was inadequate, and also because the sun could not penetrate the thick canopy of palm fronds. Vehicle traffic had to be confined to roads already constructed by the Seabees.

It was the understanding of the division headquarters section that there was a completed camp ready for the division's occupation, but when the men arrived they found a bivouac—not a camp. A temporary command post was set up in an old plantation house that overlooked Macquitti Bay. There was a kitchen attached, and the Seabees had placed screening on the front and rear porches. Water had to be obtained from wells; engineers eventually drilled seven wells, with a capacity of two hundred thousand gallons per day.

Smith moved into the plantation house with Rupertus. "The front porch was used as a living room and bar. On one side of the house were two small bedrooms occupied by General Rupertus and myself. On the other side beyond the hall was a large room in which the staff was billeted. We ate on the back porch. The house was surrounded by a hedge of croton bushes. At the front was an arbor of yellow hibiscus. Along one side of the house were single and double hibiscus. In the yard was a large mango tree, a flame tree, lime trees and bougainvillea" (RI, 53). The gardens and flowers around the plantation house were described in some detail; his experienced eye picked up on those things, about which he had more than a working knowledge.

General Geiger had chosen Pavuvu as an area to rejuvenate the First Marine Division by flying over the site. From the air it looked like an ideal location, but had the general been on the ground, he might have changed his mind. The entire division, to a man, was discouraged at the conditions it found itself in after a period of prolonged combat.

The physical shortcomings of Pavuvu proved to be a hindrance to the restoration of the fighting spirit that the "Old Breed" had always been noted for. The camp lacked mess halls, galleys, showers, and roads, and the wells were only in the planning stages. The marines would have to build the camp themselves.

Training for the next operation was almost impossible, because of the lack of adequate space in which to maneuver, a vast shortage of equipment, and the need to construct the camp. Units were staging movement training among the tents of their neighbors. The shooting ranges were badly congested, because of the limited number that could be built. Also, the beaches could not be utilized to the fullest extent, due to the coral reefs that surrounded the island. Only cleared sections could be used by the LCVPs.

The first priority, as viewed by Smith, was an increase in the quality and quantity of rations.

The food had been bad at Cape Gloucester, with very little variety and very few fresh provisions. The men were not in very good physical condition. The purpose of the move to the Russell Islands was to rehabilitate the division for future operations. Authority was granted to increase the ration by twenty-five percent. It was assumed that fresh provisions in reasonable quantities would be furnished. We built reefer boxes on the beach to receive these stores but the reefer boxes were generally empty.... We obtained permission to slaughter the cattle which had previously belonged to the plantation on the islands and which were grazing in the coconut groves. There were about 600 head of these cattle.... They were sorry looking animals. We used LCM's as cattle boats. From various units we obtained cowboys who rounded up the cattle.... The slaughter was located in one of the buildings near the plantation house. The chief executioner was a hospital corpsman who was armed with a mallet.... The beef was stringy and tough, but it was fresh. After the slaughter house was operating at full capacity the Australian government decided it did not want to engage in that type of reverse lend-lease operations and we were directed to cease operations. (RI, 54)

Thereafter, most supplies came from depots on Banika Island.

General Rupertus left for Washington on 9 May after approving the plans to set up his CP on the hill overlooking West Bay and Hooper Bay. He instructed

Smith to set up an independent mess for himself, as well as some of the junior members of the staff, in the plantation house. Rupertus was living up to his reputation as "difficult" at best.

In order to set up a mess, Smith had to find an aide to run it for him. In his own words, "From the candidates for the job I selected First Lieutenant Burdette F. Bevan. He had been a Marine from 1930 to 1934, then he had gone back to college and gotten his law degree. When the war broke out he came in again and obtained a commission via the Officer Candidate School and the Reserve Officers' School. He had been a platoon leader, a legal officer, and a battalion quartermaster. In the field it is not essential that an aide have all the social graces. The essential qualification is to be a good forager. I never regretted the choice of Bevan as an aide" (RI, 55).

Food became the main preoccupation of the division. Large gardens had been established on Guadalcanal, which gave an occasional treat of fresh vegetables. Visiting ships were also a source of supplies. The natural thing for the marines to do was to fish, not only for food but for relaxation. Smith had caught two barracudas on one fishing expedition, using the same crash boats he had used off Talasea. He and Bevan had selected a cook, Sgt. Brown Smith, who had ten years' experience in the restaurant of the Supreme Court of the United States. Their choice was a fortunate one and the envy of other messes.

The men had to be constantly reminded not to use grenades to obtain fish, as they had done in Iceland. One delicacy peculiar to the area was the meat of alligators. The tails were considered delicious and highly desired for steaks. The local pigeon was hunted for food, but Smith complained that it had to be parboiled for six hours in order to be edible.

Smith and Bevan attended church services every Sunday. After trying out several of the Protestant denominations, they decided to attend the services conducted by a Chaplain Oakie. Oakie put a lot of energy into his sermons and talked a language to which most of the men could relate. On 30 May, a joint memorial service for the division's dead was conducted by the three faiths represented in the Chaplain Corps—Catholic, Jewish, and Protestant. The Catholic chaplain conducted a Mass, the Jewish chaplain recited several prayers, and the Protestant chaplain delivered a short sermon. Smith described what happened: "The Protestant chaplain was a very serious minded young fellow who inveighed against the futility of war and the uselessness of the sacrifices. We were honoring the dead of the Division and it was not particularly appropriate to question before the men the value of their sacrifice" (RI, 57).

Most of the marines would recall Pavuvu with disfavor, mostly for the rotting coconuts and for the large number of rats that inhabited the island. The coconuts were eventually cleaned up, but the rats were never brought under control. After the camp was organized, it was easy to see its merits. It was true that Pavuvu lacked much room to train and maneuver troops, but it was an island that the men might have seen as very pretty, if they had been farther away from the reality of war. The most rewarding aspect of Pavuvu was the fact that it was free of malaria. The veterans had something to be thankful about.

Even though Pavuvu was supposed to be malaria free, the division surgeon, a believer in atabrine tablets as a preventative measure, prescribed six tablets per week for every man in the division. Very shortly, most of the men were showing the well-known atabrine tan. Smith stopped taking the tablets, but it took over a month for the yellowish color to disappear from his skin.

On 15 May, Smith took a trip to Guadalcanal to renew some old acquaintances. He stayed with Brig. Gen. Pedro A. del Valle, who at that time was corps artillery officer for the Third Amphibious Corps. Smith also visited with Generals Roy S. Geiger, Merwin H. Silverthorn, and Allen H. Turnage, and he was asked to observe a training session of the Third Marine Division for the coming invasion of Guam. The availability of amphibian tractors would make the capture of Guam easier than when the Marine Corps Schools had tackled the problem in the late thirties, when landing forces had had to rely on the old-style naval boat to get ashore. Now the Third Amphibious Corps was stressing the importance of transferring from lcvps to the amphibian tractors. The same technique was to be used at Peleliu and at Okinawa.

Smith always enjoyed the company of other marine officers, especially those of his own generation, and the exchange of ideas about the new tactics demanded by new situations and circumstances. The development of new equipment had rendered some of the older Marine Corps School solutions obsolete. For instance, the early plan for the assault on Guam included initial landings in the inlets of Talafofo and Inarajan, because of the reefs surrounding the good beaches. As it happened, the Third Amphibious Corps actually went over the reefs with the amphibious tractors and landed at Asan and Agat, where there were excellent beaches near vital objectives.

The 26th of May was a busy day on Pavuvu. First the commanding general of First Marine Air Wing, Gen. James T. Moore, made a short visit with Smith in the morning. Later in the day Smith went to a farewell party for Admiral Halsey. It seems that the dividing line between the South Pacific Area and the Southwest Pacific Area had been moved from the northern Solomons to the Russells. Naval establishments in the South Pacific were no longer needed, and Halsey was making the rounds to say good-bye to people he had worked with. Smith would recall, "On behalf of the Island Command of the Russells, he was presented with an inlaid ebony cane. It was apparent that Admiral Halsey was quite affected in bidding good-bye to the South Pacific" (RI, 59).

The tempo of activity increased when Col. Dudley Brown, head of the Planning Section of the Third Amphibious Corps, arrived to start planning for the Palau operation. Supplies were arriving at last, and the division was starting to take on a more positive outlook. The arrival of replacements was most welcome. The replacements meant reliefs for several of the officers and men who had been with the division for over twenty-four months. Lt. Col. R. P. Ross was assigned as executive officer of the First Marines, commanded by Lewis B. "Chesty" Puller. According to Smith, "It had taken a long time to convince him [Puller] that in a unit the size of a regiment a staff was essential and should be used. I had had Ross in the First Battalion, Sixth Marines. For a short period he had been my Executive Officer and he was an exceptional one. He was exactly what Puller needed" (RI, 59–60).

Early in June, the Joint Chiefs of Staff had sent their concept of the Palau operation to Third Amphibious Corps on Guadalcanal. Smith went there personally to get a copy of the plan and to plead for LCVPs to be used for training purposes. He returned to Pavuvu with the promise of forty boats. The original plan included the invasion of Peleliu, Anguar, Babelthaup, and Yap. An army corps plus the First Marine Division would be assigned the task. Shortly after the plan was issued, Halsey's Third Fleet found that Leyte was not heavily defended; when Halsey so reported to the Joint Chiefs, they decided to cancel all of the above operations, except Peleliu and Anguar. An army corps, made up of the Seventh, Seventy-seventh, and Ninety-sixth Divisions, was loaned to MacArthur to speed up his timetable for the Leyte operation. The main reason for taking Peleliu was to set up air bases to support an invasion of Mindanao, some five hundred miles away. Control of the Palaus and the Marianas (which were to be attacked first) would cut off the Japanese bases that remained in the Central Pacific. Finally, the Palaus would provide several excellent anchorages. Once the Leyte invasion was under way, Peleliu was no longer needed, but the directive for the First Marine Division never changed; it was its responsibility to take Peleliu, so Smith started to work on the plan to do just that (OH, 124–26).

By the time Rupertus and Selden returned to Pavuvu on 21 June, Smith had completed plans for the landings on Peleliu. He submitted them to Rupertus, who approved them without much comment and detailed Smith to locate a suitable site for a rehearsal landing. Smith found a place called Kaylan Point, and on 30 June a rehearsal landing was carried out by the Seventh Marines, who went over the reef in the amphibian tractors. Smith and Rupertus were observing the landing exercise from different boats. When Smith went ashore he was told that Rupertus had been injured. "I found him on the beach receiving first aid and in considerable pain. He had gone ashore in an amphibian tractor and debarked. After witnessing the exercise for a short time he decided to re-embark in the amphibian tractor. While climbing aboard . . . the hand-hold had given away and he had fallen backwards on the rough coral where the amphibian tractor was parked. He thought he had a badly sprained ankle. It developed that he had a broken ankle, which laid him up for a couple of months" (RI, 61).

Smith was carrying out the duties of assistant division commander in an exemplary manner, but serving under Rupertus was difficult in the best of times. The ankle injury only made things worse. Rupertus had had a varied career in the Marine Corps and had served in many different stations, and he had performed to satisfaction. While he was stationed in China in 1929, his wife and two children, a son and a daughter, had died in a scarlet fever epidemic. Rupertus had turned from a congenial associate to a surly introvert with a reputation for being moody and unsmiling. His best-known characteristic affected Smith directly—Rupertus had a long-standing dislike of and distrust for subordinates.[4]

According to Smith, "General Rupertus had a fixation about Assistant Division Commanders; he didn't like them underfoot, and he told me when I got to Pavuvu 'Now I am setting up this new command post up on the hill here. . . . I suggest you set up a separate mess over in the plantation house.' So, I . . . told him, 'General, I should keep abreast of what's going on in the Division, so you should let me take some of the junior members of the staff section to live with me so I can keep abreast'" (OH, 128–29).

Smith went on to say, "I was only a guest at Division Headquarters. I was never consulted about anything tactical, or anything like that. I went around, inspected the training, and periodically I'd come in and tell the general what I saw. Our relations weren't buddy-buddy, but there was no bitterness or anything like that. He treated General Shepherd exactly the same way on Cape Gloucester. He didn't allow General Shepherd to eat in the Division mess. . . . The only time I ever went over to the mess was when some VIP was there and he thought he ought to have me over" (OH, 129). Queried further about why Rupertus acted as he did, Smith answered, "It may have been the way General Vandegrift treated him. I don't know [hearty laughter can be heard at this point on the recording]. I haven't the least idea" (OH, 129).

It was common knowledge that many of the men in the division had a very low opinion of Rupertus, especially for his poor performance on Guadalcanal. Vandegrift had awarded Rupertus the Navy Cross for his conduct on Tulagi, but the men saw Rupertus in a different light. He was arrogant and had acted in a panic, without justification, when the battle for Tulagi was just starting. A battalion commander (later a retired brigadier general) observed, "He [Rupertus] just sat on his duff in a bunker and let others do the dirty work."[5]

Left: Smith's aide-de-camp, Lieutenant Bevan, and a king mackerel on Pavuvu, July 1944. *Courtesy of* MCUA.

Below: Lt. Gen. Alexander Vandegrift, Commandant of the Marine Corps, arrives at Pavuvu Island, Russell Islands, to visit the First Marine Division, August 1944. *From left:* Brig. Gen. E. E. Hall, Brig. Gen. Gerald G. Thomas, Vandegrift, Colonel Selden, Admiral Fort, and Brigadier General Smith. *Courtesy of* MCUA.

Rupertus may have needed to rest his ankle, but a division preparing for battle needed its commanding general. Nonetheless, Rupertus was ordered to the United States for temporary duty as head of a promotion board for colonel and lieutenant colonel. Marines who remember that time and place feel that it was simply an act of kindness on the part of the commandant toward his friend of many years. Rupertus had remarried shortly before going overseas and had a new son, whom he had never seen.[6]

The command ship, USS *Mount McKinley,* dropped anchor off Pavuvu on 2 August with Rear Adm. George H. Fort on board as commander of the Western Attack Force. He was there to coordinate planning with the division. During the month of August, much effort went into the planning of the invasion of Peleliu. After an initial scheme of maneuver was approved by all command levels, landing exercises were carried out, and newly issued equipment was broken in for the ordeal ahead.

By 10 August, Guam had been secured. Shortly after, General Geiger flew into Pavuvu, where he reported to Admiral Fort on the *Mount McKinley.* Fort had received no orders naming Geiger to the post of Commanding General, Western Landing Force. With a flurry of communiqués back and forth from Pearl Harbor, the snafu was corrected; the appropriate authority was forthcoming to redesignate Geiger as the commanding general. From this point on, the staff of Third Amphibious Corps took over the planning of the Palau operation. Smith was sent to Pearl Harbor to secure permission for changes in the plans. He stayed with Gen. Julian Smith while at Pearl Harbor and enjoyed an evening at a large country estate, where life seemed to continue as if there were no war.

On his return to Pavuvu, Smith passed through Tarawa; he used the stop to observe the island and visualize the vicious battle that had taken place there. What amazed him most was its small size, that a full division could actually fit on the island for the seventy-two hours that the battle had raged. One of the casualties of the costly battle had been Col. H. R. Amey, who had been the adjutant to the First Battalion, Sixth Marines when Smith commanded it in Iceland. Smith found his grave in one of the small cemeteries where the dead had been buried as they fell. He was especially touched to see that the graves were well cared for and that the white sand had recently been groomed and reshaped.

The Peleliu operation was the first time that three of the generals of the Marine Corps with the last name of Smith came together to be a part of the same campaign. The senior Smith was Lt. Gen. Holland McTyeire Smith, nicknamed "Howling Mad" for his temper, which was not as bad as the press liked to portray. He was a strong personality and was America's foremost expert in conducting amphibious landings. His decision to relieve an army general under his command on Saipan remains a subject of debate. Gen. H. M. Smith was "a fighting general[,] . . . a patriotic warrior, the fiercely loyal, concerned, compassionate leader to whom his country was an obsession and his men a religion."[7]

Maj. Gen. Julian C. Smith had served in the Marine Corps for thirty-two years and had commanded the Second Marine Division at Tarawa. He was well liked by subordinates and superiors, especially for his willingness to be a team player. His quiet demeanor kept him from getting as much credit for his accomplishments as his performances warranted. He was known within the Corps as an expert rifleman, and he helped foster the fine art of marksmanship throughout his tenure as an officer. Upon retirement, he became president of the National Rifle Association.

The three General Smiths were often confused with one another. Several characteristics were common to all of them. The most obvious were their love of the Marine Corps and their respect for the individual marines who carried out their orders. All three had entered the Marine Corps shortly after college. All had served with dedication, and all had been sent to command and staff schools. They were all strong leaders of impeccable character and personal integrity. They were not "ass kickers," in the vernacular, yet nobody ever had a problem understanding who was in charge.

The operational plan for Peleliu prescribed five landing teams abreast going ashore on the southwest coast on D day. Naval gunfire and air strikes were to start nine days before D day and support the troops until they were well established ashore. The First and Fifth Marines were to pivot to the left (north) and advance up the island. The Seventh Marines was to pivot to the right and sweep south to the coast. A reinforced battalion was scheduled to take the island of Ngesebus after the capture of Peleliu. As soon as the islands had been secured, airdromes were to be prepared and naval bases developed. The division was to stay until relieved by army troops.

By late August, training exercises had been completed, replacements assigned to units, and new equipment inspected. It was at this point that O. P. Smith was involved in a necessary but distasteful part of command—the relief of a fellow officer. When Smith left the Fifth Marines, Lt. Col. Henry W. Buse had been the temporary commander of the regiment until Col. William S. Fellers had become available. Fellers had come to the regiment after a brilliant stint as division G-4. Vandegrift had promised him a regiment, but it was a poor choice, according to Smith:

In observing the training of the Fifth Marines, I had noted that Fellers was irascible and pretty hard on his subordinates. Although I would not have run the regiment in the manner he did, I considered he was acting in character. He had always been given to sounding off. Walt (Lt. Col. L. W. Walt), the Executive Officer of the Fifth Marines, who was very close to Selden, came to Selden and stated that he was considerably concerned about the regiment; that it was impossible to get decisions out of Fellers; that he was unreasonable; and that the officers and men were losing confidence in him. Selden talked to me about the affair, and I agreed to watch Fellers more carefully to check on Walt's report. . . . I came to the conclusion that it would be to the best interests of the regiment and the Division to relieve Fellers. Selden and I then put the question up to Rupertus, who decided to send Fellers home under the rotation policy. . . . Fellers might have made it, but the chances are that he would have cracked up. (RI, 76–77)

When General Vandegrift visited the division before it embarked for the Peleliu campaign, Smith took him and his entourage to all the bivouacs, because Rupertus was unable to leave his quarters. Rupertus presented an air of optimism to the commandant, who left for Pearl Harbor feeling good about what he had seen (RI, 77).[8] One has to wonder about what has been left unsaid on the part of the commandant. Could he have really been satisfied with Rupertus's condition on the eve of a potentially hard campaign, when so many young lives were at stake?

During one of the training rehearsals, Smith was confronted by a gravely concerned General Geiger, who had not been informed of Rupertus's ankle injury and consequent inability to go ashore with his staff on the training exercise. Smith said, "I assured General Geiger that in the remaining two weeks before the landing I felt General Rupertus's ankle would mend sufficiently to permit him to carry on" (RI, 83). General Geiger's reaction was, "If I had known I'd have relieved him." Smith had felt that it was up to General Rupertus to tell General Geiger about his limitations, and out of loyalty to Rupertus, Smith had said nothing (OH, 130).

Smith had been quiet about the accident ever since it happened, but his position as assistant division commander made him worry about Rupertus's incapacity, perhaps more than Rupertus himself. Asked what his function was, Smith answered: "To observe the training and to stand by in case the division commander breaks his leg. The humorous thing was that it did happen on Pavuvu. I said nothing to anybody about this incident, but I began to worry as D day approached. I went to Dr.—whatever his name was—and I said, 'Look, doctor, frankly, is the General going to be able to make it for Peleliu?' He told me he thought he would, but he would have to use a cane. I said okay. And I never said anything" (OH, 129–30).

Late in August, the division embarked for the invasion of Peleliu. With 1,489 officers and 26,995 men, it was slightly over its authorized strength (RI, 81–82). After a great deal of discussion, the role of the assistant division commander was clarified:

> General Rupertus told me that at Peleliu he wanted me to function as General Shepherd had at Cape Gloucester. The situation at Peleliu, however would not be comparable. . . . Three regiments were landing in assault at Peleliu. If I were sent ashore in advance of the Division Headquarters, it was logical and proper that I, as senior officer ashore, should coordinate the attack of the three regiments until the arrival of Division Headquarters. I told the General frankly that to send me ashore in advance of himself with no authority to control the situation ashore put me in a very anomalous situation; I could not escape responsibility for what transpired ashore. I suggested that he organize two command groups, a skeleton group with me, and the bulk of the staff with him. I would go in early and set up an advance command post. . . . After considerable discussion, the General agreed. (RI, 71)

Smith embarked on a troop transport, the USS *Elmore,* with a small command group that included Colonel Hankins. General Rupertus's leg was not well enough to make the landing. A final rehearsal landing was scheduled for the last "fine tuning" of the sequence of events ahead of the division, with a final critique at Third Amphibious Corps headquarters. The critique would give everybody a chance to get acquainted and to do any last-minute adjustments. In general, most of the participants thought that the rehearsal went as well as could have been expected. On 8 September, the convoy departed for the Palau Islands.

5

PELELIU

The Palau Islands were to be an important part of the navy's forward base structure for operations against Ulithi, Truk, and Yap. General MacArthur wanted them neutralized also in order to secure his right flank as he pursued his much-heralded "Return to the Philippines." By the time the First Marine Division assaulted Peleliu, however, its significance as a military base had been eroded. Just days before the assault was to take place, Admiral Halsey requested that the operation be canceled, but Admiral Nimitz disagreed and ordered its capture as planned. Thus one of the most costly battles the First Marine Division ever fought was also an unnecessary one.

In many respects, Peleliu is the forgotten battle of World War II. The armed services edition of the *Complete History of World War II,* which was made available to most veterans shortly after the war, gives only a cursory mention of the horrific battle.[1]

Smith's voyage from the Russells to Peleliu proved to be a pleasant experience. The ship's captain was an accommodating and innovative officer who had indoctrinated his crew with the importance of the assault troops, which ensured good relations between the troops and the sailors. Cordial relations were not always the norm between the two naval services.

Smith was assigned bunk space in the flag (admiral's and general's) quarters, sharing a double-room suite with Col. Joseph F. Hankins and Col. William Harrison. They frequently ate at the captain's mess, where they had some interesting discussions. "There were some lively arguments in the mess; the captain was definitely anti–New Deal and 'Willie' Harrison was very much pro–New Deal. Hankins stuck to the proposition that you should never argue over religion and

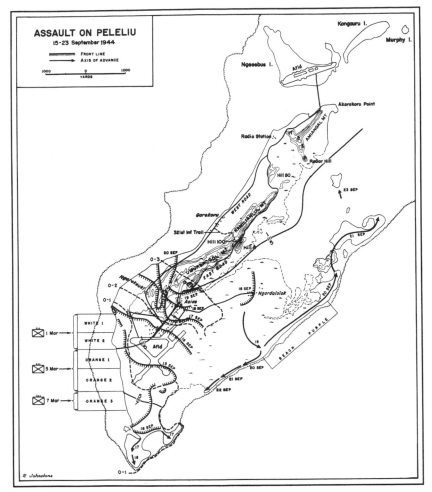

Peleliu. *Courtesy* MCHC.

politics [Smith doesn't tell us about his own views]. . . . I read or played cards. My official reading consisted of a review of the Division and Task Force orders for the operation. When that was finished I resorted to the ship's library. During the trip I was able to read *A Yankee from Olympus* and *The Late George Apley*" (RI, 3).

Documents captured on Saipan were an important source of information about the defenses on Peleliu, but aerial photos did not give much indication of the disposition of the troops, and they gave even less information about the extremely rugged terrain. Consequently, the planners assumed that Peleliu would be defended in the same way as the islands that had been captured. The Japanese tactic was to use a strong force to oppose the landing, hoping to drive it back into the sea. The logic was not faulty; the most vulnerable part of an assault is the first few minutes the troops start ashore.

The planners could not know that new tactics awaited them. The Japanese would fight from a series of defensive lines, which would prove extremely costly to the marines. Consequently, the division should have used siege tactics shortly after it came ashore, instead of the costly assault-and-maneuver tactics that most of the battalions employed.

A marine officer later wrote, "The new [Japanese] doctrine discouraged the traditional grandiose suicidal attacks in favor of limited but stinging counter-attacks. The objective was to play for time, bleed the enemy and fight a protracted battle of attrition. The deadly significance of these revised tactics would become evident during the Marine's last three great battles of the war: Peleliu, Iwo Jima and Okinawa."[2] Or, put another way, "It was easier, and less costly, to mow down *banzai* attacks than to dig stubborn defenders out of fortified positions."[3]

Peleliu never received much attention from the press, because Rupertus had sent letters to all of the correspondents and to his regimental commanders (Smith never received a copy!) predicting what a "quickie" Peleliu was going to be—probably faster than Tarawa. Smith disagreed with such optimism, but as it turned out, many correspondents, seeing little sense in covering such a small operation, left for the Philippines. At the time of the Peleliu operation, the navy's best amphibious landing team—Gen. Holland H. Smith, Adm. Richmond Kelly Turner, and Adm. Raymond A. Spruance—was away in the Marianas, its attention not on Peleliu but on the next operation, Okinawa.

O. P. Smith was scheduled to land ninety minutes after H hour to set up an advance command post. The group consisted of Smith and his aide (Lieutenant Bevan) and representatives of G-1 (personnel), G-2 (intelligence), G-3 (operations), and G-4 (supply). Col. James Smith was communications officer, and Col. Joe Hankins functioned as headquarters commandant. They were accompanied by a dozen enlisted men.

Smith left the *Elmore* for one of the boat-wave control vessels closer to shore. "The target was practically blanketed with explosions. Yet the Japanese in their caves lived through it. The naval gunfire ships by this time had shifted their fire to the north flank and the high ground behind the northern beaches. Columns of smoke were coming up from the area hit by rockets and naval gunfire and also, unfortunately, from some of our own burning amphibian tractors. This was not a very pleasant sight[;] . . . 26 of the amphibian tractors had been hit and put out of action" (RI, 17).

Smith set up the CP in a deep antitank ditch with a high bank facing the en-emy; it was on a road leading to the airfield, just inland from the coast. He quickly assessed the situation and then set about his first priority, that of making contact with his regiments. He was able to hook into the radio link for the Fifth Marines (Col. Harold "Bucky" Harris) and Seventh Marines (Col. Herman H. Hanneken), but he was unable to make contact with the First Marines (Col. Lewis B. Puller).

Within a couple of hours after setting up operations ashore, Smith was sur-prised by a visit from General Gieger, who had a tradition of being at the front lines when a battle was under way.

> I told General Geiger that the Corps Commander, according to the book, was not supposed to be on the beach at that early hour, with which he agreed but he said he had come ashore to find out why so many amphibian tractors were burning on the beaches. He also wanted to see the airfield. I told him that by climbing up the bank he could see the airfield about 200 yards ahead. . . .While General Geiger was on top of the bank, the Japanese sent over a couple of their 150 mm mortar shells. . . . General Geiger did not stay on the bank long. . . . With the sketchy reports we had, General Geiger and I esti-mated that there were approximately 250 casualties up to that time. In view of the fact that later reports showed that there were over 1200 casualties the first day, we were far short of the mark. (RI, 21–22)

The First Marines landed two battalions in assault against rugged wooded terrain that increased in elevation a thousand yards inland. The high ground dominated the airfield and the beaches, and losses were heavy in the leading as-sault units. Twenty amphibious tractors were lost on the first day; of the eighteen tanks assigned to the regiment, seventeen were knocked out en route to the beaches or on the beach. "As Puller prepared to leave the ship, [Captain] Talbot [com-mander of the transport] inquired if he, Puller, would be back for dinner. Puller pointed out that he expected to be fighting for some days to come. Captain Tal-bot claimed that the bombardment they had seen would allow the regiment to walk to its objectives unmolested. . . . Puller suggested that the Captain come ashore about 5:00 P.M., for dinner, and pick up a few souvenirs" (RI, 25–26).

The Fifth Marines landed two battalions in assault, against scattered resis-tance. The Third Battalion had cut a swath around the southern end of the airfield and had reached the eastern coast.

The Second Battalion, Seventh Marines had been selected as the division re-serve. The regiment's other battalions were to land to the right of the Fifth Ma-rines and swing to the right against a promontory in the southwestern portion of the island. In the event, fire from a small island on their right caused a lot of casualties with the amphibious tractors. However, the Third Battalion pushed across the island with the Fifth Marines, while the First Battalion ran into rugged terrain on the right of its sector and made little progress. The division reconnaissance company tried to assist the First Battalion, but it suffered heavy losses. Smith was not happy with the situation. "This was an improper use of the Reconnaissance Company, as there later developed several opportunities for employment of this company in the manner for which it had been trained" (RI, 30).

The first day ashore, the Seventh Marines had fallen short of its objectives but had secured, in conjunction with the Fifth Marines, enough room to deploy artillery. Smith finally got a telephone line to Puller later in the day. "He [Puller] did not ask for help and seemed confident that he could hold his own" (RI, 31–32).

"The first five days at Peleliu," said Smith, "were just as tough as Iwo Jima, but then it tapered off, and Iwo Jima kept on going. And of course, Peleliu was a smaller operation because we only had one division in assault and they had two and two-thirds divisions on Iwo Jima" (OH, 133). The casualties for the first day were ninety-two killed and 1,148 wounded, with fifty-eight missing, according to Smith. "These were very heavy losses and could not have been sustained for many days in succession without destroying the combat efficiency of the division" (RI, 34).

On the second day, 16 September 1944, General Rupertus came ashore and assumed command. Smith was thankful for the relief; "After orienting him on the situation, I gave a little thought to body comforts and began to look for rations and coffee" (RI, 37).

Rupertus later moved the CP to an old administration building closer to the airfield. Smith wistfully commented, "I remained down in the ditch. I was there on November 1st when I came back to Pavuvu. I did a lot of traveling around the division, and went in periodically to tell the General what I'd seen. I never sat in on any conferences on planning or anything like that. I just went around and talked to the battalion commanders" (OH, 139). Smith used an old litter for a bed. The ditch had been mined toward the beach. When the division engineer, Col. Frank Fenton, moved in with Smith's group, the mines were taken care of. Also, several Japanese bodies had to be buried deeper to kill the stench.

The marine attacks for each day followed an established routine. They started about 0700 with heavy artillery barrages. Usually the fighting ended around 1700, when the marines dug in for the night. Smith later wrote, "Long experience with the Japanese in rugged and overgrown country had taught us to eschew night attacks and be prepared for night counterattacks and infiltration efforts" (RI, 43).

The high ground north of the airfield was a maze of deep ravines with sides fifty to a hundred feet high, made up of coral formations; it was impossible to dig in for protection. Within the ravines were hundreds of caves, each with several exits and with connecting tunnels between. The Japanese were skilled in using the caves to advantage by firing their artillery or mortars and then rolling the weapons back into the interior of the caves before the marines could locate or attack them. "As an example of the density and character of the fortifications on Peleliu, an examination of the results of the six-day assault by the 1st Marines is revealing," explained Smith. "During this period, the 1st Marines overran and liquidated the occupants of the following installations: 3 block houses with 4-foot reinforced walls[,] 17 pill boxes[,] 144 prepared caves. . . . The 1st Marines engaged [here] in one of the bitterest fights in the Pacific War" (RI, 46).

Smith was kept outside of the inner circle of officers who conducted operations during the battle for Peleliu. Rupertus used Smith the same way that he had used his previous ADC, General Shepherd—that is, ignored him.

Once the Division Commander is operating in his CP, the Assistant Division Commander becomes a contact man whose job is to visit the combat units and the rear areas and keep the Division Commander advised as to the condition of the troops, the status of the unloading, and the progress being made by the troops. The Division Commander, of course, makes similar visits, thus doubling the observations. The Assistant Division Commander is also available for odd jobs where a senior officer is needed, for example, to attend conferences or take charge of a detached operation. After General Rupertus had come ashore and taken over at the CP I started to move about. (RI, 59–60)

Smith continues his narrative: "To visit 'Lewie' Puller and the 1st Marines was always an adventure. Puller believed in keeping his CP well forward. . . . It was a hot day and Puller was stripped to the waist. He was smoking his battered pipe; characteristically he held the pipe between his incisors and talked out of the side of his mouth. . . . A day or so later . . . I was able to replenish Puller's supply of pipe tobacco from a supply which Captain Graham had very kindly sent in from the *Mt. McKinley*" (RI, 61–62).

Maj. Gen. Julian C. Smith and Adm. Theodore S. Wilkinson, CO, Third Amphibious Force, toured parts of the southern end of the island that had already been secured. O. P. Smith carried out the unenviable job of escorting these dignitaries in such a way that they could see how difficult the fighting was and at the same time stay out of harm's way.

Smith's command post was called "Sleepy Hollow," because the artillery blasts were deadened by the high banks around it. His staff made the best of what it had. A mess tent was set up along with tents for the entire staff, and a well was dug (fresh water could be found by digging three feet in the sand) to provide for showers. Smith shared his tent with his aide, Lieutenant Bevan. The staff received occasional treats from Captain Harrison of the uss *Elmore* and Captain Graham of the uss *Mount McKinley* in the form of ice water and ice cream, which was sent ashore in large metal milk jugs.

"When the 321st RCT [regimental combat team] came over from Anguar on September 21st, Brigadier General Marcus Bell, the Assistant Division Commander of the 81st Division, came to Peleliu for liaison purposes. He was accompanied by his aide, Captain Clayton. General Bell had no facilities for taking care of himself, and General Rupertus asked me to put him up at my mess. He, therefore, pitched his small blackout tent in our area and he and Clayton ate in our mess. Clayton had a lot to learn about being an aide in the field and Bevan gave him a few pointers" (RI, 69).

Smith had argued with General Geiger that though the First Marines did need to be relieved, it could be done by the Fifth Marines, which had completed its mission on the east shore. "I suggested to General Geiger that he give us an opportunity to do this, but he was adamant. We really needed another regiment to finish the job" (RI, 81). The First Marines were relieved on 23 September by the 321st RCT and departed for the Russells on 2 October.

Col. Chesty Puller fought his regiment until it was a shattered force. He was fearless in combat and demanded the same from all under his command. He demanded, and got, total obedience to his orders. He was not, however, universally respected by his own men, or by his peers, especially after his performance at Peleliu. Many marines thought that he had overreached his abilities as a regimental commander. Many believed he displayed a callous disregard for the lives of his men.

Smith had this to say about Puller on Peleliu: " Lewie banged his head against the opposition. I went over the ground he captured, and I didn't see how a human being had captured it, but he did. He believed in momentum; he believed in coming ashore and hitting and just keep on hitting and trying to keep up the momentum until he'd overrun the whole thing. . . . No, no finesse. When he destroyed 140 defended caves that's quite an operation, plus a blockhouse or two. No, there was no finesse about it, but there was gallantry and there was determination" (OH, 140–41).

On 20 September, Rupertus ordered an attack by the First Marines against a section of Bloody Nose Ridge known as "Walt's Ridge." The attack used every resource available to Puller, including maximum air support. Maj. Henry J. Donigan wrote the following analysis for the *Marine Corps Gazette*:

> The attack failed. Heavy losses were incurred, and the exhausted survivors fell back to where they could safely cover the enemy positions.
>
> What happened next was possibly the most significant and dramatic event of the battle. General Rupertus, realizing that the First Marines was spent, was in a state of despair. He had no more replacements to give to the fight for the ridges. Regardless, he refused to request assistance and strongly argued against bringing in army troops. Puller had lost all touch with reality in his frenzied determination to fight the Japanese to the last man, if necessary. He was too proud to admit that his regiment was finished. It took the judgment and courage of General Geiger to assess that something was terribly wrong and desperately needed to change. Geiger . . . ordered the 321st Infantry Regiment of the 81st Division . . . to relieve the 1st Marines.[4]

Puller had been given one of the toughest missions ever handled by the Marine Corps. He also sustained "the heaviest losses ever suffered by a regiment in Marine Corps history."[5]

An interesting operation took place 28 September against Ngesebus Island, northeast of the northernmost tip of Peleliu. It was within six hundred yards of the mainland and could be reached at low tide by amphibian tractors. The Third Battalion of the Fifth Marines was used to assault the island.

> The operation against Ngesebus presented an opportunity of seeing at close hand a complete landing operation in miniature. All of the generals and admirals in the area were present: Admiral Fort [Peleliu task force commander], General J. C. Smith [expeditionary troop commander], General Geiger [Third Amphibious Corps commander], General Rupertus [First Marine Division commander], General Mueller [Eighty-first Infantry Division commander], General Bell [assistant division commander of the Eighty-first], and myself. . . . We had an unobstructed view of the landing beaches and most of the water gap. . . . Naval gunfire ships . . . worked on the northern end of Ngesebus and continued to fire on that part of the island throughout the landing. Promptly on schedule the artillery started its preparation. . . . The southern and western shores of Ngesebus were smothered with artillery and shell bursts. The planes then came over to strafe and bomb the southern shore. . . . This, I believe, was the first time marine planes had supported an assault landing conducted by Marines. The aviators apparently wanted to

show us what they could do. . . . The bombing planes dropped their bombs at 300 feet. The strafing planes came in so low that they had to zoom to clear the trees on the 30-foot ridge on the western side of the island. (RI, 88–89)

Ngesebus was secure that evening. The original plan called for its capture so that its uncompleted airstrip could be finished. The soil on the island proved to be so sandy and soft that it was deemed unfit for operational use, but when topped with crushed coral the airstrip was acceptable. It served to allow marine air components to perform close-support missions for the marine ground troops for the first time in the war in the Pacific.

Marine air had played an important role in the war to date, but it had been separated from its ground elements. Late in the war, close marine air support of marine ground troops took place. Naval air components rendered some support to the marines on Tarawa and the Marshall Islands. Marine close-air support was used extensively in the Philippines and impressed the army ground troops with its efficiency. Marine air was not used for ground support of marines as much as infantry officers thought it should be. When it did accompany the infantry, it was much appreciated for its skill and audacity. The respected correspondent Robert Sherrod, however, criticized it: "Top Marine aviators were too deeply interested in shooting enemy planes out of the wild blue yonder, so they lost sight of their primary mission."[6]

The west-shore road on Peleliu came under sniper fire from the caves overlooking the roadway. Vegetation hid the Japanese from view, and they were able to fire on anyone using the road. At one particular curve in the road, about a thousand yards from the airfield, there seemed to be a large concentration of deadly sniper fire. Colonel Hankins took it upon himself to do something about the menace. He had been on several prewar rifle teams and intended to do some counter-sniping from the road itself. When he got to the point known as "Dead Man's Curve," he was confronted with a traffic jam. "Standing upright in the middle of the road, Hankins shouted commands and gave hand signals that, between pings of sniper fire, unsnarled the roadblock. The convoy just started to move again, northward towards Garekoru Village, when a single shot from the ridge ripped through Hankins's chest. He was killed instantly."[7]

O. P. Smith would explain the incident much the way Bill D. Ross described it above, stating simply, "As he dismounted from his jeep he was hit in the stomach by a Japanese sniper bullet and died almost instantly" (RI, 95–96). It's significant that Smith recounted the basic details of Hankins's death without further comments about the man or incident. His oral history, taped at his home in California on 9, 11, and 13 June 1973—eight years before his death and twenty-five years after the incident—gives a more detailed accounting of this personal loss. It also gives us a glimpse of his private feelings toward Hankins. The two men had first met in Iceland. Hankins had been a coal miner in civilian life, so he had volunteered to teach a demolitions class.

> Arthur Worton was more social than I was, and he had had Joe Hankins as his exec. Joe didn't handle a tea cup very well, and Arthur wanted a more acceptable socialite, . . . and they sent Joe Hankins over to me to relieve Baldwin who had been promoted and gone up to be the executive officer of the regiment. Joe did a good job for me, but I could not persuade him that a reserve had any chance [of assignment to key jobs and promotion to senior rank] in the Marine Corps. We lived together in a hut all winter long, just the two of us and there I talked and talked and talked to him; I don't think I ever made any impression, he just felt that the reserves didn't have a chance. Then later on I came to Cape Gloucester [where] he was commanding a battalion and had won a Navy Cross, and I talked to him and said, "Hankins, what is this about the reserves not having a chance?" He had to admit he'd done pretty well. . . .
>
> He was going out as an individual to get a sniper and he was killed. He was a good shot, but he was killed before he could get in a position to watch. I was very fond of Hankins. That's one loss during the war that affected me. I never quite got over it—losing Hankins. I was very fond of him. When he was provost marshal there he picked up a young Jap—just a boy—who had been one of those people who had been sent down to swim into the beach with explosives strapped around their waists to blow up the airfield or something, and he was captured. Hankins made him his orderly, and would come around to my place with this Jap three paces behind. The Jap would watch everything Hankins did; if he sat down the Jap would set down. He only knew one word of English—okay. Finally Hankins got tired of the okay and put him back in the stockade. Nice little Jap. (105–6)

This Japanese prisoner of war was very upset by the death of Hankins and pleaded for the privilege of digging Hankins's grave.[8]

By 27 September, Peleliu was secure enough to raise the same flag that had been raised at Cape Gloucester and Talasea. By 29 September, elements of the First Marines were being evacuated. In the second week of October, it was the turn of the Fifth Marines to be relieved of combat duties. On 20 October 1944, Gen. Paul J. Mueller relieved Geiger and Rupertus of their responsibilities on Peleliu, and both officers left the island. Smith was left behind to bring out the remaining marines and their equipment. He and a small staff were attached to

Briefing for Peleliu at III Amphibious Corps' headquarters on Guadalcanal, September 1944. *Front row, from left:* Brigadier General Smith, General Rupertus, and Commodore Brittain. *Courtesy of* MCUA.

the Eighty-first Division pending the arrival of suitable transport. They departed Peleliu on 1 November 1944.

Before Smith left Peleliu, he had occasion to watch the army institute siege tactics against the remnants of the Japanese left on the island. Rupertus, as noted, had refused to change the assault-and-maneuver tactics of the marines to deal with the changed Japanese defense; siege tactics would have saved many lives against the well-dug-in enemy. J. Robert Moskin, a prominent Marine Corps historian, is outspoken in his criticism: "The first week raised serious questions about the marine doctrine that pounding straight ahead as fast as possible conserved American lives. Marines advanced with infinite courage when ordered to, but these bullheaded tactics against a skillful enemy who could not retreat and would not surrender simply did not work. Finally, somebody had to call a halt to the slaughter and start looking for a smarter way to invade the Umurbrogol ridges."[9]

Smith's own words summarize the Palau assault: "The Palau Campaign was not by any means the largest amphibious operation in the Central Pacific Campaign, but for the concentrated fury of the fighting it was only exceeded by Tarawa and Iwo Jima. . . . The cost of casualties for the capture of Peleliu was high, but in

Brigadier General Smith and Maj. Gen. W. H. Rupertus in the Division Command Post near the airfield at Peleliu. Smith used the antitank ditch when he first came ashore with an advance element of the Division Command Post before Rupertus took over, September 1944. *Courtesy of MCUA.*

comparison with the number of Japanese killed, the cost was not as heavy as at Tarawa or Iwo Jima" (RI, 119). Geiger called Peleliu the toughest fight of the war.[10]

When Smith returned to Pavuvu, he discovered that Rupertus had left for the United States, having been relieved of command by Maj. Gen. Pedro del Valle. Smith was ordered to serve on the staff of the proposed Tenth Army. Asked years later what he thought about the assignment, Smith replied:

I wasn't too happy about it. I would rather have stayed with the Division. As a matter of a fact Jerry Thomas wanted to clear me out of Peleliu to come back and command the Marine Corps Schools. And I wrote Jerry and said, "Look, Jerry, it took me a long time to get out to the Pacific and I want to stay out here for a while. I realize that probably I've got the qualifications to command the schools, I've taught there several times, and maybe eventually it'll be a nice job, but not now." Then General Rupertus got hold of me before we sailed to Peleliu, and he wanted the job of Commandant of the Marine Schools, and he wanted me to say that I didn't want it. I told him that I'd written Jerry Thomas that I wasn't interested in going back at that time. Then he told General Vandegrift that I absolutely didn't want the job—which was not quite it, I didn't want it at that time. So he [Rupertus] was ordered to the Marine Corps Schools. (OH, 149–50)

Rupertus was ordered home by General Vandegrift, who wrote: "I decided now to bring Bill Rupertus home. . . . Bill was already tired when I saw him in the Pacific, and I let him stay on only because of the personal request of Admiral Halsey. I knew the Peleliu Campaign must have nearly exhausted him. . . . Late on March 25 I was at home, Colonel Kilmartin, . . . telephoned to report [that] Bill [was] *in extremis.* I hastened to his side. He was dead when I arrived. Bill's death came as a low blow. After we buried him I wrote General Holcomb: "The Marine Corps has lost one of its finest officers and I have lost one of my best friends."[11]

Gen. Raymond G. Davis, a Medal of Honor recipient, as a young major commanded the First Battalion, First Marines on Peleliu. He later recalled, "We could have saved a lot of lives by not trying to take the whole island. After we secured the airfield, we should have pulled back, got into a siege stage, got our guns up and just pounded the place."[12]

Two impressions of the battle for Peleliu remain. The first is admiration for the heroism of the marines in some of the most intense fighting of the war against Japan. The second is a question: why was Rupertus allowed to stay in command, when his ineptness was so apparent? He botched the battle of Peleliu and cost American lives. General Vandegrift must bear some of the culpability in keeping Rupertus on the job, when many of his peers scorned the man's leadership capabilities. O. P. Smith must also share some responsibility for keeping Rupertus on the job. It would have been possible for him to bring the subject of Rupertus's limitations (caused by his broken ankle) to the attention of General Geiger. Instead, Smith chose to be loyal to his superior. It was a misplaced and costly loyalty.

6

OKINAWA

Brig. Gen. Oliver P. Smith arrived at Pearl Harbor on 7 November 1944. Brig. Gen. Merritt A. Edson, Chief of Staff, Fleet Marine Force Pacific, arranged for a car to pick up Smith at the airport and take him to quarters temporarily vacated by Gen. Holland Smith.

It was during this visit with "Red Mike" Edson that Smith discovered that the Tenth Army was being formed. No one knew just where it would be utilized, but Okinawa was prominently mentioned. Spruance and Turner wanted to give that command job to Holland Smith, but Nimitz, as Commander in Chief Pacific (he also "wore the hat" of Commander in Chief Pacific Ocean Area, or CincPOA), was determined to have an army officer command the increasingly large operations that were ahead of the Allies as they got closer to Japan proper. Nimitz's reluctance to give Holland Smith further command of operations in the Pacific can be attributed to the overwhelming increase in interservice dissension that had followed Holland Smith's relief of an army general on Saipan. The army was expanding its role and capabilities to the point where the marines' total of six divisions would most likely be used in joint operations under army command. Before Smith arrived at Pearl Harbor, Lt. Gen. Simon B. Buckner, named Tenth Army commander in June 1944, had already met with Nimitz, Spruance, Lt. Gen. Millard F. Harmon, and Adm. Ernest J. King, the Chief of Naval Operations, to discuss strategy. King was enthusiastic about a Formosa operation and argued forcefully in favor of it. Buckner opposed it, pointing out that Japanese troops from the elite Kwangtung Army were garrisoned on Formosa. Its capture would take at least nine divisions and cost up to fifty thousand casualties.[1]

Okinawa Shima. *Courtesy* MCHC.

The proposed strategy through Okinawa and the Philippines to the Japanese homeland was arrived at by Admiral Nimitz taking into consideration the light losses MacArthur predicted for his attack against Luzon. The capture of Luzon, Iwo Jima, and Okinawa would also interrupt the flow of oil to Japan from Borneo and Burma.[2] The decision seemed to silence, at least for the time being, the increasingly abrasive rivalry between the army and the navy.

Nimitz urged Smith to use every effort to ensure that the mix of army and marine divisions would be a workable force. He asked Smith specifically to use his influence, as the marine deputy chief of staff for the Tenth Army, to keep the army's service troops and equipment to a bare minimum, so that available shipping could handle the operation.

The logistical needs of the marines in assaulting island strongholds were small compared to the support required for the large-scale, prolonged land battles the army was used to fighting. However, when marines were assigned roles similar to those of army divisions, they necessarily developed much larger logistical bases also. Nimitz was concerned about the requests for additional shipping by the island command at Peleliu; allocating priorities was one of his biggest problems. Smith reassured him that he was of the opinion that much of the shipping requested for Peleliu could be disregarded without hindering the mandates of the island command.

When Smith left CincPOA headquarters, he was pleasantly surprised to obtain the services of a driver and a Buick sedan for his official use during his stay in Hawaii. The first trip he took was to Schofield Barracks, where he reported to General Buckner. Smith found Buckner, a graduate of the Virginia Military Institute and West Point, to be a proud infantryman in remarkable physical condition. Piercing blue eyes beneath a crop of snow-white hair readily got people's attention. He had commanded American forces in Alaska for five years before coming to the Tenth Army. He had observed the amphibious assaults upon Kiska and Attu, but he had very little firsthand experience of commanding troops in combat.[3]

Buckner had functioned well with other services while in Alaska and planned to live there after the war.[4] Reporters called him "The Stallion of Alaska," in recognition of his energetic and forceful command in the region, and of his stress on physical conditioning. An 8 May 1943 article in the *Saturday Evening Post* described Buckner: "Physical fitness and discipline, blunt speech and strict adherence to the rules have always been a fetish with him. He makes such a *bravura* display of toughness that it is almost as if he is trying to hide the fact that he is also one of the scholars of the Army: a former commandant of the Military Academy at West Point, honor graduate of the Command and General Staff School, former executive of the Army War College."[5]

Smith admired Buckner, with whom he had much in common. Buckner was well known for his "contempt for indecisive bureaucratic officialdom regardless of service."[6] Smith was one of the leading theorists in the Marine Corps and, like Buckner, did not suffer fools gladly. Smith thought Buckner had character and integrity; "His methods and judgments were somewhat inflexible, but you always knew where he stood" (TA, 3).

Formation of the Tenth Army under Buckner's command had originally been part of Operation Causeway—the invasion of the Pescadore Islands and Formosa. The planners were not happy with the outcome of the plans, so they scrapped it in September 1944 because Formosa would require troops beyond the logistical resources available.[7] Smith's reception to the staff of the Tenth

Army was cordial and sincere. Buckner let it be known that he was going to have a command that functioned without friction. The Tenth Army's chief of staff and Smith's army counterpart are described in Smith's own words:

> Brigadier General E. D. Post, a West Pointer, was chief of staff to General Buckner and had served with him in various capacities for several years, first at West Point and then in Alaska. Post had served with the General so long that he could forecast his reactions to any given situation. The relationship between the General and his chief of staff was very close, almost that of a father and a son. Post himself was a pleasing personality and a very even temper. It would have been hard not to get along with him.
>
> Brigadier General Lawrence E. Schick was the Army Deputy Chief of Staff. I was designated as the Marine Deputy Chief of Staff. Schick was a West Pointer who had started out in the Cavalry, then, as the cavalry arm had diminished in importance, had transferred to the Adjutant General's Department. He was a small, wiry man, quick of speech and action. There was always a snap in his eyes. He had come from Alaska with General Buckner. After watching him work for a few months I came to the conclusion that he was the finest staff officer with whom I had ever had the pleasure of serving. He had his finger on every detail of the administration of the Tenth Army. In the field he was to become my tent mate. He was intensely proud of the Army, as I was of the Marine Corps, and we had many heated though friendly arguments. (TA, 3)

One of the marine officers, Col. James Roosevelt, the president's son, had requested assignment to Tenth Army in order to get back into the combat zone. He was popular with the other staff members, and Smith was of the opinion that he did excellent work. As soon as Smith arrived, Roosevelt came to him for permission to transfer to a combat command. Smith suggested that he make his request through channels, and the young Roosevelt was shortly notified of a change of orders. He returned to his former position on the staff of Adm. R. O. Davis, who was charged with mounting out the Twenty-fourth Corps for the Okinawa operation.

Smith and his aide, Lieutenant Bevan, were assigned to quarters near the Schofield Barracks hospital. It was a three-bedroom bungalow with two bathrooms, a dining room, servant quarters, and a living room, all sparsely furnished. Two orderlies were assigned to take care of housekeeping chores.

Schofield Barracks is situated in a mountainous region several hundred feet higher than Honolulu, so the average temperature is much cooler, especially at night. Smith had his household staff draw firewood from the army's stockpile so that he could enjoy a fire in the fireplace. One nuisance that surprised him at such an elevation was the preponderance of mosquitoes, day or night. However, spraying with "Flit" took care of the problem. There was a beautiful officer's club near the bungalow, with a large lawn, which functioned as a landing field for the small Piper Cubs. The club served excellent meals, and many members of the Tenth Army staff ate there whenever they could. Buckner decided that Tenth Army would set up its own mess in a nearby barracks, and Smith was assigned a place at Buckner's table.

Smith admired the scenic vistas of his mountainside quarters. When writing to Esther, he paid particular attention to the different crops being raised on the islands and the diversity of colors. The pineapple fields fascinated him most of all. Smith was a knowledgeable and a detailed observer of anything that grew from the soil, dating from his college days when he worked as a gardener.

An extensive and demanding physical conditioning program was underway by the time Smith arrived at Tenth Army; Buckner's commitment to physical fitness was responsible for the activity. Buckner was probably in better shape than anybody else on his staff, even though he was sixty-two years old. He wanted his staff to be tough, and he tolerated no excuses. Smith disagreed with his boss:

I believed at the time and still believe that he was on the wrong track. The program General Buckner devised was suitable for battalion commanders but not for staff officers, many of whom had passed their fiftieth birthday [Smith was fifty-one at the time]. An Army staff officer is subjected to considerable mental strain but he can do with a reasonable amount, only, of physical conditioning. For the older officers the program resulted in broken collar bones, broken arms, sprained ankles, and charley horses. Included in the required conditioning were the running of the Combat Course (for which Buckner held the record), firing all infantry hand and shoulder weapons, soft ball and conditioning hikes. The conditioning hikes were laid out by General Buckner. No. 1 hike was six miles in length and involved a climb and descent of 1500 feet. The hike started in the pineapple fields, then followed a valley into the mountains, then, after a considerable climb, followed a trail along the side of the mountains, then descended to the pineapple fields again. There were plenty of trees along the route and the view from the mountains was superb. In the winter it was pleasant and cool, and, except for a couple of short, stiff climbs, one did not even get up a sweat. Bevan and I enjoyed this hike and took it several times. Hike no. 2 was eight and one half miles in length and involved a climb and descent of 2000 feet. Part of the climb and descent had to be made hand-over-hand. I looked over this route and decided to pass it up. . . . I had joined the Tenth Army eight days after leaving Peleliu and the Army probably considered I was fit for combat duty. As a matter of a fact I was rather thin [Smith's normal weight was about 150 pounds—with his six-foot, one-inch height, he always looked underweight] and had a very heavy atabrine tan, which is not a particularly healthy looking tan. What I needed was food and relaxation. (TA, 7–8)

The social atmosphere at Schofield Barracks was active, with nurses, Red Cross workers, and WACs accompanying men to dances, beach parties, and cocktail parties. Smith's puritanical instincts and professional commitment to the tasks at hand were evident when he wrote, "You had the feeling that you were half in the war and half out of it. My own opinion is that staging areas should be located in areas where there are no distractions" (TA, 8).

A directive from the Joint Chiefs of Staff prior to 1 October 1944 was the genesis of the Okinawa operation. The directive authorized CincPOA to organize a task force to occupy one or more positions in the Nansei Shoto, a chain of islands that included Okinawa, with a target date of 1 March 1945. Its purposes were threefold:

(1) Establishment of secure bases which could carry the attack to the Japanese homeland, support other operations taking place in and around the East China Sea, and to destroy any line of communication that still existed between mainland Asia, Formosa, Netherlands East Indies, and Malaya to the Japanese Empire.

(2) Establish sea and air lines of communication throughout the East China Sea to the coast of China, and eventually up to the Yangtze Valley.

(3) All of the preceding was intended to bring unremitting military pressure against Japan.

Planners for the operation thought that it would be done in three phases:

Phase I: Capture the southern portion of Okinawa including small adjacent islands, and develop base facilities.

Phase II: Seize the remainder of Okinawa and Ie Shima and develop additional necessary base facilities in favorable localities.

Phase III: Exploit our position in the Nansei Shoto. (TA, 10–11)

Admiral Spruance would serve as "Officer Conducting Operations," Admiral Turner as joint commander of the expeditionary force, and General Buckner as commander of the expeditionary troops. The directive spurred a flurry of activity at Tenth Army headquarters.

On 9 November, Tenth Army submitted a tentative task force organization. It called for an additional seventy thousand men above what had been authorized by a CincPOA joint staff study of 15 October. Most of the increase was in service and supply troops, which could be used effectively on Okinawa. However, the size of the force that could be transported across the ocean was limited by shipping and the capacity of the beaches to accommodate the men and supplies. The army did not seem to understand the restrictions as well as the Marine Corps. When Admiral Nimitz asked Smith to do all that he could to limit the manpower requirements of Tenth Army, there was a reason behind his request.

Most of Okinawa was surrounded by coral reefs, except for river mouths, so the planners were concerned that any assault would have to be conducted over them. An early decision of the planning staff was to select the Tagushi beaches in southwestern Okinawa as the landing location. A landing there seemed most likely to allow the capture of an airfield site within the first few days.

On 9 November, Tenth Army staff presented its plan (Plan Fox) for a landing on the Tagushi beaches to Admiral Turner and his staff at Amphibious Force Pacific headquarters at Pearl Harbor. Turner ultimately accepted the plan, with the proviso that two other locations be taken as well in the initial stages of the operation: the small island of Keise Shima south of the Tagushi beaches, and the islands of Kerama Retto, which should be occupied a week before the assault on Okinawa proper. Turner wanted to make sure that his ships had a protected anchorage where they could be rearmed and resupplied without danger from Japanese submarines or bad weather. The day of the assault was designated "Love" (or L, for landing, in the military phonetic alphabet of the time) day by the planners, to avoid confusion with the Iwo Jima operation, for which the day of the landing had already been designated "Dog" (for D) day.

Buckner's was designated Task Force Fifty-six. The chain of command passed up through Admiral Turner as joint commander of the expeditionary troops to Admiral Spruance as commander of the Fifth Fleet (Task Force Fifty), then on to Admiral Nimitz as Commander in Chief Pacific Ocean Area. As soon as the Tenth Army was well established ashore, Admiral Turner planned to withdraw. Buckner would then report directly to Admiral Spruance. At the conclusion of the assault phase, Buckner would report directly to Nimitz. (As it happened, the operation took much longer than originally anticipated, and Admiral Turner, who had previously been scheduled for a transfer, was replaced by Adm. Harry W. Hill, who, in turn, reported directly to General Buckner.) The Tenth Army, since it contained two corps, was technically an "army," but actually it was a naval task force created by and controlled from CincPOA headquarters.

The armada that Spruance commanded during the Okinawa operation numbered over 1,300 seagoing vessels and over five thousand small landing craft, as well as hundreds of specialized ships bringing supplies and equipment from Ulithi. Spruance positioned his Fifth Fleet between Okinawa and the Japanese homeland so that he could cover and protect the operations taking place. The Fifth Fleet was the one that "came to stay."

The staff at Tenth Army was ordered to draw up task organizations for the assault phase and for the garrison phase of the Okinawa operation (the garrison stage is beyond the scope of this book). The task organization of Tenth Army for the assault phase was as follows:

CTF 56, Expeditionary Troops—Lt. Gen. S. B. Buckner, Jr., USA
(a) TG 56.1 Army Troops Lt. Gen. S. B. Buckner, Jr., USA
    Headquarters
    Special Troops
    Antiaircraft
    Engineers
    Signals
    Medical
(b) TG 56.2 III Amphibious Corps Maj. Gen. Roy S. Geiger, USMC
    Corps Troops
    1st Marine Division Maj. Gen. Pedro A. del Valle, USMC
    6th Marine Division Maj. Gen. Lemuel C. Shepherd, Jr., USMC
(c) TG 56.3 XXIV Corps Maj. Gen. John R. Hodge, USA
    Corps Troops
    7th Infantry Division Maj. Gen. Archibald V. Arnold, USA
    96th Infantry Division Maj. Gen. James L. Bradley, USA
(d) TG 56.4 77th Infantry Division Maj. Gen. Andrew D. Bruce, USA
(e) TG 56.5 2d Marine Division Maj. Gen. Thomas E. Watson, USMC
(f) TG 56.6 27th Infantry Division Maj. Gen. George W. Griner, Jr., USA
(g) 99.1 Naval Forces Rear Admiral C. H. Coob, USN
    (Advance Echelon only)
(h) TG 99.2 Tactical Air Force Maj. Gen. F. P. Mulcahy, USMC
(i) TG 99.3 Island Command, APO 331 Maj. Gen. F. G. Wallace, USA. (TA. 23–24)

Smith found the army staff members competent and professionally well qualified. His only misgiving was that most of the men had come directly from Alaska with Buckner and had little or no experience in combat. He thought that they performed well, considering that the staffs of the two corps commands were veterans, with considerable combat experience, which sometimes intimidates individuals with less experience.

Smith was the senior marine on the Tenth Army staff. Some of his colleagues were exhibiting the resentments marine officers harbor when they feel that the Corps is threatened by one of the other services. Gen. Merritt Edson was trying to enhance the Marine Corps's leverage in amphibious affairs by recommending larger numbers of marine officers on the staffs of the army formations then operating in the Pacific. This would have been fine if it had been meant to impart the wealth of experience that the Marine Corps had gathered in amphibious operations, but placing as many marine officers as possible, irrespective of their usefulness to the staffs that they served, became an obsession. Nimitz had already made it clear, after Saipan, that FMF Pacific would not hold command positions in the field for the rest of the war; therefore, the marines would have to work more closely with the army.

Smith had this to say about the marines on the Tenth Army staff. "Upon my arrival at Tenth Army Headquarters I found that CincPOA had already approved the marine augmentation of the Tenth Army staff. It did not take long to see that the list was somewhat padded. This padding would result in marine officers doing clerical duty at Army Headquarters as there were manifestly not enough bona fide billets to take care of all the Army officers on the staff as well as the marine and naval officers. After considerable discussion with the Army staff, I succeeded in getting the number reduced from 48 to 34 and I still considered this latter figure high" (TA, 25–26).

Jon T. Hoffman, Edson's biographer, accuses some marine officers (especially Smith, since he is the only marine singled out by name) of joining the "enemy."[8] Smith was never as outwardly aggressive as Edson, but he did not believe that the presence of high-ranking marine officers doing clerical work for the army could in any way advance the position of the Marine Corps.

Third Amphibious Corps planners completed a plan, Plan Fox, for the Okinawa Operation and arrived at Schofield Barracks for a planning session with Tenth Army planners. The chief of staff of Third Amphibious Corps, Col. Merwin J. Silverthorn, was an old friend and stayed with Smith at Schofield Barracks. General Geiger stayed at Pearl Harbor with Holland Smith. O. P. Smith and Silverthorn shared some pleasant moments, especially attendance at a celebration dinner at a hotel in Honolulu in honor of Silverthorn's promotion to brigadier general. Smith and Silverthorn had served together on the staff of the Marine Corps Schools in the late thirties; they had cemented their friendship at that time. Silverthorn was a distinguished career officer who, like Smith, worked tirelessly to cultivate a foundation of excellence in the Marine Corps.[9]

The corps plan proposed using the Sixth and First Marine Divisions in the assault phase, with the First Marine Division on the right or south flank of the Third Amphibious Corps boundary. The First was still in the southern Solomons, while the Sixth was on Guadalcanal, so the two divisions could readily coordinate with each other. The Second Marine Division, located on Saipan, was scheduled to be used as the army reserve. If resistance in front of the First and Sixth Marine Divisions became heavier than planned, Smith had arranged with Buckner for the Third Amphibious Corps to have first choice on the use of the Second Marine Division after the landing. The Second was scheduled to make a diversionary landing on the southeast coast of Okinawa on Love day and L day plus one. It was assumed that their assistance would not be needed before that time.

Planning for the Okinawa operation increased in tempo after Christmas. An alternate plan, called Baker, was approved by Buckner on 3 January. No one seemed to like it; it provided for a landing by Third Amphibious Corps on the southeast corner of the Chinen Peninsula, and for the landing of Twenty-fourth Corps at Nakagusuku Bay, north of the Chinen Peninsula. The approaches to southeastern Okinawa were more direct, and weather would be less of a problem than on the west coast. However, its disadvantages included the presence of several small islands that would interfere with fire control, the absence of an airfield nearby, and the fact that the two corps could not be mutually supportive of each other. Smith disliked the alternate plan. "I am convinced that in the event of bad weather on the west coast, landings would have been delayed rather than resort to the east coast landing as provided in the alternate plan" (TA, 30).

The three reserve divisions—the Seventy-seventh Infantry Division, Twenty-seventh Infantry Division, and the Second Marine Division—were factored into Plan Fox. The Twenty-seventh Division was to capture Kerama Retto. The Second Marine Division, as noted, was to carry out a series of diversionary landings on the southeast coast area on Love day. The Seventy-seventh Division would capture Ie Shima and support the two corps in the assault phase. All of these plans assumed that Fox (the west coast landing) would be the operative plan.

Base-development planning for Okinawa after the island had been seized was carried out concurrently with assault planning. Okinawa would become the supply base, staging area, and training facility for the invasion of the Japanese homeland. The plans were complex and constantly being upgraded as L day approached. The proposed island commander, Maj. Gen. F. G. Wallace, was an artilleryman and a contemporary of General Buckner. Early in his career, a horse had fallen on Wallace and fractured his leg so badly that he had had to fight against retirement for many years. In order to strengthen his leg he usually wore high-topped riding boots. He had not been successful in obtaining a combat command, and he seemed to lose his spirit when he learned of the death of his son in Europe. Smith thought that Wallace lacked the qualifications to do the job but felt that the chief of staff, Colonel Jones, could supply the necessary drive.

The island commander was to plan for the construction of two airfields by L day plus five, and two more by L day plus twenty. Other responsibilities were preparation for an advance fleet base in Nakagusuku Bay, improvements to Naha Harbor, and construction of a rehabilitation and staging center. As the plans expanded and became more developed, over twenty-two airstrips were planned.

On 21 December 1944, Lt. Charles Calvert Benedict, Jr., Smith's son-in-law, was killed in action while flying a mission near Mukden, Manchuria, as part of the 468th Bomber Group of the Twentieth Air Force. Lieutenant Benedict was married to Smith's older daughter, Virginia, and his death came eight months after the birth of their daughter, Gail. Smith must have been devastated by the news of his son-in-law's death, but he did not mention it in his diary or letters.

Smith went on 1 January to the Fleet Marine Force headquarters at Pearl Harbor, where he was awarded the Legion of Merit by Gen. Holland M. Smith. The citation was officially forwarded to O. P. Smith at Tenth Army. Normal protocol would have had Buckner make the presentation, but Smith had talked the situation over with his roommate, Brig. Gen. Lawrence Schick, and they concluded that since Gen. Holland Smith had signed the citation, it would be more appropriate for him to make the presentation. Schick explained the situation to Buckner, who was pleased to agree, another example of his wish to foster interservice cooperation and harmony.

Buckner understood the need for him to designate a second in command before the operation got under way. It was not, however, a simple decision. Buckner and Geiger had attended the army's Command and Staff School at Fort Leavenworth at the same time during the early 1920s. They had become very close friends and had taken a mutual interest in each other's careers over the years between the world wars. Buckner wanted Geiger to be his second in command, but he ran into problems with the army's senior officer at Pearl Harbor, Gen. Robert C. Richardson. Smith relates what transpired.

General Buckner felt that a second-in-command of the Army should be designated prior to the operation. General Wallace, the prospective Island Commander, was the senior major general and Geiger was the second senior. General Buckner did not feel that General Wallace was capable of handling a field army. He did feel that General Geiger was capable of doing so. Since General Geiger was junior to General Wallace, the succession of command would not be automatic but would have to be prescribed by higher authority. General

Buckner, therefore, decided to write a letter to CincPOA recommending that General Geiger be designated as second-in-command. As General Buckner was still at Schofield Barracks, and since his Army superior was General Richardson (ComGenPOA), the General thought that he should forward the letter via General Richardson. The letter was duly forwarded but was returned by General Richardson with a note stating that the second-in-command of the Tenth Army was one for the War Department to decide and that no member of the Tenth Army staff should even mention the matter to any member of CincPOA's staff. General Buckner was considerably put out, but let the matter rest, with the idea of making the designation after landing on Okinawa, over which General Richardson had no control. I was apprised of these various maneuvers and advised Silverthorn by officer courier mail with the request that he inform General Geiger. I felt that General Geiger would like to know of the confidence General Buckner reposed him. (TA, 34–35)[10]

Circumventing Buckner's temporary senior in command was simply a matter of waiting until the force was at sea, where it would no longer be in the jurisdiction of the army commander on Oahu. In due course, Buckner communicated with Admiral Nimitz and received confirmation. On 18 June 1945, when Buckner was killed in action on Okinawa, General Post, the chief of staff, immediately notified General Geiger that he now commanded the Tenth Army.

There was no intent to turn over command of the Tenth Army to Geiger simply because he was Buckner's longtime friend. Geiger was one of the finest officers to serve in World War II. He had performed brilliantly as an aviation commander on Guadalcanal before his assignment as a corps commander, which was a rarity for an airman, in any of the services. Geiger had served with or personally knew all of the army division commanders scheduled to be a part of the Tenth Army. "In prior campaigns of Geiger's III Corps, there had been a notable lack of friction between them [army and Marine Corps units], particularly at the higher echelons, for Geiger would under no circumstances condone any unnecessary inter-service rivalry nor did he play favorites. And his attitude in those respects was common knowledge."[11]

The operational plan (OpPlan 1-45) for the capture of Okinawa was completed during the first week of January. Buckner's command now consisted of 375,000 officers and men, with approximately 170,000 combat troops in the assault phase, approximately half marines and half army. Buckner wanted to see what his command looked like in the field, so he collected several members of his staff so that they could confer individually with each division staff. Smith accompanied Buckner and his aide, Lt. Col. Hubbard, in the general's well-equipped c-54 aircraft. Their first stop was at Tarawa, where Buckner and Smith toured the battlefield. The war had long passed away from the tiny coral atoll, but the island was still littered with smashed amphibious tractors and pock-marked remnants of defender's blockhouses. The cemeteries stood in silent tribute to the horrific cost of capturing the island.

The next stop was Espiritu Santo, which was the home of the army's unfortunate Twenty-seventh Infantry Division, commanded by Gen. George Griner. During the Saipan campaign the division had been commanded by Gen. Ralph Smith, a classmate of O. P. Smith at the École de Guerre. Ralph Smith's removal from command by Holland Smith had led to a rift between the army and the marines, one that lingers to this day. In the 10 September 1944 issue of *Time*, Bob Sherrod had described the Twenty-seventh as a division that did not like to leave the safety of its foxholes. Griner and his staff were trying to overcome that stigma, but Buckner and Smith were not impressed with what they saw.

Next on the list was New Caledonia and a visit with the Eighty-first Infantry Division, commanded by Maj. Gen. Paul J. Mueller. Smith was favorably impressed with the division's location and thought that compared to the Twenty-seventh, it looked "very good." The 321st Regimental Combat Team of the Eighty-first had performed well on Peleliu. After the war, Mueller would become MacArthur's chief of staff in Tokyo.[12]

On Guadalcanal, Buckner and Smith were guests in Maj. Gen. Pedro del Valle's quarters. The Sixth and the First Marine Divisions both had excellent training facilities on Guadalcanal. The First Marine Division was still bivouacked on Pavuvu, but Maj. Gen. del Valle frequently rotated the regiments to Guadalcanal for training exercises. Both divisions were full of campaign veterans. General del Valle, a Puerto Rican of aristocratic Spanish antecedents and a 1915 Naval Academy graduate, had accompanied Benito Mussolini's army in Ethiopia and North Africa as an observer in the late 1930s. He was a brilliant artilleryman and had commanded the Eleventh Marines on Guadalcanal. He was also, however, a fanatical anti-Semite and segregationist. In 1953, after his retirement, he would organize the Defenders of the American Constitution, Incorporated.[13]

Maj. Gen. Lemuel C. Shepherd, Jr., commanding general of the Sixth Marine Division, was a graduate of the Virginia Military Institute. He had served with the Fifth Marines in World War I and had performed extremely well at Guam and Cape Gloucester, and he would culminate a distinguished career by becoming the Corps's twentieth commandant. Buckner was impressed with the readiness of the marine divisions and exempted them from time-consuming status reports about the state of their training.

Buckner's staff landed in Tacloban, on Leyte, and had to travel twenty miles by jeep to the headquarters of the Twenty-fourth Corps. Smith shared a tent at the corps's compound with Colonel C. D. Sullivan, who had been a classmate at college and was now writing the history of the Twenty-fourth Corps. Lt. Gen. John R. Hodge, commanding the Twenty-fourth Corps, had served with distinction on Guadalcanal as commander of the Americal Division and would later serve in Korea. "Hodge earned a reputation as a 'soldier's soldier,' sharing hardships with his troops at the front."[14]

When Buckner and Smith visited Leyte, rains had turned the ground into a morass that caused untold hardships for the troops. The Seventh and Seventy-seventh Infantry Divisions had been campaigning in the mud for three months and were actively fighting at the time of Buckner and Smith's visit. Both were good divisions and competently led, but they were desperately in need of new equipment and replacements when they came off the line in Leyte. Smith, always an astute observer of troops, was quick to credit the excellent performance of the army divisions on Leyte and later their continued excellence on Okinawa, even though each division was about eight hundred men short of its normal complement. Some of the deficiency in army replacements at that time was directly attributable to the losses sustained in the Battle of the Bulge in Europe.

After Buckner and his staff completed the inspection tour, they made a short stopover on Guam and Saipan. The Second Marine Division, commanded by Maj. Gen. Thomas E. Watson, was stationed on Saipan. Buckner trooped the entire line of the Eighth Marines, and he was very impressed with what he saw. He talked with each of the battalion commanders, later telling Smith that the division had the most alert group of battalion commanders he had ever seen. After Buckner's return to Schofield Barracks, his G-3 reported at a staff meeting that "the Marine divisions visited were in magnificent condition and splendidly trained" (TA, 53).

The Third Amphibious Corps and the Twenty-fourth Corps came under Tenth Army jurisdiction on 14 January. Plans for the operation were issued 11 March, with the invasion day (Love day) set for 1 April 1945—April's Fool Day and Easter! Over four hundred ships were required to transport the Tenth Army.

Smith and other senior officers of the command detachment went by plane to Guam, where on 12 March they joined Admiral Turner aboard the USS *Eldorado*. Turner was coming from the Iwo Jima operation. The staff boarded the *Eldorado* on the 12th. Smith was given a stateroom, which he shared with the future island commander, Major General Wallace. Smith found him to be a fine shipmate. During one of their many conversations, Wallace asked Smith "what the Marines had against General MacArthur[.] I told him frankly that our unfavorable opinion of him was compounded of several things, some important and some minor; that we appreciated his ability but just did not like him" (TA, 70).

Smith and General Post were assigned to the mess shared by Admiral Turner and General Buckner. Buckner and Turner cautiously felt each other out in the wardroom. Turner was especially anxious to find out where Buckner stood in regard to MacArthur, but Buckner, ever the gentleman, would not commit himself.

After picking up the Twenty-fourth Corps at Leyte, landing rehearsals were held off Rizal. Turner was not well pleased with the performance of his small control craft, and he let the participants know that he was displeased in language that could not be misunderstood. The Southern Attack Force, carrying the Twenty-fourth Corps, headed north from Leyte on 19 March. The Northern Attack Force, carrying the First and Sixth Marine Divisions, also headed for Okinawa, from Guadalcanal. The Second Marine Division left Saipan on 27 March.

Before either attack force left for Okinawa, the Fifth Fleet initiated air and surface strikes against the Ryukyu island chain. Underwater demolition teams started operations against the Kerama Retto group on 25 March. As planned, the Seventy-seventh Infantry Division landed on several of the small islands south and west of Okinawa. These islands were secured so that (in addition to protecting the anchorage) they would not pose any threat to the main landings and so that they could be used for artillery installations to support the assault. The FMF reconnaissance battalion landed on Keise Shima on 26 March, and by 31 March a battalion of 155 mm guns was in place to aid the invasion sector a few miles to the north.

On 31 March, Admiral Turner announced that the weather was suitable for the landings to begin the next day. Over 1,300 craft converged on Okinawa. It was an undertaking that exceeded the invasion of Normandy on D day in the number of assault forces and the extent of naval gunfire support. It was also the greatest test that the American navy faced in World War II, applying the amphibious doctrine of force projection thousands of miles from a base of supply.

On Love day, 1 April 1945, at 0830, the landing forces headed for the Tagushi beaches. By 0900 thirteen thousand troops were on the beaches, without resistance! Smith was assigned an observation position on the *Eldorado* on the searchlight platform above the superstructure, but he could see very little. The assault troops landed as scheduled, with the Sixth Marine Division positioned on the northern flank, the First Marine Division on its right flank. The Seventh Infantry Division landed to the right of the First, and the Ninety-sixth Infantry Division took the extreme right flank. By midday the Yontan and Kadena airfields were secure. Resistance was remarkably and unexpectedly light. Buckner, who had experienced the embarrassment of finding no Japanese ashore in the invasion of Kiska, was not anxious to be associated with another such debacle.

The Second Marine Division suffered more casualties than the other marine divisions combined during the first two days; its convoy was aggressively attacked by kamikazes. The unfortunate division was playing a diversionary role and, except for the Eighth Marines, never set foot on the island of Okinawa.

By 3 April the Seabees had made the Yontan airfield operational, while the army engineers were at work on the Kadena airfield. The Third Amphibious Corps was making extraordinary gains in its dash to the northern part of the island, and by 4 April it had completed Phase I of the plan, twenty days ahead of schedule. However, resistance in the north was light compared to the increased opposition the Twenty-fourth Corps was experiencing in its drive to the south of the island. It appeared that the main battle for Okinawa was going to be in the south.

Smith went ashore for the first time on 7 April. He visited the Third Amphibious Corps and spent some time with his old friend, General Silverthorn. Smith observed what was taking place and offered recommendations when asked to do so. Otherwise he spent most of his time observing the troops and acting as a liaison between the ground troops and the Tenth Army headquarters.

The marines had successfully overrun all of the northern portion of the island, including the Motobu Peninsula, which contained a large concentration of enemy troops. Smith proudly commented, "The campaign in the north should dispel the belief held by some that Marines are beach-bound and are not capable of rapid movement. Troops moved rapidly over rugged terrain, repaired roads and blown bridges, successfully opened new unloading points, and reached the northern tip of the island, some 55 miles from the original landing beaches, in 14 days" (TA, 82).

In the meantime, the Twenty-fourth Corps had run into heavy resistance and had slowed to a crawl. The Twenty-seventh Infantry Division was put into the line on the extreme western flank, on the right of the Tenth Army line. Smith was surprised to learn that a delay had been imposed on the Twenty-fourth Corps by Tenth Army headquarters. He asked when the advance would resume and was told not until more artillery had been assembled and until the Twenty-seventh Division was actively committed to the battle. Smith was probably correct in assessing that the army was too dependent on artillery support to reduce cave and underground strongholds. The experience of the marines indicated that infantry eventually had to take every position, with whatever supporting arms, such as flamethrowers, were available. Waiting for artillery to do the job alone caused delays that meant more casualties in the long run. The Twenty-fourth Corps was to learn that lesson the hard way. When the delayed attack of 19 April failed to produce the expected gains, Smith wrote, "This sounds like hindsight, but, in substance, this advice [his preceding paragraph] was given to the Tenth Army. They, at that time, did not believe it. Even after the failure of the attack . . . , I am not sure that the staff was entirely convinced" (TA, 83).

Several days before the 19 April attack, Smith was asked to talk to the correspondents on the USS *Eldorado*.

So much talk had been passed around about the tremendous air, naval gunfire, and artillery support which would back up this attack that I was concerned lest the correspondents would be too optimistic about the gains which would be made. I pointed out that the concentration of artillery behind the XXIV Corps (27 battalions), for the narrow front on which it was attacking, was greater than that employed on the Western front in World War I, but I also pointed out the limitations of artillery employed against an enemy dug in as the Japanese were. . . . But in the final analysis, it would be the infantryman who would have to dig the Japanese out of his caves. In the press dispatches only my statement regarding the amount of artillery was reported, not the qualifications regarding its effect. (TA, 85–86)

On 18 April, the Tenth Army command post moved ashore, south of Kadena airfield. Twenty-fourth Corps still had not moved; after four days of aggressive fighting and it still had no gains to show. Tenth Army was discouraged at the intensity of the Japanese resistance and the rugged terrain that confronted it in the south.

On 21 April, Nimitz and Vandegrift paid a visit to Okinawa. Smith met them with the official welcoming committee at Yontan airfield and accompanied Vandegrift to the Third Amphibious Corps, while Nimitz was most anxious to visit Tenth Army headquarters. While Smith was at Third Amphibious Corps, a warning order was received from Tenth Army for the First Tank Battalion of the First Marine Division to be made available for the Twenty-seventh Infantry Division in the south. Geiger was not pleased with the order, because tank-infantry teams were vital to marine divisions. He proposed instead that the whole division be used if help was needed. Smith immediately proceeded to Tenth Army, where he took up the matter with General Buckner, who never issued the order for the tanks. Instead he relieved the Twenty-seventh and substituted the First Marine Division, which went into the lines with Twenty-fourth Corps and under its command.

After the marines secured the northern portions of Okinawa, the focus of attention shifted to the southern end of the island where the Twenty-fourth Corps was still facing strong resistance. The lack of progress triggered controversy that continues today. The press was very critical of Buckner, because there was no end in sight for the capture of the island. The navy was being brutalized offshore by the kamikaze suicide planes. Something had to be done to move the situation along more rapidly. Admiral Hill, who had relieved Admiral Turner, later said that Buckner "felt [the criticism] very keenly. They were all doing their best."[15]

Admiral Spruance, who commanded the largest and most powerful fleet in history, despaired over his losses. He was impatient for the rapid advances he had experienced with Gen. Holland Smith, in contrast to the negligible progress of the Tenth Army. However, Okinawa was a different type of land battle; different tactics were required, and they took time. In his biography of Spruance, Thomas Buell states, "Whether Holland Smith with an all-marine force could have seized Okinawa more rapidly is doubtful. . . . [T]he struggle for Okinawa was more suitable to the Army method. Spruance's deprecation of the Army was unfair and was motivated by his growing impatience and his concern over his continuing loss of ships."[16]

Criticism of the slow-moving battle for Okinawa came from several sources, claiming that Buckner lacked competence or was not flexible enough to consider an amphibious end-run to the southern shore, thus forcing the enemy to fight on two fronts. However, the critics failed to take into consideration that an amphibious assault from the south had already been studied. When Gen. A. D. Bruce, commander of the Seventy-seventh Infantry Division, had completed the Ie Shima operation, he had proposed that his division be used for that purpose. The proposal had been carefully investigated, and the staff had concluded that an end run to the south could not be supplied, that no force larger than a division could be put ashore because of the rugged and steep cliffs that lined the shore, and that support vessels would be vulnerable to kamikaze attacks.

The issue of a southern landing was raised again when the First Marine Division moved south. The Tenth Army then resisted an end run on the same grounds—that a landing could not be supported logistically. The army divisions already on the line were at a low state of efficiency by 24 April, and it was more prudent, in Buckner's opinion, to replace them with fresh troops than to risk an amphibious assault away from any supporting arms.

After the war, while Smith was serving as commandant of the Marine Corps Schools at Quantico, he received a long letter from Gen. Harry J. Malony, who was writing a history of the battle of Okinawa for the army. He included a general summary of the controversy regarding the end run in the south and asked for Smith's comments. Smith's reply to General Malony was detailed and comprehensive:

Prior to 24 April, the date on which the 1st Marine Division was placed in Army reserve, I, at different times, informally discussed the question of a southeast coast landing with General Geiger and his staff, with a member of the staff of Admiral Spruance, and with members of the staff of the Tenth Army. . . . [M]y own recommendation was for a landing by a Corps of two divisions (1st and 2nd Marine Divisions). My recollection now is that this was the consensus of the officers of the III Amphibious Corps with whom I talked. The Army staff, as I remember, advanced the following arguments in opposition to the proposal:

(a) The beaches on the southeast coast would not support two divisions;
(b) The complexity of naval gunfire support would be increased;
(c) The terrain favored a strong defense by the Japanese;
(d) The time element. It would require an appreciable time to obtain ship-
    ping for the 1st Marine Division and mount it out.

The 2nd Division, in mid-April, still had its shipping but would have to be brought over from Saipan. If marine divisions were to be committed to the southern front it was quicker to move them one at a time by road to the established front. It required only two days to commit the 1st Marine Division after the decision was made. . . .

The opinions I have expressed are my own. . . . My opinions are also probably influenced by hindsight.

The Tenth Army, in my opinion, did a magnificent job and made a major contribution toward winning the war.[17]

Buckner told Nimitz that instead of a southern attack, which could be another Anzio, that with fresh troops in the form of the Third Amphibious Corps, added fleet support for the existing front, and introduction of the new army flamethrowing tanks, "he would be able quickly to blast the enemy out of his stronghold. Nimitz . . . said that he would accept Buckner's tactics 'provided they produced early results.'"[18]

By 1 May the First Marine Division had already replaced the Twenty-seventh Infantry Division in the south. Buckner had placed most of the Third Amphibious Corps's artillery under the command of Twenty-fourth Corps. Smith approved of the moves, because the northern sector required only minimal amounts of supporting fire. The Twenty-seventh Division took over the patrolling duties of the Sixth Marine Division in the north, freeing it to move to the south, where it joined the line to the west of the First Marine Division. Now Buckner had five divisions on the southern front with which to break the stalemate, but ferocious battles would be the order of the day before the island of Okinawa could be secured.

The Japanese counterattacked several times during the first two weeks of May. In the Sixth Marine Division's sector, a bitter fight was raging against Sugar Loaf Hill, northeast of Naha. For days the hill was contested, alternately captured and relinquished in a bitter engagement that saw the marines gain the crest of the hill five different times before they were able to secure it. It was one of the hardest-fought battles of the campaign.

Stormy Sexton was commander of "King" (K) Company, Third Battalion, Fourth Marines, a reactivated regiment formed from the four Marine Raider battalions, which had been disbanded in February 1944. The original Fourth Marines had been captured in 1942 when the Philippines surrendered to the Japanese. Captain Sexton had seen a great deal of combat with the Marine Raiders previous to his tour in Okinawa, and he would later serve with distinction as Smith's aide-de-camp in Korea. He would also command the Fourth Marines in Vietnam. He had this to say about Sugar Loaf: "It was the site of the most brutal combat I witnessed in my entire career. On the 18th of May, I relieved a company on the hill, and we suffered 70 casualties just effecting the relief[,] and the subsequent days were no improvement."[19]

During the Oroku Peninsula campaign, the Sixth Marines erected a Bailey bridge over the Kokuba River and attached at either end signs that proudly proclaimed, "The Longest Bridge Built by the Marine Corps." A picture of the bridge and its sign was circulated throughout the Tenth Army. The First Marine Division could not refrain from a response; Col. "Bigfoot" Brown placed a piece of metal matting across an irrigation ditch, built large approaches on both sides, and placed signs on the ends that said, "The Shortest Bailey Bridge in the World." A photograph was taken of it and sent all over the Tenth Army. General Shepherd was reported to be "burned up" about the joke, but it got a few laughs from the troops (OH, 166).[20]

Organized resistance on Okinawa was beginning to disintegrate by the second week in June, although fighting would continue until all of the enemy had been killed or committed suicide. The press was continuing to be critical about the progress on Okinawa, however, and on midnight of 17 June Nimitz, concerned about the adverse publicity, defended Buckner's position and tactics in a strongly worded statement. Admiral Hill, aware of how Buckner was affected by the negative reporting, sent his army liaison officer, a Colonel Thompson, to deliver a copy of Nimitz's press release to Buckner in person. When Thompson arrived at Tenth Army headquarters, he was told that Buckner was in the field and that the staff would see to it that he got the message as soon as he returned. General Buckner never returned.

On 18 June, Buckner decided to see the Eighth Marines in its first action after being attached to the First Marine Division. He was pleased with its performance. He was standing between two coral rocks watching a rifle company move forward when a Japanese 47 mm gun fired three rounds and hit the base of one of the rocks. A large chunk of coral went right through his heart. Buckner never regained consciousness, even though a doctor was at his side within a few minutes after he was hit. "It was a cruel turn of fate. Not only did he miss seeing this wonderful endorsement of his conduct of the Okinawa Campaign, but also the satisfaction of seeing this campaign come to a victorious conclusion within the coming week."[21]

Memorial services were held for General Buckner the next day, and Smith attended as an honorary pallbearer. "The ceremony was very impressive and very sad. Buckner had been a very active man and it was difficult to adjust oneself to his passing" (TA, 136). After the war, Buckner's remains were reburied in Kentucky, and Smith once again served as an honorary pallbearer. A memorial service was also held on the same day in Washington, D.C.

With Buckner's death, command of Tenth Army passed, as arranged, to Roy Geiger, who now directed the mopping up of the southern sector. Geiger was relieved of that command on 22 June by Gen. Joseph Stillwell, but by then the battle for Okinawa was finally over. Organized resistance of the Japanese forces on Okinawa was officially declared at an end. A flag-raising ceremony on 21 June 1945 celebrated the occasion.

The capture of Okinawa made it possible for the Allied forces to use the island as a gigantic staging area for the invasion of Japan. Okinawa was transformed into a massive military complex with thirteen airfields and over twenty-two airstrips. Supplies were stockpiled at an unprecedented rate. Plans were under way to give Okinawa a port capacity the same as that of Honolulu. All of this endeavor was preparation for what was expected to be the mightiest and bloodiest invasion of the war, the assault of the Japanese home islands.

The cost in human life for the capture of Okinawa was staggering. Japanese losses amounted to over one hundred thousand killed and ten thousand taken prisoner. U.S. Army and Marine losses were almost eight thousand men killed in action and thirty-two thousand wounded. Kamikaze attacks cost the navy an additional 4,300 deaths and 7,300 wounded. Casualties for Iwo Jima had amounted to about twenty-six thousand; on Okinawa the figure rose to seventy-three thousand. It was the largest, costliest, and the most bitterly contested battle of the Pacific war.[22]

The costs on both sides were cause enough to reflect about the future conduct of the war. The Japanese faced almost total annihilation if the war continued, especially if they did not modify their attitude toward surrendering. American leaders were also faced with the stark reality that the invasion of the Japanese home islands would be bloody beyond anything experienced so far in the war. Winston Churchill made a chilling prediction for the destruction of the Japanese homeland after reviewing the results of the battle for Okinawa: "the loss of a million American lives and half that number of British troops."[23]

Admiral Hill later reflected, "As I look back on Okinawa, my first reaction is one of admiration for the far-sighted and accurate planning which had provided such a solid and practical foundation for its success. Never in history had an amphibious operation of this scope been undertaken, 5,000 miles from its nearest repair base, and 7,000 miles from its logistic base in the homeland."[24] Col. Joseph H. Alexander confirms Buckner's legacy: "The battle of Okinawa represented joint service cooperation at its finest. This was General Buckner's greatest achievement. . . . Okinawa remains a model of interservice cooperation to succeeding generations of military professionals."[25]

Brig. Gen. Oliver P. Smith was a key player in the planning and invasion of Okinawa. He was able to observe intimately the complexity of commanding large formations of divisions from two different branches of the armed forces. His keen eye and curious intellect are readily discernible in the detailed narrative that he prepared about the battle of Okinawa and in his opinions about its conduct.

Smith received orders from CincPOA on 15 June to proceed to Quantico, Virginia, where he would assume the duties of commandant of the Marine Corps Schools. He departed Okinawa on 23 June, on the same plane that had brought General Stillwell to the island to take command of the Tenth Army. Smith landed in Washington, D.C., where his wife, Esther, was waiting for him at the airport with the family car (TA, 152). The war was over for General Smith.

7

Post-World War II

Brig. Gen. Oliver P. Smith arrived in Washington, D.C., on 27 July 1945. He had been in the Pacific combat zone for a year and a half. The war was still raging as he settled into his new job as commandant of the Marine Corps Schools. One week later, the first atomic bomb was dropped on Hiroshima. Three days later a second bomb was dropped on Nagasaki, which brought Japan to accept unconditional surrender terms. The instrument of surrender was signed on the deck of the USS *Missouri* on 2 September 1945. The guns were finally silent.

World War II was a time of individual and collective sacrifice that may never again be equaled. Men and women in the armed services, our citizen-soldiers, answered the call to serve. Professional soldiers, such as O. P. Smith, formed a cadre around which those thousands of men and women coalesced into an American fighting machine.

With the war over, thousands were discharged from military service as rapidly as they had been inducted. Smith immediately began evaluating the accomplishments and lessons of the conflict, incorporating them into the curriculum of the Marine Corps Schools so that the students could benefit from the hard-earned experience of their predecessors.[1]

Smith was responsible for much of the instructional material that was used during and immediately after World War II, when the Marine Corps Schools eventually reached a parity with counterparts in the army. A part of Smith's contribution was his skill as a teacher. Many of those who knew him would remember him as a teacher first, only secondarily as an inspiring leader of troops in combat.

Brigadier General Smith reviews candidates for the Marine Corps Schools, Quantico, June 13, 1946. *Courtesy of* MCUA.

On 28 January 1946, Smith was also given the responsibility of forming and outfitting the First Special Marine Brigade at Quantico, in conjunction with his duties at the Marine Corps Schools. He formed a headquarters group and two battalions from troops stationed at Quantico, supplementing them with some of the students already enrolled in the schools. Another battalion was formed at Camp Lejeune in North Carolina. The brigade was meant to be a combat-ready unit available on forty-eight-hour notice for deployment anywhere in the Atlantic or the Caribbean. There simply were not enough trained troops on active duty should an emergency arise.[2]

The brigade was to be moved to Camp Lejeune after it was organized; Smith was given temporary command. Most of the manpower came from the schools, and the commandant of the Marine Corps knew that there could have been strong protests about robbing the classrooms had someone other than Smith been given the command of the brigade. As it was, the brigade was staffed and equipped in a short period of time. When it was transferred to Camp Lejeune, on 4 March, Smith was relieved by General Vandegrift, who informed Smith that it had never been intended that he would command the brigade after it had been formed.

In mid-1946, Lt. Gen. Clifton B. Cates was appointed commanding general of Quantico Barracks and commandant of the Marine Corps Schools. Smith became the Assistant Commandant, Marine Corps Schools. The changes that then took place were implemented by Cates. The next year and a half was an important time for the Marine Corps and for Smith. Cates, as base commander, took the opportunity to observe Smith at close quarters, while Smith carried out his duties with his characteristic dedication and efficiency.

The Marine Corps was fighting for its very existence in the immediate post-war period. A plan to streamline the armed forces provided for air force parity with the army and navy, as well as for a national defense secretary, with separate secretaries for the army, navy, and air force. The Marine Corps was striving to obtain an official mandate for its own existence, a mission that could be uniquely its own. The air arm of the Marine Corps and naval aviation were most in jeopardy, because the newly created U.S. Air Force wanted to incorporate all air activities under its own tent.[3]

An organization of young ambitious marine officers took it upon itself to develop the means of countering any threat to the Corps from the other services. Their efforts were encouraged by Brig. Gen. Gerald C. Thomas, a veteran of the First World War and the Guadalcanal campaign, where he had served with distinction as the First Marine Division G-3 (operations officer). Thomas was acting as Vandegrift's personal representative in all matters pertaining to the defense reorganization negotiations. These officers became known as the "Little Men's Chowder and Marching Society." Most of the members of the society were working at Quantico, with Smith as their nominal boss. Smith frowned upon their more extreme statements in defense of the Marine Corps. Lt. Gen. Victor H. Krulak, an organizer of the society, wrote:

We were often misunderstood by our peers and sometimes by our superiors. Twining [Col. Merrill B. Twining] and I, for example, were working at the Marine Corps Educational Center in Quantico, Virginia, as members of a Marine Corps Board assigned to study amphibious concepts. To a much greater degree, we were engrossed in analyzing Army, Navy, and Joint Chiefs of Staff documents, writing memorandums for others to use to educate the public and members of Congress as to the hazards of the proposed legislation, composing speeches for senior marine officers and later organizing some of the congressional lobbying effort. Our immediate commander was Brigadier General Oliver P. Smith, a quiet, straightforward, God-fearing gentleman who found it hard to ascribe antagonistic motives to others who deplored our behind-the-scenes activity. "Wheels within wheels," he called it.[4]

Smith's tour of duty as commandant of the Marine Corps Schools (January 1946 to April 1948) challenged his knowledge and experience in military affairs, and it had long-term ramifications for the future of his service. The commandant of the Marine Corps, General Vandegrift, asked Smith to serve on a board with Lemuel Shepherd, assistant commandant, and Gen. Field Harris, director of aviation, to study the influence that atomic weapons would have on amphibious doctrine. The formation of the board was the result of a report to the commandant from Roy Geiger after he had watched the atomic bomb test at Bikini on July 1946. Geiger had written, "It is trusted that Marine Corps Headquarters will consider this a very serious and urgent matter and will use its most competent officers in finding a solution to develop the technique of conducting amphibious operations in the Atomic Age."[5]

On 16 December 1946, the Shepherd Board recommended a revolutionary new concept, "vertical envelopment," made feasible by the invention and improvement of the helicopter. Specifically, it recommended: "1. that an experimental squadron should be organized and equipped with 12 helicopters of the first available type; 2. that a study of techniques, tactics, logistics, and other phases of ship-to-shore movement by helicopters be made to include military requirements for the future helicopter design."[6] On 22 December the commandant directed Smith to implement the helicopter development program and to study further the feasibility of large transport seaplanes in amphibious operations. A special committee of the Academic Board from the MCS Education Center (Quantico), which became known as the "Helicopter Board," was to write the new doctrine for the helicopter.

Smith's report, submitted to General Vandegrift on 10 March 1947, was entitled, "Military Requirements of Helicopter for Ship-to-Shore movements of Troops and Cargo."[7] On 1 December 1947, "Marine Helicopter Squadron One (HMX-1) was established at Quantico . . . to test this new concept of vertical envelopment and the new flying machine that would make it work."[8]

When Cates learned that he would be selected as the next commandant of the Marine Corps, he told Smith, confidentially, that he wanted him to be his assistant commandant. However, the position required a major general; since Smith was only a brigadier general at that time, he remained at Quantico for the time being. When Cates left Quantico for Washington, Smith took over as commanding general of the Marine Barracks, Quantico, as well as commandant of the Marine Corps Schools. On 2 April he was promoted to major general, and on 15 April he left Quantico to become assistant commandant and chief of staff of the Marine Corps.

As assistant commandant, Smith was again embroiled in the unification fight. The "Chowder Society" had provided Cates with a letter to be presented by him to Congress. Smith would recall, "I went over with Gen. Cates to the congressional hearing. Twining and his crowd [had written] the letter, and I objected to the content of the letter because it impugned the motives of the Joint Chiefs of Staff. It just said they were trying to do away with us. I pointed out to Twining that if you mention Joint Chiefs of Staff these people will say, 'Who do you mean?' And then you just say [Lt. Gen. J. Lawton] Collins [Chairman, Deputy Chief of Staff, U.S. Army] or something like that and you get involved—you should avoid impugning motives" (OH, 181).

Benis Frank, the interviewer of Smith's oral history, asked him, "But someone has told me that you weren't happy with this. . . . He used the terms wheels within wheels."

Smith replied:

I didn't like the letter they wrote. As a matter of a fact, Cates changed the letter. Those bitter things were taken out. You could fight for your life without impugning the motives of these people. We do know that General Eisenhower wrote this memorandum that we be in regimental strength and man the landing boats. That's what we were up against. What he'd done—been over in Europe and seen the Royal Marines and that's what they were doing. They had nothing and they did man the landing boats, so he thought that would be a good idea for the U.S. Marines, who happened to have six divisions in the Pacific war.

We just laid our case on the line—why there should be a Marine Corps. . . .

[Question:] Do you think there was a place for what they were doing down in Quantico—for all of these preparations, and the studies, and the background?

Oh yes, [Smith answered] but you have to be very careful how you use that information. Some of these young officers could write these sharp letters, but they didn't have to take the responsibility of following through with them. The Commandant of the Marine Corps had to follow through. If he had accepted wholeheartedly what these young fellows wrote, he'd have to follow through with it, and that would have been a little difficult. . . . How would Cates prove that Collins was out to destroy the Marine Corps? . . . General Collins merely had a plan for an overall chief of staff who would run the whole works. I don't remember anything he ever put in writing about that. (OH, 182–83)

Late in 1948, Smith was asked by General Cates "to head a second board to examine measures which the Marine Corps should take to meet its responsibilities for leadership in amphibious warfare. The board recommended: (1) that until major advances were made in helicopter technology, few advanced tactics could be developed, and (2) that the time was rapidly approaching when helicopter squadrons should be organized to support the Fleet Marine Force."[9] Little did he know that his command in Korea in 1950 would be the first to use helicopters extensively in combat.

In February, when he was still president of Columbia University, General Eisenhower made a fact-finding trip to Washington, D.C., to determine how the new Defense Department was functioning. Cates asked Smith to brief Eisenhower about the organization and missions of the Marine Corps. Smith spoke for about an hour, concluding, "If I have not made it clear I would like to reemphasize now that our major effort revolves around the maintenance of adequately trained Fleet Marine Forces, prepared at any time and on short notice to extend the power of the fleet ashore in the seizure of objectives which are vital to the prosecution of a naval campaign or in the protection of American interests abroad."[10] Eisenhower asked a few questions but did not question the presentation and seemed pleased at its thoroughness and clarity. Smith was a good spokesman for the Marine Corps. His natural conservatism did not lead him to "make a lot of noise," but when he had something to say that he felt strongly about, such as his beloved Marine Corps, his sincerity and passion got one's attention.

Early October 1949, Smith submitted a memorandum to Cates about the congressional unification hearings, a five-page document that logically and succinctly summarized the positions that the commandant should take before Congress. It said, in part:

> An all-out investigation will engender bitterness on the part of the Army as well as the Air Force. There will be testimony in rebuttal. We will be attacked and we may have some weak spots. Nevertheless, I believe the Commandant should set forth his case before the committee for the two principal reasons:
>
> (a) To reassure all hands in the Marine Corps that the Commandant is protecting their interests.
>
> (b) To make certain that the case of the Marine Corps as a whole is considered.
>
> I do not believe that the Commandant should be put in the position of pressing to be heard. The invitation should come from the Committee and the presentation made by the Commandant should develop from testimony already given.

6. Following are a few comments and recommendations regarding lines of action:

(a) Admiral [Arthur W.] Radford's presentation [as Chief of Naval Operations] was kept on a high plane. The public and Congressional reaction was favorable. We should continue to keep the investigation on a high plane.

(b) We should soft-pedal "impaired morale" and play up "concern and apprehension."

(c) We should indicate that we are not only concerned about our own future but also about national security.

(d) We should not be put in the position of opposing unification. What we are concerned about is the implementation of unification contrary to the letter and intent of the law.

(e) We should not impugn the motives in the Army or Air Force. We should do our best to give them credit for having honest convictions.

(f) We should avoid criticism of the Navy.

(g) We should avoid loose use of the term "general staff." The Army has a perfect right to have a general staff if it wants one. What we object to is the concept of an over-all chief of staff and a national general staff. This concept is, of course, approved by many members of the Army General Staff.

(h) The Committee is apparently very much interested in the impact of present defense policies on the Navy Department budget. We should exploit this.[11]

The National Security Act of 1947 reaffirmed the position of the Marine Corps within the Navy Department, with the mission of seizure and defense of advance bases and land operations incidental to naval campaigns. The Marine Corps achieved statutory protection for its air, ground, and reserve organizations. The act also made amphibious warfare doctrine the unique responsibility of the Marine Corps and gave the Corps representation on the Joint Chiefs of Staff. That was a triumph for the Corps; up to that time, the commandant had attended JCS meetings only on an invitational basis. On 1 March 1950, "the House Armed Services Committee . . . recommended the inclusion of the Marine Corps Commandant in the Joint Chiefs of Staff and rotation of the group's chairman ship."[12] For now, the merger fight could be put on hold.

Smith had spoken to General Cates very early in 1950 about his desire to command the First Marine Division. He and Cates had agreed that Smith would stay on as assistant commandant for two years, and it was approaching the end of that stint (April 1948–March 1950). Gen. Graves E. Erskine had been commanding general of the First Marine Division for two years and was ready to be relieved. On 14 April 1950, Cates confirmed Smith's appointment as Commanding General, First Marine Division and as base commander of Camp Pendleton, effective 31 July 1950.

While Smith was making preparations to go to Pendleton, Adm. Forrest Sherman, now Chief of Naval Operations, asked Smith to go to Southeast Asia to determine what the French needed to complete their nasty little war in Indochina. Sherman knew that Smith had attended the prestigious École Supérieure de Guerre and was fluent in French. Smith was most anxious to be with troops again and did not want the job in Asia, so he convinced Admiral Sherman that General Erskine should have the assignment. Consequently, Erskine went to Asia, while Smith thankfully headed for Camp Pendleton.

On 25 June 1950, the North Korean People's Army swept across the thirty-eighth parallel and invaded South Korea. The United States was at war.

8

INCHON AND SEOUL, KOREA, 1950

Gen. Douglas MacArthur, commander of Far East Forces, was ill prepared to counter the invasion of South Korea. He had four poorly trained and grossly undermanned divisions in Japan. It was perhaps fortunate that it was MacArthur in command of the Far East Forces in 1950. He was a powerfully popular military leader who demanded and usually received what he asked for from the Joint Chiefs of Staff, who tended to stand in awe of him. He was a strong believer in the amphibious assault, and he had earlier received permission from the Joint Chiefs to establish an amphibious training unit in Japan under the able command of Adm. C. Turner Joy. The commander of Amphibious Group One was Rear Adm. James H. Doyle, who one day prior to the invasion of South Korea was visited by Gen. Omar N. Bradley, chairman of the Joint Chiefs of Staff, and Secretary of Defense Louis Johnson. Bradley was no admirer of the Marine Corps or the navy and had gone on record as saying that amphibious operations were a thing of the past. Doyle relates what took place: "Bradley asked me what I was doing there. . . . [I replied,] 'I'm here to give amphibious training to units of the Eighth Army at General MacArthur's request.' . . . Bradley simply looked scornful. No reply. Shortly after, during a visit with Turner Joy in General MacArthur's office, I mentioned the incident in connection with Bradley's prediction. It was then MacArthur's turn to be scornful. He said: 'Bradley is a farmer.'"[1]

MacArthur realized, after intelligence reports confirmed the magnitude of the invasion, that he did not have enough troops in the area to stop the enemy, much less push them back across the thirty-eighth parallel. At first he asked Washington for a brigade of marines, then followed with a request for a full

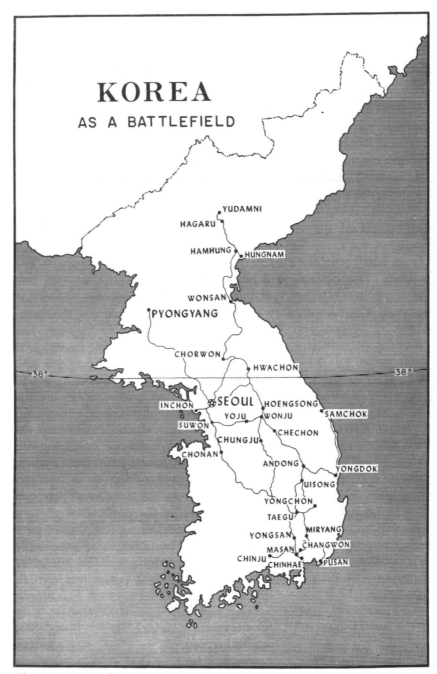

The Korean Peninsula. *Courtesy MCHC.*

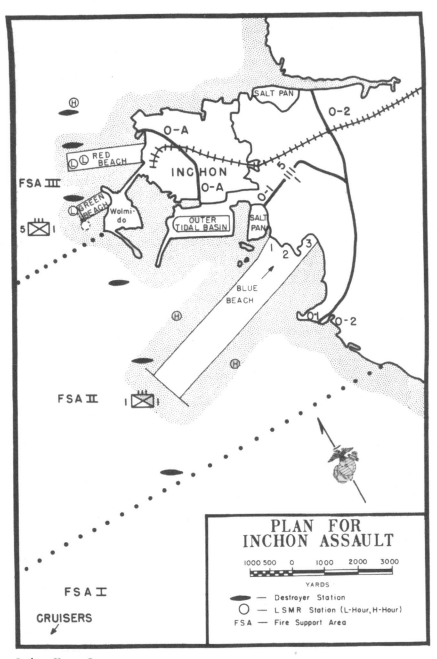

Inchon, Korea. *Courtesy MCHC.*

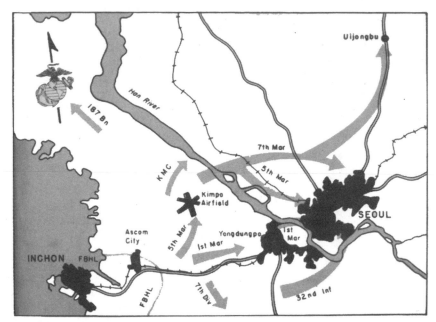

Seoul, Korea. *Courtesy* MCHC.

marine division with its attached air wing. In the meantime, he was forced to put the troops at his disposal in a defensive posture so that he could buy some time for a counterstroke. MacArthur knew that his plan for pinching off the North Korean troops already fighting in the South could become a reality if he had the First Marine Division under his command.

In Washington, the military establishment was in disarray after the debilitating unification fights. General Cates, the commandant, could not fulfill MacArthur's request without calling up the reserves. Equipping and manning the First Provisional Marine Brigade had already severely strained the resources of the Marine Corps.

That brigade was activated at Camp Pendleton on 7 July 1950, under the command of Brig. Gen. Edward A. Craig, assistant commander of the First Marine Division. The division commander was Maj. Gen. Graves B. Erskine, with Craig being responsible for most of the training schedules. (Craig had been born in Danube, Connecticut, in 1896, and had joined the Marine Corps in 1917 after graduating from the St. John's Military Academy at Delafield, Wisconsin. He was a tall, slender man with prematurely gray hair, an inspiring leader who had received the Navy Cross for his actions during the recapture of Guam.)[2]

Craig received the very latest in tanks for the brigade, and new and powerful 3.5-inch rocket launchers. The nucleus of the brigade was the Fifth Marine Regiment, commanded by Lt. Col. Raymond L. Murray, a young, hard-driving, introverted man who had served in Iceland with the Sixth Marines and as a forceful and effective leader in the Pacific. Craig later commented, "I received quite a bit of pressure to take a full colonel, but considered that he [Murray] was the best man available to command that regiment, and he was one of the outstanding regimental commanders of any regiment in Korea."[3]

When O. P. Smith left Washington on 18 July for Camp Pendleton, he was unaware that MacArthur had requested that the First Marine Division arrive in the Far East by mid-September at the latest. The Joint Chiefs of Staff (JCS) and MacArthur were frantically exchanging messages about bringing the division up to full strength. Many of the battalions had only two companies, while the platoons generally consisted of two squads each instead of the standard three. MacArthur was adamant in his request for a fully manned division for the proposed amphibious landing, and it was a golden opportunity for the Corps to prove that its claim of amphibious expertise was not an idle boast.

The provisional brigade was originally scheduled to disembark in Japan, but the deteriorating situation in Korea changed the schedule, and it landed at Pusan, much to the relief of Gen. Walton H. Walker, commanding general of the Eighth Army. The brigade went immediately to the front, a defensive arc around the port of Pusan, where it was desperately needed.

Events were moving rapidly, driven by the ugly prospect that the Eighth Army might be driven to a Dunkirk-like retreat from the Pusan perimeter. The Marine Corps was authorized to call up its reserves on 19 July, and several emergency measures were instituted that increased the flow of officers and men to the staging area around Camp Pendleton. The Second Marine Division at Camp Lejeune lost most of its men, and the security forces at several posts around the United States were reduced to a bare minimum; Congress helped by passing legislation that authorized the president to extend all enlistments for a year.

In the First Marine Division, matching up men and equipment with their units was a monumental administrative task. Men were arriving every hour, literally from all points of the compass. Smith calmly and methodically established priorities. In his words, "The Division proceeded on the basis that divisional elements should be built up to war strength faster than the attached Force [combat-support, such as engineers] and Service Command [logistical] units; and that, within the division, initial priority should be given to the buildup of combat units, keeping in mind the desirability of being prepared to mount out

Major General Smith talks with Tenth Corps commander, Maj. Gen. Edward M. Almond, in the Seoul Capital Building. Maj. Gen. Field Harris, CO, First Marine Aircraft Wing Far East, is directly behind Almond, wearing the flight jacket, September 29, 1950. *Courtesy of MCUA.*

an RCT [regimental combat team, a specially reinforced regiment] in advance of the remainder of the division" (AM, 10–11).[4] Smith selected the principal staff officers and unit commanders from men already available to him at Pendleton. The provisional brigade had taken 32 percent of the division staff, which did not become integrated as a single body until after the Inchon landing.

Training activities during the buildup period were limited to physical conditioning and test-firing of weapons. Some of the equipment taken from the large stockpile of World War II supplies stored at Barstow, a hundred miles north of Pendleton, had to be refurbished and tested. The piecemeal arrival of units made any training schedule tentative at best. Units from the Second Marine Division started to arrive by 3 August. The reserve units made it by the 4th. By 10 August, general cargo and ammunition were being loaded aboard the ships.

Prior to embarkation, all units were issued directives that covered such items as fire-support coordination, air defense, and antimechanized defense techniques. It was hoped that the information would help the troops in the absence of intense training that had been denied them in the rush to get to the Far East.

While the division was being formed, Washington was still sorting out its options. There had been a reluctance on the part of the JCS to authorize the additional (third) regiment for the division, as every move in Korea had to be evaluated in respect to its impact upon China. Gen. J. Lawton Collins, Chief of Staff of the Army, told MacArthur, "'General, you are going to have to win the war out here with the troops available to you in Japan and Korea.' MacArthur . . . smiled and shook his head. 'Joe, you are going to have to change your mind.'"[5] Finally, the Seventh Regiment was formed out of troops in the Mediterranean, Camp Lejeune, and various other sources. An air support group was given to the division only after forceful demands by MacArthur; he argued, "There can be no demand for its potential use elsewhere that can equal the urgency of the immediate battle mission contemplated for it."[6] It should be realized that the JCS had other things to be concerned about. They were especially afraid that the buildup in Korea had weakened the United States in the rest of the world to the point where the Russians and their allies might make a bold strike somewhere in Europe.

The First Marine Division required nineteen ships to embark the balance of the men and equipment. Most were loaded by 18 August, although some late-arriving ships did not finish loading until 22 August. A detachment was left behind to see that the balance of the necessary equipment was loaded and shipped to Japan at a later date.

The division staff was ordered to the Far East by airlift in two groups. Smith and his aide, Capt. Martin Sexton, remained behind until Smith was convinced that the most essential equipment was loaded and under way. He closed the command post and departed from Camp Pendleton on 18 August.

Sexton had played on two national intercollegiate championship soccer teams at the University of Maryland, where he had graduated in 1941. He had joined the Third Marine Raider Battalion late in 1942, participating in the Russells and Bougainville campaigns. After the Raider battalions were disbanded, he had served in the Emirau, Guam, and Okinawa campaigns. On Okinawa and Guam he had commanded a rifle company in the Fourth Marines. Sexton looked upon himself as a warrior, and he was not too pleased about the prospects of being an aide for a general officer. "I . . . recall when I was interviewed as a possible Aide-de-Camp I said: 'General [Smith], I appreciate the honor but I don't like to push cookies.' He replied 'I don't either, and where we are going we won't have to worry about that.'"[7] The two men were a good match, and Sexton became a staunch supporter and admirer of the general.

In view of the fact that I was his Aide for approximately a year, I had an opportunity to observe him under a full range of circumstances. And under all of the trying situations that the 1st Marine Division faced during the Korean war, General Smith was always in control of his emotions. I never saw him lose control of his emotions, or let his true feelings overwhelm his common sense or reasoning. And there were numerous times when giving vent to his true feelings would have been understood. In view of this, General Smith's courses of action were the result of proper staff functioning and logical command decisions. Even under the most adverse circumstances, his decisions were made in a calm, confident and professional manner.[8]

Smith was a pipe smoker in private moments and especially when he was in fatigues. He rarely smoked in conferences or meetings. As Sexton recalled, "General Smith smoked Sir Walter Raleigh smoking tobacco. One of the first things that he emphasized after he selected me as his Aide was that he smoked that brand, and that it was my task to insure that he never ran out. This was solved by my maintaining a large supply among my personal effects. Once we were in Korea, I would write my wife sufficiently in advance to keep our supply in a satisfactory state. Thanks to her cooperation, the General was satisfactorily resupplied throughout the tour that we spent together."[9]

The division G-3 (staff operations officer) was Col. Alpha L. Bowser, a calm, knowledgeable veteran who contributed a great deal to the masterful performance of the division in Korea. He later wrote that "all of the Division staff G's had performed the same jobs during World War II. . . . The general's eyes twinkled as he said, 'I wasn't born yesterday, I knew that in this case we had no time for on-the-job training.'"[10] Smith had a reputation for using his staff to the fullest; he expected and got maximum effort from its members. "I don't want an officer on my staff who never makes an error or a mistake because I will strongly suspect that he isn't doing anything or [that he is] blaming his mistakes on someone else."[11]

The scramble to assemble the division within a deadline was reason enough to question whether a smoothly running military force could result from such pressures. As Sexton commented after he left Korea, "There was perhaps a great deal of confusion apparent to the majority of the men and officers who joined Camp Pendleton during this period, but . . . no more . . . than is normal in such a situation. Time and space were against the division. I think the net result answers this question of confusion; for certainly out of confusion, a smoothly functioning division developed and there were few complaints in the field."[12]

Admiral Doyle met Smith at the Haneda airfield in Tokyo on 22 August and escorted him to the landing force commander's quarters on the USS *Mount McKinley*. Before Smith left the ship to report to MacArthur, Colonel Bowser briefed him on what he had already learned about their mission. Smith was only now informed that the division was scheduled to land over the seawall at Inchon on 15 September. Bowser reviewed some of the objections to the location, such as a tide of thirty-two feet or more, a vast area of mudflats surrounding the invasion site, and most of all, the compressed time element. The division would not land at Kobe, Japan, until 1 September at the earliest. That left no room for training or for rehearsing the landing, and the ships had to be unloaded and reloaded for combat.

Smith reported to MacArthur's headquarters in the Dai Ichi Building, where he was made to wait for an hour and a half for Maj. Gen. Edward M. Almond. Almond was MacArthur's chief of staff and was slated to command Tenth Corps, composed of the First Marine Division and the army's Seventh Infantry Division. Smith's "first impression of General Almond was not very favorable. He was supercilious in manner. He discussed the forthcoming operation with me. I voiced the objections noted above. With a wave of the hand he said there was no organized enemy anyway, and that our difficulties were purely mechanical, and that the date was fixed. Then he questioned me as to my command experience. He insisted upon calling me 'son'" (KL, 6).

When Almond ushered Smith into MacArthur's office, Smith thought that MacArthur looked his seventy years. Apparently Almond had briefed him on Smith's objections, because MacArthur immediately went into a discourse on the importance of Inchon. A landing at Inchon and the capture of Seoul, twelve miles to the east, would be a decisive blow that would isolate the North Korean forces from their logistical base in the North. Tenth Corps would cut their line of communications and act as an anvil as the Eighth Army drove northward. He remarked that Gen. James Wolfe's bold proposal in 1759 to land troops at the cliffs of Anse du Foulon, resulting in his capture of Quebec and defeat of the French army under General, the marquis de Montcalm, had all met with similar disapproval from his contemporaries, much like Inchon. MacArthur also declared to Smith that the successful invasion of Inchon and consequent capture of Seoul could not help but secure the future for the Marine Corps. Finally, he promised that the troops would be out of Korea by Christmas.

The next day Smith attended a meeting conducted by Maj. Gen. Clark L. Ruffner, future chief of staff of Tenth Corps. At this meeting Smith learned that the division was to "land at Inchon, seize a beachhead, then rapidly capture the Kimpo Airfield, then cross the Han River, capture Seoul and the high ground north thereof, then fortify a line north of Seoul, which was about 30 miles in extent" (KL, 7). Later the same day, Almond called another meeting with Smith, Maj. Gen. David G. Barr (commanding general of the army's Seventh Division), and assorted other staff officers. Smith mentioned the possibility of alternative landing sites but was abruptly told by Almond that he was interested only in Inchon. Now Smith was convinced that he would need the First Provisional

Brigade, and he made an initial request for its detachment from Eighth Army. Almond told him it would depend on the tactical situation at that time.

The next day, 24 August, Smith, General Shepherd (Commanding General, Fleet Marine Force Pacific), and Admirals Joy, Sherman, and Doyle attended an "indignation meeting," where concerns were expressed about Inchon. Many alternative sites could cut the North Korean line of communications, but they agreed that the landing would probably take place at Inchon, if for no other reason than that the capture of Seoul was a main objective. Smith left the conference convinced that the assault would be on Inchon on 15 September, even though it had not yet been authorized by the JCS. Time was slipping by. As Stormy Sexton later recalled, "Inasmuch as the ever present time-space factor was again making its presence felt because of the lateness of receipt of directives from X [Tenth] Corps, it was necessary for the 1st Marine Division to initiate and complete nearly all plans and orders *prior* to receipt of any orders or instructions from X Corps."[13]

The only approach to the city of Inchon was via a dredged channel that threaded through huge mudflats, with little room for maneuver or navigational error. At high tide the water was about thirty feet deep on the mudflats, barely enough for a tank landing ship (LST) loaded with troops and equipment. It was obvious to Smith that Wolmi-Do, an island that dominated the waterfront area, would have to be taken first. Twice a day the tides covered the mudfields, so Wolmi-Do would be taken on the earlier tide and the main assault on the mainland completed on the second tide, just before nightfall.

The decision to secure Wolmi-Do first meant a nighttime transit of the tricky channel, and the navy was reluctant to do it. Smith remained strong in his belief that the island was the key to success in the operation. The navy searched for a solution to the problem, an excellent example of the spirit of cooperation and professionalism that existed between Smith and Doyle. The navy came up with the idea of using destroyers, high-speed transports (APDS), and dock landing ships (LSDS) for the assault approach on Wolmi-Do. These powerful ships were maneuverable enough to handle the erratic currents and were equipped with state-of-the-art radar navigational instruments. Doyle's chief of staff acted as the task force commander, leading the "point" ship up the channel.

Aside from eliminating Wolmi-Do as a threat to the main endeavor, seizing the island would provide an excellent location for placement of artillery. Consequently, an artillery reconnaissance group came ashore with the assault forces. The Third Battalion of the Fifth Marines, under Lt. Col. Robert D. Taplett, one of the best battalion commanders in Korea, was scheduled to land on the first tide of the day. The follow-up tide could bring in the artillery, if the "recon" group decided that the island was a suitable place to site the guns.

Admiral Joy had no objections to the plans. General Shepherd expressed a concern that the assault forces, the Fifth Marines and the First Marines, could not link up before nightfall. Smith told him that it would be impossible, because there were not enough daylight hours available if Wolmi-Do was to be taken on the first tide of the day; Shepherd let it ride.

Three landing areas were selected: Red Beach (to be assaulted by RCT 5), Green Beach (on Wolmi-Do, by Battalion Landing Team 3/5—that is, Third Battalion of the Fifth Marines, specially reinforced), and Blue Beach (RCT 1). Blue Beach was located southeast of Wolmi-Do, on the southern shore of Inchon. Red Beach was north and slightly east of Wolmi-Do, in the heart of the dock section. Taplett's battalion was scheduled to land early in the morning and secure the high ground on Wolmi-Do. Then it had to sit tight until the next tide, late in the afternoon, when the artillery and reinforcements could come ashore. The First Marines, commanded by Col. Lewis B. Puller, was to land at Blue Beach on the afternoon tide, seize the high ground immediately inland from the assault beaches, and then consolidate before nightfall. The Fifth Marines was to do the same—that is, seize the high ground inland from Red Beach and consolidate its perimeter for the night. The Fifth Marines was being reinforced by the First Korean Marine Corps Regiment, which was to mop up the interior portions of the city.

On the second day, the Fifth Marines would move south around Inchon for as early a linkup as possible with the First Marines. Both regiments were then to advance and seize the southeast portion of the port, while the "ROKs" (South Koreans) secured the city proper. Smith later wrote, "From the start, we gave up any idea of getting wheeled or tracked vehicles, other than LVTs [amphibian tractors], over the mud flats. Our problem was to get men ashore with minimum equipment, seize an initial beachhead, and entrust to the SeaBees the problem of providing means to get our heavy equipment ashore" (A-M, 64).

Red and Blue Beaches were not true "beaches," like those of the Pacific campaigns. At Inchon, the assault troops got to the "beaches" via ladders placed against the seawalls that fronted the tidal basin. On 30 August, Smith once again queried Almond about the release of the Provisional Marine Brigade. Almond informed him that General Walker would be accommodating; as Smith would recall, "GHQ does not want to send a dispatch to Eighth Army requesting release of the brigade. The attitude is that Gen. Walker will be reasonable and Gen. Craig can arrange for release of the brigade at the proper time. It is, of course, not fair to General Craig to put him in the position of requesting release from combat commitments. I decided to put myself on record regarding the brigade and sent a dispatch to Tenth Corps requesting that the Brigade be released from combat commitments on 1 September in order to plan for the forthcoming operation and mount out" (KL, 14).

The next day a serious attack against the Pusan perimeter jeopardized the chances of the brigade's being available for Inchon. MacArthur had ordered the brigade out on 4 September but rescinded the order in face of the new threat. Smith was concerned "to know whether the Brigade is going to be available. There is no move to call off the operation, but it does not appear feasible without the Brigade" (KL, 15).

With time running out, Smith spoke to Admirals Joy and Doyle about the feasibility of having the Chief of Naval Operations intercede to get the brigade released. It was decided to use that as a last resort. Col. Edward S. Forney, a marine on Almond's staff, suggested that they use the Seventh Marines instead. However, it would not arrive from the Mediterranean until 15 September. Another proposal that seemed to be unrealistic, according to Smith, was the substitution of the army's Thirty-second Infantry Regiment, which was in Yokohama.

On 3 September, a conference was held at Almond's office to discuss the brigade. Those present were Smith, Joy, Almond, Doyle, Ruffner, and Brig. Gen. Edwin K. Wright, operations officer for the Far East Command. The discussion was potentially explosive, because so much was at stake. Almond reiterated that 15 September was still firm and declared that if the Fifth Marines could not make that date, for whatever reason, the Thirty-second Regiment would be substituted. Admiral Joy tried in vain to tie Almond down to specifics about the brigade but succeeded only in heating up the discussion more. Smith now took a firm stand. "I told General Almond frankly that in complicated amphibious operations such as the one we were to engage in, last minute substitutions could not be made; that it was unfair to the troops so substituted; that if the substitutions were made I would call off the Blue Beach landing and give the mission of the 5th Marines to the 1st Marines, and have the 32nd Infantry follow in. I told Almond, however, that to make this change would be going beyond the point of considered risk" (KL, 16).

Adm. Arthur D. Struble, commander of the Seventh Fleet, broke the impasse by suggesting that a regiment of the Seventh Division be embarked immediately and sent to a position off Pusan, where it could act as a floating reserve for General Walker and at the same time permit the release of the Provisional Marine Brigade on an hour's notice. After some hurried calls to Walker's headquarters, Smith was assured that the brigade could be released on midnight of 5 September. No sooner was the news received than another worry arrived on the scene: weather forecasters predicted that a typhoon was going to be off Kobe at the same time as the invasion fleet was leaving for Korea.

Smith attended another conference on the *Mount McKinley* with Doyle and Brig. Gen. Doyle G. Hickey, Far East Command deputy chief of staff, and Col. Louis B. Ely, who was pushing for a commando-like raid on the Kimpo airfield, about sixteen miles inland from Inchon. The proposed raid was another of Almond's unrealistic schemes. He had discussed it with Shepherd, who, surprisingly, seemed favorable to the operation. Shepherd told Smith to set aside a hundred well-trained men to be turned over to the army for the "raid." Smith told Shepherd that he had known Ely on Okinawa, that he had little faith in his capabilities, and that he was not very enthusiastic about the plan; however, he would pick the men if he was ordered to do so.

Ely also had a plan for the capture of Wolmi-Do by stealth at night; then the marines could come ashore the next day! Smith firmly informed him that Wolmi-Do was a part of an assault plan already fixed in place. The commando raid would have been a costly fiasco. Smith had not received any directives on the matter, but he could not afford to divert any more men from their original tasks. After hearing about the commando strikes, Smith also lost some of his confidence in Tenth Corps headquarters. He listened to yet another proposal the next day, from Brig. Gen. Henry I. Hodes, assistant commander of the Seventh Division. Hodes suggested that a battalion of the Thirty-second Infantry borrow five tanks from the marines and go "barrcling down the road" to capture the high ground south of Seoul. Smith lamented, "This was another one of the fantastically unrealistic plans that are generated at the Corps [headquarters]" (KL, 25). Smith was not the only one to be concerned about Almond. Walton Walker also believed that "Almond's knowledge of combat fundamentals and principals [*sic*] was limited. . . . His impetuous nature led him to underestimate the enemy while overestimating his own competence."[14]

The typhoon resulted in a warning broadcast on 10 September. Rear Adm. Arleigh Burke, deputy chief of staff to Admiral Joy, feared that the invasion fleet might be jeopardized by the powerful typhoon, then developing around the Marianas. If the initial schedule of the fleet was adhered to, the storm would hit just as the ships rounded Kyushu on their way to the Yellow Sea. (Burke was a most forceful personality and later one of the great Chiefs of Naval Operations.) When MacArthur asked him what might be done, Burke suggested that the fleet sail a day early, on September 11th. "Arleigh [Burke] was impressed by the alacrity with which the general grasped a situation and acted upon it."[15]

The fleet avoided the direct path of the storm, but it had a night of heavy seas. On 12 September the *Mount McKinley* pulled into Sasebo to pick up MacArthur and his party, which included Generals Shepherd, Almond, and A. P. Fox; Maj. Gen. Courtney Whitney, intelligence officer for the Far East Command; and Wright. Smith later explained what took place: "Admiral Doyle conducted a tour of the *Mt. McKinley* for the benefit of the embarked generals. The tour was a technique employed by the Admiral to impress Army officers with the fact that amphibious operations require specialization. The tour produced the desired impression" (A-M, 129).

The armada included over 130 ships from the U.S., Canadian, British, New Zealand, Australian, French, and ROK naval forces. In general, the American ships carried the troops and most of the supplies and conducted very effective gunfire support, screening, and blockading operations so as to isolate the invasion site. The First Marine Division (Reinforced) now included twenty thousand marines, and three thousand more once the provisional brigade arrived from Pusan.

Omar Bradley later wrote, "Ned Almond had never commanded a corps— or troops in an amphibious assault. However, he and his staff, mostly recruited from MacArthur's headquarters, were ably backstopped by the expertise of the Navy and marines, notably that of Oliver P. Smith, who commanded the 1st Marine Division, which would spearhead the assault."[16] Smith sent the following message to all hands: "The operation which the First Marine Division, Reinforced, will soon conduct is one which will involve unusual known and potential difficulties. Its successful execution is of vital importance to our country and the United Nations. The Division Commander is confident that Marines will display their traditional ingenuity, aggressiveness, and devotion to duty in overcoming all obstacles" (A-M, 143).

Edward A. Craig, the brigade's popular commander (as well the First Division's assistant commander), was a contemporary of Smith's and was of similar deportment and disposition. They now came together as the division commander and assistant division commander, even though they were not able to talk face to face about operations until the division was heavily committed in combat. Craig described Smith as a

great Marine and his fine record is an inspiration to all who served with him. . . . I first met General Smith while I was a student at the Marine Corps Schools, Quantico, Va. It was 1937, and I was a member of the Senior Class. He was an infantry tactics instructor and highly regarded by his students. I will always remember one of the problems he gave us. It involved a critical command decision, and we had to solve it in fifteen minutes. This included reading the problem and writing and turning in the answer. Gen. Smith was never one to give an order and then [say] . . . how to do it. This was impressed on me in Korea. I was with the 1st Brigade in the Pusan perimeter. Gen. Smith was in Japan, preparing for the Inchon landing. I was to embark the Brigade and join the rest of the 1st Marine Division at sea. I saw him about two days after the Inchon landing. The enclosed letter is interesting because it shows how he delegated authority and gave a general mission to his Assistant Division Commander.[17]

Smith had never discussed the Inchon landing with Craig. Smith's handwritten letter reads:

OFFICE OF THE COMMANDING GENERAL
FIRST MARINE DIVISION
(SECRET)   8 September 1950
Dear Eddie:—

I am sending over this note by Lt. Col. Moore. I had already talked to [Col. Edward W.] Snedecker [brigade chief of staff] and [Col. Joseph L.] Stewart [brigade G-3] about the operation but I believe it would be well to repeat my ideas about your participation.

If everything goes all right on Wolmi-Do during D-Day I would like for you to go ashore on the evening tide and set up an advance CP [command post]. We will give you a dispatch to that effect some time during the day of D-Day. I would expect you to function at discretion. There may be decisions to be made which you can best make on the spot. If there is time and you feel that the matter should be referred to Division, do so. In any event, keep us advised. In this connection I am thinking primarily of Red Beach. I believe we will be better able to handle the situation at Blue Beach from the *Mt. McKinley.*

Depending on the situation it is my intention to land on Wolmi-Do on the evening tide of D+1 [the day after D day]. We do not want to clutter up the island with a lot of CP vans, etc. What we hope to do is soup up your communications and bring in a minimum of personnel. At the first opportunity, we will displace the CP beyond the City. At this time we will move forward the rest of the personnel from the *Mt. McKinley* and personnel and equipment from the other ships. I appreciate the beating you are taking in coming out of action and mounting out. Only Marines could do what you are doing. We had a narrow squeak in getting you at all. We had 100% backing of the Navy in finally putting it across. Within a week after we land, the 7th Marines will be with us.

The Brigade has done a splendid job in South Korea and we are all proud of you. You have put the rest of us on the spot. I am confident we can all give a good accounting of ourselves, when the chips are down.

I regret that I could not get down to see you, but I could not work it in. I am looking forward to seeing you on Wolmi-Do.

Sincerely,

[Signed] Oliver P. Smith[18]

On 13 September, the first exchange of fire took place on Wolmi-Do, involving six U.S. destroyers that had gone up the channel to bombard the Korean defenses. Soon after the destroyers opened fire, they took several hits from artillery on Wolmi-Do. It was difficult for the hardy "tin-can" sailors, but now they knew where the enemy guns were located. Admiral Struble ordered a vigorous shelling from the big guns of the heavy cruisers and battleships, which silenced the opposition.

MacArthur was in an expansive mood aboard the *Mount McKinley,* and he actively engaged his messmates in conversation in the wardroom. After a particularly lengthy monologue, Smith confessed to his diary, "Admittedly General MacArthur has had a remarkable career and has to his credit many outstanding accomplishments. However, the pomposity of his pronouncements is a little wearing" (KL, 28).

Smith and Admiral Doyle established H hour as 1730 (5:30 P.M.) on 15 September 1950. Water height over the mudflats would then be adequate for the LCVPs (personnel landing craft) and the LVTs. The landings on Wolmi-Do were scheduled for 0630 that morning. First light came on D day at about 0530, and a deafening, hour-long bombardment of Wolmi-Do commenced. The first landing craft reached Green Beach at 0633, and Taplett's battalion took the island with only light casualties. Taplett had a knack of "getting things done," but he occasionally had shouting matches with his commanding officer. Norman Kingsley recalls that "Bob Taplett could be contentious and argumentative. He physically kicked me out of his CP once (I [had] snuck in to look at his Sit[uation]-Maps)—and told me many years later, 'You're lucky I only threw you out; 'cause I was really steamed that day after a screaming match with the regimental commander[,] Ray Murray.'... He [Murray] was no milquetoast either; young, tough, but shrewd and cagey. He could out-argue the best lawyer."[19]

MacArthur took the admiral's chair (a raised, padded seat on the port, or left-hand, side of the pilothouse) of the *Mount McKinley* to observe the shelling of enemy installations ashore. He silently watched the amphibious operation that he calculated would quickly draw the war in Korea to an end. His visionary strategy had been expertly implemented by Smith and Doyle, a testament to the skill and industry of the men who had crafted such a complicated assault in such a compressed period of time, and against a "beach" where the assault troops had to use ladders to climb from their landing craft.

Doyle, Shepherd, Almond, and Smith gathered around MacArthur when Taplett's messages started coming in. MacArthur asked about casualties and was told that they were minimal. He turned to Doyle and told him, "Say to the Fleet, 'The Navy and the Marines have never shone more brightly than this morning.'" MacArthur then announced, "That's it. Let's get a cup of coffee"[20] The marines on Wolmi-Do were now on their own. The mudflats became visible as the tide started to recede, leaving ships high and dry in a sea of mud, until the tide returned later in the day. Smith sent a message to Craig to establish the advance CP.

At 1730, the assault battalions of the First Marines landed on Blue Beach and attacked inland to secure the high ground commanding the beaches. Blue Beach had been selected in order to avoid the city proper and to threaten the rear of any enemy units that attempted to hold the city. Puller's men charged ashore against minimal resistance. It was imperative that they seize high ground so that the assault troops could consolidate and assume a defensive posture before nightfall. The first objective was readily taken. Red Beach, north of Wolmi-Do, aimed straight at the heart of the city of Inchon. The Fifth Marines, less the Third Battalion on Wolmi-Do, would form on the mainland in columns of companies and drive inland to secure Observatory Hill.

The Fifth Marines, which had left the Pusan perimeter after disengagement from the enemy and had embarked for the assault on Inchon, was briefed on its objectives on board ship. It assaulted over Red Beach without skipping a beat. It is powerful evidence of the quality of leadership that existed at every level in the RCT and the provisional brigade. Attached to the Fifth Marines was a battalion of ROK marines to assist in maintaining a secure perimeter when darkness descended. Observation Hill was not taken until late in the evening.

Artillery was established on Wolmi-Do on the late-evening tide. It was soon in business, supporting landings on both Red and Blue Beaches. D day went according to the plan, and Smith wrote: "Casualties for 16 September were as follows: KIA 2, MIA 1, WIA [wounded in action] 23" (KL, 32).

For the remainder of the time that Smith was in Korea, a tally of casualties was the last entry in each of his daily log entries. He knew that success or failure in a military enterprise is purchased with the lives of young warriors, and he always evinced respect and affection for the men who met the enemy one on one. He would pen a tribute to them five years before his death: "There is one resource of the Marine Corps that has always been fully developed[:] the individual Marine.

What made a good Marine during the Revolutionary War still makes a good Marine. A competent, loyal, highly motivated Marine is an asset far exceeding in value all the developments of a technological age."[21]

The morning after the assault, Craig notified Smith that Wolmi-Do was too crowded and that he was moving the division command post to the outskirts of the city. Smith responded that he would meet Craig at the new location in the early evening of the 16th, and he made his farewells to colleagues on board the *Mount McKinley*. His good-bye to Admiral Doyle was especially meaningful and heartfelt. The two men had worked together for twenty-five days under the most harmonious of circumstances, and they had created a successful instrument of amphibious force projection that is still studied by military students throughout the world.

Craig was waiting at the CP when Smith arrived, and the two immediately went over the events of the day and what lay ahead. Smith announced to Admiral Doyle that he was taking command of the troops ashore as of 1800 (6 P.M.). The ramshackle building that the command post occupied was typical of the locations Smith would use throughout his stay in Korea. Craig later recalled that Smith "was frugal in his habits and never demanded the little extras that many officers of rank did. We messed together with some members of his staff and always ate only the issue rations. After we occupied the City of Seoul, the US Army delivered a six-wheel command truck to Smith. It was equipped with a bunk, desk, shower, etc. A true luxury in the field. He used this vehicle just once. He normally slept on a folding cot and continued this practice all the time I served as his ADC."[22]

The battle for Inchon was going better than planned. The First and Fifth Marines made contact at the southeast corner of the city, and the ROK marines were turned loose to clean out the heart of the city; they were better able than Americans to differentiate between the North and South Koreans. It turned out that they were extremely brutal, yet effective, as they cleared the streets. Murray drove his regiment toward the Kimpo airfield, while Puller headed easterly toward Yongdung-po, on the main road from Inchon to Seoul. On the first full day of the invasion, by nightfall, the two regiments progressed about five miles from the coast.

The next day MacArthur, Almond, and Struble attended a briefing at the First Marine Division CP. Smith thought everybody was pleased with the progress. The party started out, via jeeps, for Puller's CP; Puller was a favorite of MacArthur's. Later in the day they visited Murray's CP and were treated to a spectacle of six smashed North Korean tanks, compliments of Col. Harold Roise's Second Battalion. The tanks were still burning when, much to the surprise of

Roise's men, the visiting brass suddenly appeared. Since MacArthur had awarded a Silver Star to Puller earlier, Almond gave one to Murray, there beside the knocked-out enemy tanks.

On 17 September, Smith presided over the installation of a new mayor of Inchon and the reestablishment of civil government. He issued a proclamation that the city had been liberated and that the rightful government was back in power. The mayor had been imprisoned by the North Koreans. On the same day, Smith was introduced to Maj. Gen. Frank E. Lowe, U.S. Army Reserve. Lowe was a forceful character who played an important role during the early months of the Korean conflict. President Truman and Lowe were artillery veterans of the fighting in France during World War I. Between the wars, Lowe had served as president of the Reserve Officers Association and vice commander of the American Legion. He had been ordered to active status in 1940 and had been placed in charge of Reserve Officer Training Corps and reserve affairs in Washington, D.C. During the war, he had worked tirelessly for the Truman Committee (Senate Special Committee Investigating the National Defense Program) and had assumed special duties assigned by Gen. George C. Marshall in South America and the British Isles. He had retired as a major general in the reserves in 1946.

Lowe's retirement as a "gentleman farmer" at his beautiful home in Harrison, Maine, had been cut short when Pres. Harry Truman asked if he would go to Korea as his personal representative and report directly to him about the conditions in the field. The president knew from experience that his old friend had a habit of speaking forcefully and truthfully about his opinions and observations. Truman was also an admirer of the citizen-soldier concept, so it was only natural that he select an experienced National Guard officer to be his eyes and ears in Korea.

Lowe accompanied Gen. Matthew Ridgway, Gen. Lauris Norstad, and Ambassador Averell Harriman on their trip to Japan and to the meeting of 6 August 1950 in MacArthur's office, where plans for the Inchon invasion were first discussed. Lowe was warmly received by MacArthur, but privately MacArthur was not pleased to have a potential spy for the president in his sphere of influence without being able to control him. Unlike Truman, however, Lowe was a great admirer of MacArthur and had known him for twenty years. He was determined to set a high standard of performance for himself and for his tiny staff, which was generously established by MacArthur in the same office building that housed his Far East Command operations. Lowe notified Truman that it was his intention to show every communication to MacArthur before sending it to the president. He kept his word on every document, except the last one, when MacArthur had already left the Far East.

The Pentagon disliked Lowe's position, but his courage and desire to be at the front with the troops endeared him to many officers. He had no command authority, never got involved in tactics, and avoided the press as much as possible. He was an experienced and knowledgeable observer, and he let those around him know that he intended to do the job that he had come to Korea to do.[23] Lowe had observed the performance of the brigade at the Pusan perimeter before he came ashore at Inchon. The marines and the hardy old soldier from Maine were natural friends. "Stormy" Sexton had this to say about Lowe's first visit:

> I can clearly recall the first time that I heard a reference to Gen. Frank Lowe. Gen. Smith mentioned that such a person would be joining us for a while to observe the conduct of operations of the First Marine Division. Apparently all of the information that was available was a letter of introduction that was signed by President Truman.
>
> I also clearly remember the first night that our visitor joined us for dinner. Present were Gen. Smith, Craig (ADC), Col. Gregon Williams (C/S), Maj. Gen. Lowe and myself. The atmosphere was tense because none of the marines knew what to expect. The situation improved considerably as the evening wore on, and it seemed that our Army guest was truly an unbiased observer who was extremely loyal to his President.
>
> As the visit of Lowe was extended, he was constantly with the attacking battalions and regiments. And, although some called him foolish, he was never called fearful. He commented to all about his respect for the individual marine's courage and professionalism. He was heard to say on a number of occasions that, "the safest place in Korea was with a Marine Rifle Platoon."
>
> His routine was to write a letter to the president every night the tactical situation permitted.... He did not share them with anyone. As his visits stretched out the Marines seemed to welcome him as a friend.... General Smith concluded that Gen. Lowe was truly an asset who "told it like it was" and was absolutely sincere in his expressions of admiration for the U.S. Marines.[24]

Not long after the landing at Inchon, congratulatory messages started to arrive from all over the world. MacArthur's stock was at an all-time high, and he was elated with the performance of General Smith and his marines. The commandant, General Cates, wrote to Smith and Maj. Gen. Field Harris, commanding officer of the First Marine Aircraft Wing: "The Marine Corps is proud of your exploit superbly accomplished under the stress of minimum preparation and extraordinary hydrographic conditions. You have added luster to the term 'Marine.' Well done" (A-M, 206).

Admiral Doyle wrote a thorough analysis of the Inchon landing in his after-action report. One can't help but feel that he had General Almond in mind as a reader when he wrote:

> Under the circumstances, . . . it is my conviction that the successful assault on Inchon could have been accomplished only by United States Marines. This conviction, I am certain, is shared by everyone who planned, executed, or witnessed the assault. My statement is not to be construed as a comparison of the fighting qualities of various Armed Forces. It simply means that because of many years of specialized training in amphibious warfare, in conjunction with the Navy, only the United States Marines had the requisite "know-how" to formulate the plans within the limited time available and to execute those plans flawlessly without training or rehearsal. To put it another way, I know that if any other unit of our Armed Forces had been designated . . . , that unit would have required many, many months of specialized training, including joint training with the Navy, which is a regular part of the Marines' every day life. (A-M, 207)

Things were moving rapidly on the front lines by the time Smith took command of the division ashore. The Fifth Marines was at the outer perimeter of the Kimpo airfield. It was important to secure the field and make sure it was in good enough condition to accept Marine Aircraft Group (MAG) Thirty-three, which was waiting to fly in as soon as it got the all-clear signal. The field was crucial not only for close air support but to receive cargo planes from Japan. The Second Battalion occupied the airfield at 2005 (8:05 P.M.) on 17 September, after a rapid advance of about thirteen miles against moderate resistance. The next morning, the battalion beat off several sharp counterattacks against Kimpo, with heavy losses to the North Koreans.

General Shepherd, accompanied by Colonel Krulak (operations officer for Fleet Marine Force Pacific under Shepherd), was the first to land at the Kimpo airfield in a helicopter. General Craig's brigade was the first military formation to use helicopter in combat. There were only eight helicopters in Korea, and they all belonged to the Marine Corps. They had already proven themselves versatile and invaluable for resupply, reconnaissance, evacuation of wounded men, and courier duties on the battlefield. A few hours after Shepherd landed, another helicopter touched down on the runway, with Gen. Field Harris and Brig. Gen. T. J. Cushman, the new tactical air commander of Tenth Corps, as passengers. They arrived with the intention of preparing the field for MAG 33. It was planned that close air support sorties from Kimpo could be a reality by 20 September.

Northeast of the airfield, the Fifth Marines rapidly advanced to the high ground overlooking the Han River. After the Korean marines completed their mopping up operations in Inchon, Smith sent them north and west of Kimpo in a wide-swinging hook movement that formed the northern shoulder of the pincer envelopment that he had planned for the city of Seoul.

The First Marines seized the high ground east of Sosa, a small town halfway between Inchon and Yongdung-po, against increasing resistance. Its right flank was temporarily held by the division's reconnaissance company, due to delays in moving the Thirty-second Infantry into the line. When the Thirty-second Infantry, under the command of Col. Charles E. Beauchamps, had come ashore, First Marine Division had attached "Recon" Company to the Fifth Marines. The Thirty-second was attached administratively to the division for a short period of time and was equipped with jeeps and radios from marine stocks until its equipment was offloaded at Inchon. Everything seemed to be going according to plan for the capture of Seoul, a fact that is often overshadowed by the spectacular success of Inchon.

Smith moved his command post to Oeoso-ri, half a mile southeast of Kimpo, on a site previously used by occupation troops. He received a communiqué from Tenth Corps on 18 September; it "directed the 1st Marine Division to initiate reconnaissance of the Han River crossings in its zone of action and cross the River early 20 September. These instructions further directed the 1st Marine Division to envelop the enemy positions on the north bank of the Han River in the vicinity of Seoul, seize and secure the high ground thereof" (A-M, 216–17).

When Smith attended a conference with Almond the day after receiving the directive, he did so with some misgivings. Almond was pushing for a rapid crossing of the river, but Smith did not want to do it without tanks. Almond promised some bridging material, but Smith knew that the only bridging material in Tenth Corps already belonged to the marines. A crossing site was selected opposite the town of Haingju, where a ferry had operated. It contained a road system of sorts that gave access inland from the riverhead into Seoul from the northeast. Smith found out that General Lowe was planning to cross the Han with the recon company; "I told General Lowe that a 65 year old major general had no business with a Reconnaissance Company, that it was a young man's game and, furthermore, that part of the Recon company was going to swim across. I told him he would have to go with the reserve battalion. He was not very happy about it and showed me the card he had which was signed by Mr. Truman and which permitted him to go anywhere. I told him he would still go with the reserve battalion" (KL, 37–38).

Recon Company planned to have some of its men swim the river to set up a defense on the far side while the rest of the company crossed in LVTS. PFC Paul G. Martin recalls that evening: "The Recon Co. was called on the double for muster. Capt. [Kenneth J.] Houghton was displeased with us being too slow, so he ordered us to do 20 pushups. . . . The Captain told us, the President of the United States sent a major general 10,000 miles from Washington to watch the Marines cross the Han River and on to Seoul and General O. P. Smith selected the Recon Company to be the vanguard and this is a great honor for us to be on center stage."[25]

Later in the day Smith accompanied MacArthur to the same observation post, where reserve elements of the Fifth Marines were still crossing. The party, with Almond driving one of the jeeps, then went in convoy to the CP of the First Marines, in front of Yongdung-po. Smith rode with Generals Wright, Almond, and MacArthur. "From Puller's Regiment we went back to the main road from Inchon to Yongdung-po where General Barr was waiting for us. There I said good-bye to General Mac Arthur. . . . General Almond . . . is a very fast driver. On one stretch of road he drove a truck off the road and it turned over. Fortunately no one was hurt. At the end of the trip General Wright asked General Almond if he had a driver's license" (KL, 40).

Smith returned the next day to the Kimpo airfield as a courtesy, to say good-bye to General MacArthur before he returned to Japan. MacArthur had just come from a short visit to the USS *Missouri*, lying at anchor in Inchon Harbor as a part of the naval gunfire support group. The battleship had been the scene of the poignant surrender-signing ceremony at the end of the war with Japan, and the visit had had a profound impact on MacArthur; tears had rolled freely down his cheeks. He had thanked Admiral Struble, who had invited him for the visit, for "the happiest moment of his life."[26]

Just before MacArthur boarded the aircraft, he turned to Smith and, "warmed by memories of Victory in Tokyo bay and elated by impending victory in Seoul, . . . pinned the Silver Star on his green utility jacket, and said: 'To the gallant commander of a gallant division.'" When the aircraft carrying MacArthur and his staff back to Japan gained altitude and leveled off, General Shepherd, acting as MacArthur's personal advisor, wrote in his diary: "I personally believe it will take a week of fighting before Seoul is secured" (A-M, 40).[27]

The Seventh Marines arrived at Inchon as scheduled on 21 September. It had been activated at Camp Pendleton on 17 August and had sailed for Kobe, where it had picked up its third battalion, which had come from the Mediterranean, by way of the Suez Canal. Col. Homer L. Litzenberg, the regiment's commanding officer, was an energetic, hard-driving officer who was most protective of his men. Those who knew him well said he had a terrible temper but was well versed in staff requirements and tactics. He would prove to be a strong and resolute commander, and his performance in Korea was to earn him a place as one of the Marine Corps's great combat leaders.

As soon as the transports anchored off Inchon, Litzenberg located General Smith and asked him what he wanted done first. Smith told him that he needed an infantry battalion, followed by another infantry battalion for patrolling on the western and northern flanks of the division, respectively. Smith wanted to give the regiment a quiet sector in order for it to get "shaken down" and conditioned to the situation in Korea before he used it in heavy combat. Securing the left flank was perfect.

By 24 September, three battalions of the Seventh Marines were on the left flank of the Fifth Marines, which was poised to strike at the heart of Seoul from the northwest. Puller's First Marines was still driving hard through Yongdungpo; it would cross the Han River to hit the city from the south. The First Marines would complete the pincer maneuver that Smith had visualized. The Thirty-second Infantry was responsible for the right flank, south of the First Marines. Farther south of the Thirty-second Infantry, other elements of the Seventh Division were carrying out a right-hook maneuver to the east in order to carry out the envelopment of the city.

Bevin Alexander, the author of *How Great Generals Win,* is critical of Smith's handling of the battle for Seoul: "General Smith refused to undertake an envelopment from the south and insisted on throwing the 5th Marines directly against the dug-in North Korean positions north of the city."[28] Colonel Bowser has replied to the accusation in these terms: "At no time did the 1st Marine Division have any units south of Seoul nor was any such thoughts [*sic*] entertained. The 'real estate' south of the Inchon-Seoul highway had been the province of the Seventh Army Division from the beginning of the movement towards Seoul from Inchon."[29] Lieutenant Colonel Taplett emphatically stated that

if Mr. Alexander had been familiar with official accounts leading up to the crossing of the Han River, he should have known that the 5th Marines had crossed the Han on the morning of September 21, with MacArthur, Almond, Smith and other ranking personnel in full observation on a hill removed from the crossing site. I commanded the 3rd Battalion, 5th Marines which made the assault crossing of the Han.

He should have known . . . on the early morning of 21 September, that RCT-1 was still fighting for Yongdungpo and their crossing site which they didn't secure until September 23 and then crossed the Han early the next morning, September 24.

Major General Smith returns civil government to the mayor of Inchon on behalf of the United Nations, September 18, 1950. *Author's private collection.*

He should have known that by September 24, when RCT-1 crossed the Han, the 5th Marines had already fought through bitter resistance to reach the outskirts of Seoul and held all the commanding terrain and approaches to Seoul, including the landing site of RCT-1.[30]

This was the first time that Smith had his division's full complement in battle formation against a common objective. Up to this time he had worried about his open flanks, but now that the Seventh Division was scheduled to take up positions on his right and the ROK marine regiment was to fill in on the left of the Seventh Marines, he could concentrate upon the main objective—Seoul. By noon of 22 September, the Fifth Marines was on the high ground on the western outskirts of the city. The First Marines slowed its attack against Yongdung-po, because the Thirty-second failed to come abreast of its right flank (KL, 41). Litzenberg was rapidly assembling his battalions piecemeal on the left.

The days 23 and 24 September were crucial for Smith. From the moment that he and Almond first met, they had been uneasy with one another. They were opposites in temperament and style, and they probably could never have been best of friends under any circumstances. However, their differences were settled as those differences arose. There may have been lingering doubts in confidence,

Major General Smith and Brig. Gen. Edward A. Craig arrive at the Governor's Palace for raising of the Republic of Korea flag, September 29, 1950. They are accompanied by Capt. Martin J. Sexton. *Author's private collection.*

Below: While Brig. Gen. Edward A. Craig looks on, Major General Smith turns over to Cdt. Gen. C. Cates the North Korean flag hauled down from the Government Palace in Seoul, October 4, 1950. *Courtesy of MCUA.*

but the men were always civil to each other. Smith was not a man to carry a grudge or let his personal feelings interfere with his relationship, as a subordinate, with Almond. Almond had to be aware that the First Marine Division was one of the best divisions in Korea and that Smith was the star commander within Tenth Corps. MacArthur must bear responsibility for naming Almond as commander of Tenth Corps and chief of staff of the Far East Command at the same time. It was an awkward command situation, one that should never have existed.

Smith reviewed the situation as of 23 September: "From the start of planning, the First Marine Division had contemplated an initial crossing of the Han River by the Fifth Marines and an attack against Seoul by that regiment from the northwest. While this was being accomplished, the First Marines would clear the south bank of the Han River, cross the river in the vicinity of Yongdung-po, and join the 5th Marines in the assault on Seoul. The First Marine Division–7th Infantry Division boundary extended along the south bank of the Han River[,] excluding the 7th Infantry Division from participation in the attack on the city" (A-M, 262).

Almond was most anxious to have Seoul captured by 25 September, the three-month anniversary of its capture by the North Koreans. It was a political gesture dictated by MacArthur. At a meeting in Tenth Corps headquarters at ASCOM City (a Quonset-hut facility built years earlier by the U.S. Army Service Command), Almond asked Smith to guarantee the capture of the city by that date. Smith categorically stated that he could not do that but would make every effort to clear the city as soon as the tactical situation allowed. Smith viewed "MacArthur's political notions as rather whimsical, and detested Almond's demands for immediate action on that basis. Smith wanted to concentrate on the military objective—destroying the North Korean army—which he believed Almond was neglecting."[31]

In Smith's words:

The Corps Commander apparently considered that an attack from the southwest and northwest would not clear the city fast enough. At a conference at Corps Headquarters at 1700, 23 September, General Almond proposed that I send the 1st Marines around to the southeast, cross the Han River with that regiment, and attack Seoul from the southeast, while the Fifth Marines continued the attack from the northwest. General Almond felt that this pincers action would force the enemy out of Seoul much sooner than by continuing the attack in accordance with the current plan. (He was not reckoning with an oriental enemy.) I pointed out to the Corps Commander that the resistance being encountered by the 5th Marines on the western approaches to

Seoul was too much for one regiment to handle and that I desired to cross the 1st Marines northwest of Youngdung-po to assist the 5th Marines. It was further pointed out that the crossing of a regiment as proposed by the Corps Commander would greatly increase the problem of coordination of fires [artillery, air strikes, etc.].

The Corps Commander . . . modified the plan to have the 7th Division participate in the attack on Seoul. The modified plan called for the 32nd Infantry to cross the Han River and enter Seoul from the southeast. The 1st Marine Division would furnish the amphibian tractors to cross the 32nd Infantry. (A-M, 264)

Smith's refusal to accept Almond's impromptu plan electrified the atmosphere. "Almond was appalled at the tantamount insubordination of Smith's argumentative refusals. Given Almond's propensity to relieve subordinates who gave him dissatisfaction, it was obvious that Smith's globe-and-anchor saved him from a sacking."[32] The confrontation with Almond illumines Smith's inner strength. When he was convinced that he was on the right track, and when he felt that the lives of his men were at stake, he was most persistent in making himself understood. He had a large reservoir of calm courage when the situation demanded it. This aspect of Smith's temperament was frequently misinterpreted by his critics.

At the end of the day on 23 September, the First Marines had secured the southern approaches to the bridges over the Han River north of Yongdung-po. The Fifth Marines was pounding against heavy resistance at the western approaches to Seoul. The Seventh Marines was continuing its sweep to the west and north so that it could block any attempt on the part of the enemy to flee from the city. The ROK marines covered the western and northernmost flanks.

The next day, Smith checked the site where the First Marines would cross the Han River. One of the observers was Maj. Edwin H. Simmons, who would recall: "As for the crossing of the Han, Gen. Smith visited the observation post of the third battalion, 1st Marines, which overlooked the two bridge sites leading into Seoul, on the evening before the crossing. As an obstreperous 29-year-old major, I said, 'It looks like Fredericksburg, doesn't it, General?' [On 13 December 1862, during the American Civil War, Gen. Ambrose Burnside lost thirteen thousand Federal soldiers in direct assaults on entrenched Confederate defenses.] General Smith, who knew me well from Quantico, looked at me with quiet amusement, and said: 'Yes, Simmons, but we are not going to make the same mistakes as Burnside.'"[33]

Smith and Almond met at Yongdung-po in perhaps the most confrontational face-to-face meeting that the two men had in Korea. There are several versions of what took place. According to Smith:

> At 1400, 24 September, I met General Almond and General Barr in Yongdung-po for the purpose of discussing the Corps scheme of maneuver, which involved the crossing of the Han River by the 32nd Infantry. . . . In the course of the conversation, General Almond told me that he had already discussed the scheme of maneuver with Colonels Puller and Murray and that they were ready to carry out the roles which General Almond said had been assigned them. There had already been one instance where General Almond had given direct orders to Colonel Puller. As a result of this occurrence, I had directed the regimental commanders to call the Division at once for instructions if they received direct orders from the Corps. I felt now the time had come for an understanding with General Almond. I told him that I would appreciate it if he would not give orders direct to the regimental commanders; that if he would give his orders to Division we would make every effort to see that they were carried out promptly. General Almond denied that he had given any direct orders to the regimental commanders. I told him that the regimental commanders were under that impression. He then stated that he would correct that impression. There the matter rested. . . . While a senior officer in the chain of command has the right to give orders as he chooses to subordinate units, except in an emergency, this practice can only result in confusion. (A-M, 265–66)

The same meeting is further described by the historian Col. Robert Debs Heinl, Jr.

> Generals Smith, Barr, and Hodes were waiting when Almond arrived with Colonels Forney and Chiles. So was Colonel Beauchamps, on whom the crossing would actually devolve, and so was the usual cluster of correspondents.
>
>   Almond tersely announced the boundary change and his decision to send the Thirty-second Infantry across the Han at 0600 next morning (the 25th). "Dave Barr," he said. "I want you to take the 32nd Infantry across the river at six tomorrow morning; Smith, you get your amtracs on the road right now." The abrupt change of plan came as a surprise to Beauchamps. "The meeting was short," he later recounted, "and General Almond issued his orders quickly and emphatically and turned us loose."

Although the conference was short, Almond said one thing too many. At one point he assured General Smith that he (Almond) had already discussed the new plan with Puller and Murray, told them what he wanted done, and that they were ready to carry out the roles he had assigned them. General Smith was a forbearing man. But the stress of battle, combined with what he felt to be unrealistic pressure for "headway" and a scarcely concealed slap at the marines' fighting ability prompted certain feelings. . . .

In General Barr's words, "Smith just hit the ceiling."

Face to face with the fury of a patient man and looking apprehensively at the ring of correspondents and startled staff officers, Almond tried to smooth things over and told the Marine general that he would talk things over after the conference. As soon as the others left, O. P. Smith emphatically repeated his request, whereupon Almond said there must be some misunderstanding. . . . Always careful to be informed at such moments, Smith replied that Puller and Murray certainly thought that they had been given orders, . . . Almond tried to mollify the Marine by saying he would correct that impression.[34]

Smith always made a point of visiting the regiments on a daily basis if at all possible. On 25 September he stopped at the Fifth and Seventh Marines by helicopter. The Seventh was still providing flank security and conducting blocking operations. The Fifth Marines was advancing slowly against difficult resistance, but progress was being made, behind an unprecedented concentration of artillery support. Smith's use of artillery in his attack against Seoul should dispel the idea, frequently argued by other services, that marine officers are less qualified than their army counterparts to conduct land operations on a large scale. The volume of fire hurled at Seoul was the most intense ever delivered in support of a marine division up to that time. The Eleventh Marines artillery was stationed south of the Han River, giving the full support of its batteries. It was a virtuoso performance.

Murray was having trouble making contact with the First Marines on his right, and Puller was in the same predicament trying to make contact with Murray. Murray finally called division headquarters and described his problems to Colonel Bowser. It turned out that he had been using inaccurate grid coordinates issued from Tenth Corps. Bowser told Murray to go over to Puller's CP and straighten it out. When Murray got out of his helicopter, it was "the first time I [had] laid eyes on Chesty Puller. The first question he asked me was how many casualties did I have. And I said, 'Well, I've got quite a few,' and as soon as I convinced him that I had quite a few casualties, why[,] he figured[,] you can join the group then. He determined how good a fighter you were by how many casualties you had."[35]

Southeast of Seoul, the Thirty-second Infantry moved briskly against a prominent feature called South Mountain and overran most of the hill before nightfall. Almond thought that the move would make the North Koreans abandon Seoul, but it took two more days of bitter combat to control the rest of the city. "The seizure of South Mountain had no apparent effect on the defenders in the city. . . . Maneuver was provided by sending the 7th Marines from the northwest. This had a decisive effect."[36]

Smith had enough on his mind conducting the operations of his division, but he was about to inherit one more worry that was uncalled for. Almond was once again the culprit. At 2000, First Division received an order from Tenth Corps that got everyone's attention. It read as follows: "Info addressee (X Corps TacAirCommander) reports enemy fleeing city of Seoul on road north of Uijong-bu 1003-1665 and he is conducting heavy air attack and will continue same. You will push attack now to the limit of your objectives in order to insure maximum destruction of enemy forces. Signed Almond" (A-M, 288).

Colonel Bowser could not believe what he had read. The dispatch reported that the enemy was leaving the city, and Bowser knew otherwise. He called Tenth Corps for confirmation and was told by Col. John H. Chides, the G-3 (operations officer), to execute the order as it was written. Bowser gave it to Smith, who called the Tenth Corps chief of staff, General Ruffner, "for a reaffirmation of the message to attack immediately, explaining the inadvisability of attacking at night in an unfamiliar Oriental City, particularly as there was no indication of the enemy fleeing from the Division front. The Commanding General was informed that the CG [commanding general], X Corps had dictated the message himself and that it was to be executed without delay" (A-M, 289). Smith then called Puller and Murray and with some misgivings directed them to coordinate their attacks and confine their advances to locations that could be readily identified at night. Bowser called the Seventh and Eleventh Marines to pass on the order from Tenth Corps.

Recon Company was on the left flank of the Seventh Marines, north of Seoul, when the "enemy fleeing" message was sent. Private Martin was one of the scouts who observed that "near a road junction, only civilians were seen leaving the city in a northwest direction, and later, noises of tanks and other vehicles were heard coming towards the city and troop formations with civilians carrying supplies on their backs on A frames followed by carts in the rear. . . . Corporal Joseph J. Voetter and Pfc Martin were sent to Recon patrol base with a report of enemy troops and

Col. Marcel G. Crombez, USA, CO of Fifth Cavalry Regiment, talks with Maj. Gen. Frank E. Lowe, USAR (Ret.), Truman's personal representative in Korea, October 19, 1950. *Author's private collection.*

tanks entering the city. Reports were relayed to the front-line infantry units advancing into the city.... Two days later, General Smith complimented Cpl. Voetter and PFC Paul G. Martin and said, 'You were just in time.'"[37]

When Smith called Murray to inform him about the evening attack order, Murray told him, as Murray would later recall, "At that moment, my 3d battalion, Taplett's battalion, was engaged in a very hard fight for a portion of Seoul and nobody was withdrawing or retreating or doing anything else.... I called Division ... and said 'I can't pursue anybody. I'm having a helluva fight to take what I'm supposed to take right now....' General Smith came on the line and said in effect, 'I understand your problem, but I have received a direct order to launch a pursuit, and I have to issue that direct order to launch a pursuit.' I said 'Aye, aye, Sir' and continued to do just what we were doing."[38]

Almond's habit of misreading the tactical situation helped to breed distrust, perplexity, and anxiety. Ordering a night attack on two-hour notice was irrational. Said Colonel Bowser, to issue "after-dinner orders to attack a city of several million in size at eight P.M. ... was ill-advised and cost us some lives."[39] The tanks spotted by Paul Martin and his scouts were part of a concentrated

Above: Major General Smith, Major General Almond, and Rear Admiral Doyle, discussing plans on board the USS *Mount McKinley* off Wonsan, Korea, October 19, 1950. *Courtesy of MCUA.*

Left: Capt. Martin J. "Stormy" Sexton, aide-de-camp to General Smith, poses beside his jeep at the outskirts of Seoul, Korea, September, 1950. *Author's private collection.*

counterattack by the North Koreans that lasted until about five the next morning. Smith knew that the order had endangered his division; subsequently, he would scrutinize orders from Almond skeptically.

In order to secure Seoul and give some assistance to the beleaguered Murray, Smith ordered the Seventh Marines to cut across the rugged mountains to the north of the city and pinch off the area in front of the Fifth Marines. The Seventh moved with dispatch into the city; Puller raised an American flag over the American consulate building. By 28 September, the Fifth Marines had completed its mission in Seoul. The Seventh Marines had successfully taken over for the Fifth and made contact with the First Marines. Smith and Craig moved the division command post to a new location within the city.

On 29 September, the First and Seventh Marines were still dealing with remnants of the enemy within the city when MacArthur conducted a liberation ceremony at the Government Palace. The First Marine Division provided security for the ceremony and cordoned off a large segment surrounding the palace. MacArthur arrived at the Kimpo airfield at 0930 and went directly to the palace. President Syngman Rhee was an hour behind him. As Maj. Mike Capraro said of it,

> The ceremony was to "officially hand back the keys to President Syngman Rhee." General Smith and Colonel Puller were invited to attend. Colonel Puller invited the general to ride in his jeep to the ceremony, this resulted in the vehicle being full. Also in the jeep were the general's aide-de-camp and Colonel Puller's driver. The latter had an unlit and a very short cigar butt in his mouth. As we pulled in front of the palace a rigid U.S. Army military policeman, complete with white gloves and white boot laces, held up his hand and directed the driver to move out. It must be explained that the jeep had no rank insignias on it, and it listed badly to the portside because of a broken shock. Quickly sizing up the situation, Chesty muttered to his driver: "If he doesn't move, run him down!" The M.P. proved to be extremely fast on his feet, and watched in wonderment as three of the jeep occupants moved into the palace. The driver remained with his vehicle, cradling his M-1 Rifle across his lap.[40]

Smith later described the ceremony:

> At 1115 General Craig and I went to the Palace and met General MacArthur. The ceremony was strictly a U.N. affair; the division was allowed only five present. Actually we had six officers present: General Craig, myself, Colonel Puller, Colonel Murray, and two Aides. There was considerable rank present....

At 1145, the ceremony in the assembly hall of the palace began. General MacArthur made an address ending with the Lord's Prayer; the head of the U.N. Commission, a Filipino, gave a talk; then Mr. Muccio, the U.S. Ambassador; then President Rhee spoke and presented a scroll to General MacArthur. . . . All during the ceremony the rumble of artillery could be heard. . . .

It was a feeling of relief that we saw the last of the distinguished visitors depart from Seoul. The city had not yet been turned over to the Civil Government authorities and the Division was entirely responsible for security within the city. (A-M, 316–17)

Immediately after the ceremony, two of Captain Mike Capraro's public information associates got Smith's attention. Capraro would write:

General Oliver P. Smith, the Division Commander, was a model Marine leader and my respect for him was steadfast. . . . He seemed to have confidence that I knew what I was doing, although that wasn't always the case. He displayed displeasure once. On September 28 . . . the ceremony took place at Ducksoo Palace . . . attended with great pomp and circumstance. Elite U.S. Army guards [were present] in shiny helmets, spit polished boots and freshly creased olive drab uniforms. . . . Finally, as MacArthur and Rhee descended the palace stairs, two unwashed, scruffy Marines in dusty fatigues burst through the crowd with a photographer in tow and requested an interview, to which MacArthur and Rhee pleasantly agreed. General Smith looked on in horror. He turned to me and asked: "Surely these aren't Marines?" They were. . . . I replied lamely that I would look into the matter.[41]

The liberation ceremony announced prematurely to the world that Seoul had been secured. The First Marine Division took another day to complete the job of clearing out the enemy remnants north and east of the palace. Once that had been accomplished, the division took a blocking stance in the rugged mountainous areas on the road to Uijongbu, north of Seoul. On 30 September Smith attended a conference at which a possible amphibious assault was considered for Wonsan, on the east coast of Korea. On 29 September, as the campaign for Inchon and Seoul came to an end, warning orders were received that the division would be embarking for a possible landing on the eastern coast of Korea. By 7 October, the division was in its staging areas at Inchon.

The commandant, General Cates, arrived in Korea on 2 October to review the division. Smith first brought him to headquarters, where he was given a broad briefing by the staff. Then Cates accompanied Smith to the regiments in the field by way of helicopter. Smith put Cates up in the mobile van that Almond had provided for Smith. During this visit the commandant told Smith proudly that "the people from [Washington] Headquarters state that they have been embarrassed by the favorable publicity of the 1st Marine Division" (KL, 52).

The assault against Inchon and the capture of Seoul changed the course of the Korean War. North Korean troops south of the thirty-eighth parallel were either destroyed or displaced by the United Nations forces. The Inchon-Seoul campaign helped to push the invaders back to the thirty-eighth parallel, much as General MacArthur had envisioned. Smith received many congratulatory messages for his fine performance at Inchon and Seoul. One from General Almond is significant: "From CG, X Corps to CG, 1st Marine Division under date of 28 September, 1950. On this date the X Corps attained one of its distinct objectives—the securing of the city of Seoul. In recognition of the heroic efforts of the officers and men of the 1st Marine Division I extend my deepest thanks and my continuing admiration for a task well done. Signed General Edward M. Almond" (KL, 362).

The victory celebrations that followed the Inchon-Seoul campaign were not only premature but somewhat hollow. Too many of the enemy troops escaped the trap set by the Eighth Army and Tenth Corps. It was a failure on the part of the Far East Command to plan adequately for the closure. Thousands of men found their way to the north, where they would fight again.[42]

O. P. Smith, who went out of his way to avoid the press, was featured on the cover of the 25 September 1950 issue of *Time* magazine. The article reviewed the Korean War situation and was especially complimentary to Smith and the First Marine Division. On 11 October 1950, he boarded the USS *Mount McKinley* in Inchon Harbor. The first thing he did was take a shower! The greatest test of the First Marine Division and of General Smith's courage and competence was yet to come.

9

NORTH TO THE CHOSIN

The First Marine Division was en route to the east coast of Korea—thanks to General Almond, who did not want his Tenth Corps to become a part of Eighth Army, where he would have to serve under Gen. Walton Walker. He was able to convince MacArthur to send his corps to the east coast as an independent command. Part of the reason had to do with logistics; Inchon could not handle the supplies for both Tenth Corps and Eighth Army. On the eastern coast, supplies could come directly from Japan to Wonsan. The division's departure from Inchon created a congested mess at the docks, because Eighth Army was trying to come into the port at the same time. The Seventh Division eventually went overland to Pusan, where it was picked up for the trip to Wonsan.[1]

The original plan called for an assault landing at Wonsan and an advance sixty miles inland to assist Eighth Army in its drive north to Pyongyang. However, the First Marine Division could not get ashore until mines were cleared from the harbor, and the navy was having a difficult time doing that. ROK forces had already made it across the peninsula to Wonsan area, and by the time the marines landed, there was almost an end-of-the-war atmosphere. Smith received a directive stating that the division would be returning to Camp Pendleton, leaving one regiment in Japan. General Almond was scheduled to become the occupation force commander, with one division under him.

There was a great deal of discussion about the integration of Tenth Corps into Eighth Army. Smith speculates as to why it was not done: "The reasons are probably twofold: (a) There was a desire to exploit the amphibious capability of the Tenth Corps which had paid such rich dividends at Inchon. (b) The unusual command status of General Almond. He was both Chief of Staff to General

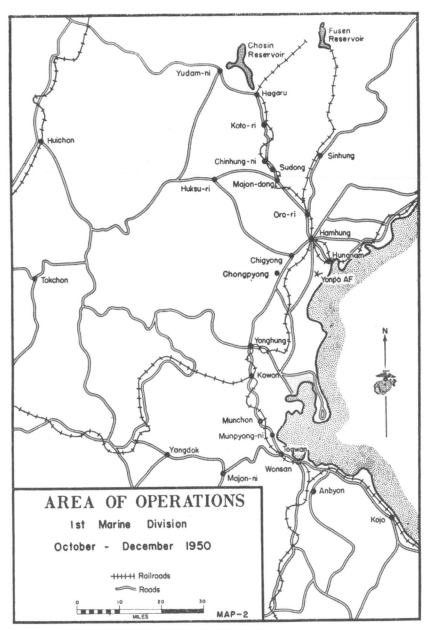

AREA OF OPERATIONS

1st Marine Division

October - December 1950

Operations north of the thirty-eighth parallel. *Courtesy* MCHC.

MacArthur and CG [commanding general] X Corps. It was entirely independent of the 8th Army and reported directly to MacArthur. There was a feeling in the 8th Army that . . . the Tenth Corps had been favored in the matter of service troops and supplies. The relations between the commands were not healthy" (A-M, 371–72).

Smith was not privy to the discussions of the higher command in Korea, but he was aware that some United Nations forces had already crossed the thirty-eighth parallel. The Joint Chiefs of Staff reluctantly gave MacArthur, who was eager to drive into North Korea, his way in a communiqué of 29 September: "We want you to feel unhampered tactically and strategically to proceed north of the parallel. Announcement . . . may precipitate embarrassment in UN where evident desire is not to be confronted with the necessity of a vote on passage of the 38th Parallel, rather to find you have found it militarily necessary to do so. [Signed] G. C. Marshall."[2]

MacArthur interpreted his authority in the following reply: "Parallel 38 is not a factor in the employment of our forces. The logistical supply of our units is the main problem which limits our immediate advance. In exploiting the defeat of enemy forces, our own troops may cross the parallel at any time in exploratory probing or exploitation local tactical conditions. . . . Unless and until the enemy capitulates, I regard all of Korea open for our military operations."[3]

American troops above the thirty-eighth parallel gave the Joint Chiefs the jitters. However, they were unable or unwilling to curb MacArthur's interpretation of their directives, and on 24 October he "issued a new battle order that stood Washington on its ear. His commanders were enjoined to drive forward toward the north with all speed and with full utilization of all their force." The Joint Chiefs were especially concerned about how operations of American forces above the thirty-eighth parallel would be interpreted in Europe. "Throughout the ordeal we believed it likely that a global war with Russia could erupt at any hour, that the free world was poised on the brink of catastrophe."[4]

The Chinese government was alarmed to the point that Premier Chou En-lai issued a warning to the United Nations, via the Indian ambassador, that China would oppose any force that came across the thirty-eighth parallel. MacArthur ignored the threat of retaliation by China, but when Arleigh Burke asked the opinion of retired admiral Kichisaburo Nomura, who had been Japan's ambassador to the United States in 1941, Nomura replied: "If you go north of the 38th Parallel, they'll come in. They'll have to do that now to save face, live up to their own words."[5]

Among the marines, the time spent aboard ship off the coast was known as "Operation Yo-Yo." The division staff was busy developing plans for several different operations—only to have them canceled by the rapid gains of the troops on the ground and the difficulty the navy was having in sweeping the waters free of mines off Wonsan Harbor. Smith left the *Mount McKinley* on 27 October to visit the First Marine Aircraft Wing, now established and operational at the Wonsan airfield. Later that same day, he visited Tenth Corps headquarters for a conference with Almond and placed the division command post at an abandoned military school in Wonsan.

The division's mission was unique for a maritime force. Some experts believe that its use as a land-fighting unit was unwise. "Trained and equipped to operate as a cohesive, balanced fighting force, undertaking primarily amphibious missions, the 1st Marine Division was, first, a bit out of its element on the Asian mainland and, second, thrown into some organizational confusion by the nature of simultaneous and divergent missions handed it by Tenth Corps.... It had not been brought back to strength following its withdrawal from west-central Korea [Inchon-Seoul]."[6] When the cold winds started to blow out of Manchuria, the troops quickly realized that they needed more adequate cold-weather clothing. Temperatures plunged below freezing, and the windchill temperatures could be life threatening.

Security became the first requirement. Elements of the Korean Marine Corps were attached to Puller's First Marine Regiment. Smith ordered Puller to send his Third Battalion to relieve the ROK troops at Majon-ni and take up a blocking position there. Puller then sent his First Battalion to Kojo, south along the coast, to secure a ROK supply dump. The division performed similar security duties in the Wonsan-Kojo area until mid-November, when it was relieved by the army's Third Division, commanded by Maj. Gen. Robert H. Soule.

The situation that Puller's First Battalion found at Kojo caused some concern at division headquarters. Smith recalls, "The reports from the battalion commander were rather disturbing. He reported his situation as critical and requested an LST as possible evacuation of the battalion. His preliminary report on casualties was 9 KIA, 35 WIA, and 34 MIA. . . . I felt the battalion commander was in a funk and it would be wise for Puller to go down and take charge. Puller was of the same opinion" (KL, 67).

The Third Battalion of the First Marines was still in a blocking position west of Wonsan, at Majon-ni. The Fifth and Seventh Marines were ordered to Hamhung, north of Wonsan on a road leading into the central mountains north of the Hwachon Reservoir. Every day that the tactical situation allowed, Smith visited the regimental command posts. He was beginning to be concerned about the fragmentation of his division. As Sexton explained: "It, of course, was the desire of all staff members . . . to keep the 1st Marine Division together as a unit, because it was felt that here was a unit with all its subordinate parts, all its supporting weapons, that was trained together to act as a unit having that purpose defeated by the wide dispersal of smaller units within the division. It was repeatedly mentioned that the great strength of the division lay in maintaining that unity. . . . When contacts were made [with the enemy] and various reports of enemy movement received, further dispersion resulted until at one time during this phase, units of the division were approximately 90 miles apart."[7] Smith maintained control of his scattered units via radio and helicopter link. Laying wire for telephone contact over such a vast area was pointless, especially in view of the heavy guerrilla activity. The helicopter proved to be extremely valuable and versatile; Smith used his daily.

Lt. Col. Frederick R. Dowsett, executive officer of the Seventh Marines, wrote his daughter: "We landed at Wonsan at dawn on 26 October 1950 and got our marching orders almost immediately. We were to relieve the 26th . . . ROK Regiment, which was somewhere north of Hamhung. The United States had been pulled into action in Korea so quickly that there was no time to do any proper reconnaissance. The maps were Korean, obtained from the Japanese, and all the Korean markings had been written over in Japanese. . . . The maps were next to useless for tactical purposes." As for the weather, Colonel Dowsett wrote, "We thought we were pretty well prepared to meet the cold. The Marines who had come with [Col. Homer L.] Litzenberg [the regiment's commanding officer] and me from Lejeune had been through cold-weather training in Labrador not long before we were . . . ordered to Inchon. We had joked about the cold-weather maneuvers when we got word we were going to the Med[iterranean]. No one was joking now."[8]

By 2 November the Seventh Marines was moving into the steep Sudong Val-. ley, south of Koto-ri, on the single road leading from the Chosin reservoir, in the mountains, eastward to the sea at Hungnam. This road became the main supply route—MSR—that was to take on such great importance in the weeks ahead. Steep cliffs rose over two thousand feet above the floor of the canyon. The First and Second Battalions of the Seventh Marines were heavily attacked that evening by Chinese forces and were hard pressed to stem the numbers massed against them. Suddenly, the next morning, the attackers disappeared as quickly as they had attacked. However, the MSR had been cut.

In its advance northward from Majon-dong, beginning 2 November, RCT 7 employed sound and proven tactics, suited to the situation. It was operating in enemy territory beyond supporting distance of other friendly units, a condition characteristic of operations in northeastern Korea, and had to be prepared to protect itself to the front, flanks, and rear at all times. It is an accepted principle that in advancing along a terrain corridor the shoulders must be occupied, or otherwise denied the enemy, before movement can safely be made along the corridor. Practically all movement in Korea was along corridors. . . . Previously in the Korean action, North Korean forces had been quick to take advantage of any failure of forces to get on the shoulders of corridors before attempting to advance along the road through the corridor. (A-M, 531)

Smith cautioned the unit to move ahead slowly.

Almond ordered Smith to pull one battalion from the Kojo area to take over security around Wonsan. Engagements encountered by every patrol were becoming sharper and more costly. A truck convoy between Wonsan and Majon-ni was ambushed with heavy losses. South of Majon-ni a patrol was hit so hard that it had to be rescued by the rest of the company.

The Seventh Marines moved farther northward on the MSR, where all the roadways north of Wonsan were being regularly attacked by North Korean guerrilla bands. Almond discounted the threats, but when Smith's predictions came true, movement by convoy was restricted to daylight hours, when Corsair aircraft ruled the air and were available to the ground troops on call (KL, 71). The guerrillas operating in the central mountain region were composed of remnants of North Korean units trying to escape northward. Large numbers were being taken prisoner, but the road between Wonsan and Hamhung was inadequately defended, especially after the Fifth Marines was ordered to the eastern side of the Chosin reservoir. The gap in security was filled by a battalion from the army's RCT 17 and the ROK Twenty-sixth Regiment, both temporarily under Smith's command.

Almond was anxiously working on ways that he could move the Fifth and Seventh Marines north without jeopardizing the security of the Wonsan area. He was not concerned about the Chinese elements in the area or about the fact that the ROK Twenty-sixth Regiment had taken Chinese prisoners. On 29 October an intelligence report from Tenth Corps disputed the significance of the Chinese in the area: "This information has not been confirmed and is not accepted at this time. . . . It is possible that entire groups of reinforcements may have been employed as groups, thereby giving rise to the erroneous impression that CCF [Chinese Communist forces] units may be engaged."[9]

Smith moved his command post to Hamhung on 4 November. The hard fight against the Chinese did not appreciably slow the advance of the Seventh Marines to the Chosin reservoir. The Fifth was on the way to the Fusen reservoir and to the power plants between the Fusen and Chosin reservoirs. Smith was anxious to have the First Marines pulled up from the south in order not to be separated farther from the center of the division.

At a meeting with Almond on 7 November, Smith complained that 170 miles separated his infantry units.

> I had been pressing for some time to lessen the dispersion of the Division, pointing out to the Corps Commander that in the 1st Marine Division he had a powerful instrument, but that it could not help being weakened by the dispersion . . . (RCT-1 was in the Wonsan area, RCT-5 was in the Sinhung Valley, and RCT-7 had moved north toward the Chosin reservoir as far as Chinhung-ni). At the conference I again urged that the situation be reviewed; that in view of the approach of winter consideration be given to stopping the advance to the north in view of the difficulty of supplying units in the mountains during the winter months. My recommendation was that during the winter we commit ourselves only to holding enough terrain to provide for the security of Wonsan, Hamhung and Hungnam, but that this not involve an attempt to hold positions on the plateau north of Chinhung-ni. General Almond had been somewhat sobered by the reverses [below] of the 8th Army. He was now agreeable to concentrating the 1st Marine Division, but he felt we should hold Hagaru-ri at the foot of the Chosin Reservoir. (A-M, 552–53)

Tenth Corps Operation Order 6, dated 9 November, directed "the 1st Marine Division to advance and destroy enemy in zone, and in addition, to be prepared for offensive operations to the west on the axis, on order, and to establish blocking positions at Hiksu-ri and Yudam-ni to protect the Corp's left [western] flank" (A-M, 492–93). In mid-November, Almond told Smith that the ROK Twenty-sixth Regiment would carry the attack toward Hiksu-ri west from Majon-dong. "As a matter of a fact, the Division was very glad to be relieved of this commitment as we might then be permitted to move RCT-1 to the MSR behind RCTs 5 and 7" (A-M, 496).

On 6 November, Gen. Frank E. Lowe again visited with Smith after spending some time observing Eighth Army's First Cavalry Division on the west coast. The division, commanded by Maj. Gen. Hobart R. Gay, had lost a battalion when ROK forces pulled out of a fight with Chinese forces, leaving the battalion surrounded by attackers. Gay had tried to effect a relief from other elements of his command but had been unsuccessful. "General Lowe felt that an attempt would be made to hold General Gay responsible for the loss of the battalion, which Lowe considered to be the fault of the Tenth Corps. General Lowe was pretty much depressed and talked in terms of the 8th Army evacuating through the port of Pusan. He probably reflected 8th Army thinking. However, the Chinese did not follow up their initial successes, and by 10 November, the 8th Army had regained its poise and started to move forward again" (A-M, 551).

It was this Eighth Army situation that Smith thought was having a sobering effect on Almond. Shortly after the first attack by the Chinese, Almond promised Smith that he could concentrate the First Marine Division. He was also "talking in terms of using Hungnam as a possible port of evacuation. (As a footnote, as soon as the situation of the 8th Army stabilized we received an order to advance to the Manchurian border)" (KL, 75). Smith still worried, however, about his open left flank. "I have continually pointed out to the Corps Commander that our advance has left our left flank wide open. . . . It is 70 miles back to the front of the 8th Army. I have been informed by the Corps that there is no enemy on our left. (. . . On November 27th the CCF came in our left flank in considerable strength)" (KL, 79).

In the meantime, before any extended advance took place, Smith authorized the implementation of some critical engineering projects. The Fifth and Seventh RCTs needed tanks in order to continue the attack. That necessitated widening parts of the MSR, because the M-26 (Pershing) tanks could not negotiate some of the turns. Another engineering project—one that saved the lives of hundreds of men and may have ensured the ability of the First Marine Division to fight its way out of the Chosin reservoir—was the enlargement of the existing OY (small observation aircraft) airstrip at Koto-ri to accept twin-engine C-47s. However, Smith wanted to check farther north on the MSR for a more suitable site. An excellent location was selected at Hagaru-ri, but when Smith tried to get Tenth Corps to construct the strip, it refused and directed the First Marine Division to use its own engineer battalion.

The 10th of November 1950 was the 175th anniversary of the Marine Corps. A modest ceremony was conducted at the evening mess at division headquarters. Smith cut the traditional cake after reading the prescribed paragraphs from the *Marine Manual.* Several messages of congratulations were received. One was from Adm. C. Turner Joy: "On the occasion of your 175th Anniversary I consider it indeed an honor and privilege to salute our courageous comrades in arms, the United States Marines, wherever they may be. You can justly be proud of your past record, of your present gallant and heroic exploits in the Korean Campaign, and, God willing, you will face the future with the knowledge that you have done much toward restoring a happy and peaceful world" (A-M, 581).

The weather was as much an adversary as the enemy soldiers. During the night of 10–11 November, the temperature plummeted to eight degrees below zero, with a wind of twenty to thirty knots. Troops were dazed by the rapidly dropping temperature. Some of the men simply collapsed, with dangerously low respiratory rates. "Stimulants were required in addition to warming in order to restore the men to normal functioning. After the initial reaction the men became more accustomed to very low temperatures, for, although even more severe weather was encountered later, the shock reaction did not reappear" (A-M, 577).

Smith was officially informed on 11 November that the objective was again the Yalu River. "Now that the situation in the west had been improved, the Corps was again anxious to resume the advance. Apparently the Chinese we met were discounted as volunteers sent in to encourage the North Koreans and it was assumed that more would not follow. The Corps was apparently still thinking in terms of driving the remnants of the defeated North Korean Army to the border of Korea before winter set in" (A-M, 581–82).

As Smith was reviewing the new orders, Chinese forces were flowing across the border in increasing numbers. The division was ordered to continue along the MSR to the Yalu, 150 road miles from Chinhung-ni. The proposed operational zone outlined in the orders was increased by about forty miles over what the division was occupying along the MSR. Heavy snowdrifts were beginning to be a problem, and the open left flank was still a worry for Smith, even though Almond continued to disregard it.

The orders of 11 November (OpOrd 6) are summarized as follows: The First ROK Corps would operate inland from the coast north and east of Hungnam. The First Marine Division was astride the MSR now and would continue northward. It was also warned to be prepared for operations west of the MSR. The Third Infantry Division was to establish blocking positions to protect the left flank of the Tenth Corps. (Smith was justifiably concerned about his left flank, because the Third Division did not penetrate far enough inland to lend much support for the Marines, who were spearheading the drive to the Yalu.) The Seventh Infantry Division would advance north on the right flank of the First Marine Division. The ROK Twenty-sixth Regiment would operate with the Third Division north of Wonsan. The Korean Marine Corps regiment was ordered to destroy the enemy in its zone of operation forty miles deep along the coast from Kojo, eighty miles south (A-M, 583–84).

By 13 November, the First Marine Division was poised to advance to the Manchurian border. The individual units involved were tasked as follows: RCT 1 was gathering its scattered units and moving them to Hamhung via Huksu-ri, where it would patrol and secure the western zone of the corps boundary. RCT 7 was to secure Hagaru-ri and be prepared to push north to Yudam-ni. RCT 5 was to protect the MSR from positions at Koto-ri, Majon-dong, and Chinhung-ni, and to be prepared to pass through RCT 7 near Hagaru-ri and continue north. The Eleventh Marines was to maintain its Fourth Battalion at Majon-dong for employment north. RCTs 5 and 7 each had a battalion of artillery from the Eleventh Marines attached. VMO [marine observation squadron] 6 supported the First Marine Division every day that weather permitted, on an "as-need-basis" (A-M, 592–93).

The orders Smith issued two days earlier had called for RCT 7 to assume a blocking position at the Funchilin Pass, between Koto-ri and Chinhung-ni, until the rest of the division could come up behind it. "At this time the separation of the infantry battalions of the Division amounted to 163 miles. The Division did not share the feeling of the Corps that there was no enemy and that the dispersion was justified" (A-M, 594).

Tenth Corps had failed to supply its formations adequately once they were ashore, so Smith ordered the establishment of supply dumps at Hamhung as soon as the Fifth and Seventh Marines left the Wonsan area. Large quantities of material were airlifted into Wonsan and Yonpo, near Hungnam, to support operations. As soon as the navy had swept the waters off Hungnam, an army engineer brigade began to operate the port of Hungnam as a forwarding and storage depot for support of the Tenth Corps. Since the marines were going to be supplied through a single, tenuous supply route, Smith authorized the First Service Battalion to place the railway to Hagaru-ri in operation. After much work the battalion located civilian operators and started shipping supplies north on a regular basis, even though rolling stock was very limited.

A railhead was established at Chinhung-ni for support of the Seventh Marines. The material was then distributed by the regimental motor transport battalions. After the regiment fought its way to Hagaru-ri, a larger railhead was established for the Seventh and the Fifth Marines, operating north toward the Manchurian border. When the First Marine Division took over responsibility for the MSR from Chinhung-ni to Hagaru-ri, approximately three hundred short tons of supplies were delivered daily to Chinhung-ni. The advance was opposed by North Korean troops that had taken sanctuary in the mountainous region between Tenth Corps and Eighth Army.

Care of the wounded was a responsibility that Smith took very seriously. A hospital was established in the outskirts of Hungnam. Each regimental combat team had a medical company attached. RCT 1 evacuated its wounded directly to the hospital ship USS *Consolation,* in Wonsan Harbor. After the First Marines left Wonsan, it used the hospital at Hungnam. Clearing stations were established at various points, from where the patients were moved either to the marine hospital or to the Tenth Corps 121st Evacuation Hospital at Hungnam. Serious cases were flown directly to Japan whenever possible.

On 15 November, Smith had a visit from Rear Adm. Albert K. Morehouse, Turner Joy's chief of staff.

For the information of Admiral Joy, I thoroughly briefed Admiral Morehouse on our situation. Since I felt that I was talking "in the family" I told him frankly of my concern over the lack of realism in the plans of the Corps and the tendency of the Corps to ignore the enemy capabilities when a rapid advance was desired. I found in my dealings with the Army, particularly with the Tenth Corps, that the mood was either one of extreme optimism or of extreme pessimism. There did not seem to be any middle ground. I have reason to believe that my concern was imparted to Admiral Joy and that he took preliminary steps to insure the rapid assembly of shipping at Hungnam where it was sorely needed some two weeks later. (A-M, 603–4)

Smith was not the only high-ranking officer to be concerned over the situation. Brig. Gen. Edwin Wright, MacArthur's operations officer, felt that Almond had spread the Tenth Corps too thin by attempting to reach the Yalu at several points. MacArthur agreed with Wright, who then directed Almond to reorient his attack from the Yalu to the support of Walker's Eighth Army. Almond accepted the decision without comment but continued his attempts to reach the Yalu River. Almond, as noted, had little respect or appreciation for Walker or Eighth Army; therefore, though Almond ordered Smith, during a visit to his divisional CP on 14 November, to attack to the west in support of Eighth Army, he allowed Barr's Seventh Division to continue toward the Yalu, where he could not support Eighth Army.[10]

The situation of the First Marine Division in Korea as of 15 November 1950 is summarized in a detailed letter from Smith to the commandant of the Marine Corps:

Dear General:

I do not know how much information you get from official dispatches of our activities here. If you depend on ComNavFE's [Commander, Naval Forces Far East, Admiral Joy] summary, which is sent to CNO [Chief of Naval Operations, Adm. Forrest Sherman] for information, you get very little. This summary covers mainly the movement of ships. I do not know what is included in the CinCFE's [Commander in Chief, Far East, MacArthur] dispatches to the Army. Possibly they are more complete.

We are fighting two types of enemy here. To the southwest, west, and northwest we are fighting bypassed remnants of the North Korean Army which are making their way north. There are several thousand of these. There has been time for them to get some semblance of organization. They are armed with rifles, submachine guns, heavy machine guns, mortars, and on occasions have produced antitank guns.

We have had several vicious contacts with the better organized elements of this force, which totals between 3,000 and 5,000 men. They move through the mountains and periodically cut in on our supply routes, probably for food. We have been spread so thin that it has been impossible to assemble sufficient force to go out and corner these people. Since October 27 we have had serious contacts with this force at Kojo, southeast of Wonsan: by 3/1 [Third Battalion, 1st Marine Regiment] halfway between Majon-ni, west of Wonsan; by 2/1 halfway between Wonsan and Majon-ni; and by 1/5 northwest of Chigyong, 48 air miles north of Wonsan.

There have also been attacks on trains on which we had guards and on truck convoys. In protecting installations and the MSR we have used all type of units: Shore Party, Amphtracs [amphibian tractors], Tanks, and Artillery, as well as infantry. The Shore Party and Amphtracs have had the responsibility of protecting the Wonsan airfield. The Amphtracs have also furnished train guards. For a while I billeted the Tank Battalion at Munchon and made it responsible for patrolling the area. They did very good work as infantry. Because of the character of the roads and bridges this is not tank country, and it is difficult to use the tanks in their normal role.

With considerable engineering assistance in building by-passes we have moved two of the tank companies north up the road to Hamhung. One is now guarding the airfield at Yonpo, south of Hungnam. The other I will push up the road north of Hamhung to assist in guarding the MSR leading to Litzenberg [commanding the 7th Marines], who is 40 miles north of Hamhung. The port of Hungnam is now open and I will bring the remainder of the tanks from Wonsan to this area.

The Artillery, not attached to regiments, was used initially to protect a portion of the MSR south of Munchon. They operated as infantry and did a very creditable job. The Artillery, less that attached to Puller [commanding the 1st Marines], is now north of here (Hungnam, our CP): one battalion of 105's with Litzenberg at the Chosin reservoir, one battalion of 105's with Murray [5th Marines], who is strung out along the MSR between Hamhung and Litzenberg, and a battalion of 155 howitzers, which with tanks will provide protection for a section of the MSR north of Hamhung. So far our MSR north of Hamhung has not been molested, but there is evidence that this situation will not continue. We are making every effort to protect our MSR.

The war in the north, in Litzenberg's zone of action, is entirely different from that of the south. He moved north from Hamhung to Sudong (about

20 miles) without great difficulty except for one serious attack on his flank. About three miles farther up the mountain valley, at Chinhung-ni, he ran into the Chinese Communists in force. He captured a number of prisoners and definitely identified the 370th, 371st, and 372nd Regiments of the 124th CCF Division. Up to Chinhung-ni the road is along the floor of a tortuous mountain valley. The rise, however, is gradual. From Chinhung-ni to the north the road takes off along the side of the mountains and heads for a mountain pass. It rises about 2,600 feet in 10,000 yards. It was here that the Chinese chose to defend. Air, artillery, mortars and infantry action were brought to bear on them and they withdrew to the north. Litzenberg estimated he had killed 1,000 of them. POW interrogations indicate that the number was nearer 1,500, with 500 desertions. The Chinese are simply not accustomed to the mortar artillery and air concentrations we put on them. I saw the air work on this mountain and they really laid it on. Litzenberg's casualties were about 50 KIA and 200 WIA for this action.

After this engagement, Litzenberg moved on up the mountain and is now at the south end of the Chosin Reservoir. On the single mountain road which is in our zone, we can use only one RCT in advance. We are moving the 5th up behind Litzenberg to protect the MSR. Litzenberg has kept his RCT well closed up in his advance. His depth had never exceeded 5,000 yards, usually two battalions forward and one to the rear, with artillery, supplies, and medical installations in the middle.

Although the Chinese have withdrawn to the north, I have not pressed Litzenberg to make any rapid advance. Our orders still require us to advance to the Manchurian border. However, we are the left flank division of the Corps and our left flank is wide open. There is no unit of the 8th Army nearer than 80 miles to the southwest of Litzenberg. When it is convenient the Corps can say there is nothing on our left flank. If this were true, then there should be nothing to prevent the 8th Army from coming abreast of us. This they are not doing. I do not like the prospect of stringing out a marine division along a single mountain road for 120 air miles from Hamhung to the border. (The road miles is [sic] nearer to 200.) I now have two RCTs on this road and when Puller is relieved by the 3d Infantry Division I will close up behind him.

We have reached a point now at the south end of the Chosin Reservoir where we will have to review the situation. The road in our zone continues to the north on the east side of the Chosin Reservoir. Another road, which was used by the Chinese in addition to the north road, comes in from the west. We will have to block it. At this point we plan to pass the 5th through the 7th and have the 5th continue to the north. The 7th will then take over the mission of blocking the road coming from the west at the Chosin Reservoir and of protecting the MSR to the limit of its capabilities. Puller will be moved up behind, although at present I am directed to establish a blocking position at Huksu-ri, about 30 miles northwest of Hamhung, and I have no other troops to call on other than Puller's. This mission should be turned over to the 3rd [Army] Division in view of my other commitments.

What concerns me considerably is my ability to supply two RCTs in the mountains in winter weather. Snow, followed by a thaw and freeze, will put out my road. We have a narrow gauge railway from Hamhung to the foot of the mountain. We are using this railroad and have a railhead at the foot of the mountain (Chinhung-ni). From this point there is a cableway to the south end of the Chosin Reservoir. It is inoperative and its repair appears to involve engineer work far beyond our capabilities. An engineer from Tokyo is coming over to look at it. From the south end of the Chosin Reservoir to the border there is nothing but mountain road. Air drop in winter is not a feasible means of supplying two RCTs. Moreover, it will not provide for evacuation. The answer, of course, is to build a strip for C-119s and C-47s. At the altitude in which we are operating the aviators require a 5,000 foot strip. The Corps thought it would be a fine idea if we built such a strip. With its other commitments, this is hardly a job within the capabilities of our Engineer Battalion. If we can find enough flat real estate in the vicinity of the reservoir to build a 5,000 foot strip, I will ask the Corps to give us a hand. Using PBMs [seaplanes, Martin Mars Flying Boats] on the reservoir is out of the question because of the ice.

I visited Litzenberg at Koto-ri just south of the reservoir. There is considerable difference in temperature where we are and where he is. Yesterday morning at 0900 it was 18 degrees Fahrenheit here and 0 degrees Fahrenheit where he is. When I visited him the small streams were frozen. Little rivulets from springs, in spots, had spread over the road and frozen. Our engineers have hauled pipe up the mountain and are making culverts to keep the water off the road. Even though the men who are up front are young and are equipped with parkas, shoepacs and mountain sleeping bags, they are taking a beating. In a tactical situation a man cannot be in his bag. We have had a few cases of frost bite. Some of our Chinese prisoners also have frost bitten feet.

As you can imagine, visiting units is rather difficult with them dispersed as they are. I have depended a great deal on the helicopter, but we are finding it has its limitations. For the last two days none has been operational because the gear box which controls the rotors froze up. The gear boxes have been drained and thinner oil has been put in. The helicopters will be operational at sea level, but they cannot reach Litzenberg with a load because of the elevation, the wind and the temperature. They simply lose control. We are building an OY strip south of the reservoir. The OY can get up, but, because of the altitude, the OY people want a strip 2,500 feet long instead of the normal 1,300 feet. We have fallen back on the jeep. It takes 3½ hours by jeep to reach Litzenberg, which means that it takes a day to visit one regiment. Craig [the assistant division commander] is with Litzenberg today.

As I indicated when you were here, I have little confidence in the tactical judgment of the Corps or in the realism of their planning. My confidence has not yet been restored. Planning is done on a 1:1,000,000 map. We execute on a 1:50,000 map. There is a continual splitting up of units and assignment of missions to small units which puts them out on a limb. This method of operating appears to be general in Korea. I am convinced that many of their set-backs here have been caused by this disregard for the integrity of units and of the time and space factor. Time and again I have tried to tell the Corps Commander that in a marine division he has a powerful instrument, but that it cannot help but lose its full effectiveness when dispersed. Probably I have had more luck than the other division commanders in impressing my point. [Perhaps Smith's luck can be attributed to the facts that he is a marine instead of an army officer and that he was persistent.]

Someone in high authority will have to make up his mind as to what is our goal. My mission is still to advance to the border. The 8th Army, 80 miles to the southwest, will not attack until the 20th. I suppose their goal is the border. Manifestly we should not push on without regard to the 8th Army. We would simply get further out on a limb. If the 8th Army's push does not go, then the decision will have to be made as to what to do next. I believe a winter campaign in the mountains of North Korea is too much to ask of the American soldier or marine, and I doubt the feasibility of supplying troops in this area during the winter or providing for evacuation of sick and wounded. Of course, a simple solution of all these difficulties would be for the enemy opposition to fold up.

I am enclosing a few photographs of the area in which we are now operating.

This letter may sound pessimistic, but it is not meant to be so. I feel you are entitled to know what our on-the-spot reaction is. Our people are doing a creditable job, their spirit is fine, and they will continue to do a fine job. Since we landed at Wonsan we have had approximately 700 battle casualties. Our non-battle casualties have been slightly higher. These non-battle casualties have been from a variety of causes. There has been some combat fatigue, but not much. The other causes of hospitalization run the whole gamut of the medical books. Operating in the mountains, as we are, there are a considerable number of sprains and injuries from falling rocks. Our 1st and 2nd Replacement Drafts have brought us up to strength, but not in excess as was first thought.

   With kindest regards.

                              Sincerely,

                              [Signed] Oliver P. Smith (A-M, 604–10)

This remarkable letter shows that Smith and his staff took the Chinese threat seriously and were actually making preparations on that assumption. General Ruffner, the Tenth Corps chief of staff, shared Smith's misgivings: "The decision for Tenth Corps to attack through the Chosin Reservoir westward to hook up with the 8th Army was made at GHQ-Tokyo. It was an insane plan. You couldn't take a picnic lunch in peacetime and go over that terrain in November and December."[11] Gen. Matthew B. Ridgway, who would soon command Eighth Army, later had high praise for Smith's precautionary measures: "As it turned out these textbook precautions were all that enabled this magnificent fighting force to battle its way out of the entrapment in one of the most successful retrograde movements in American military history."[12]

Smith continued to visit regiments and battalion command posts on a daily basis, especially the Fifth and Seventh Marines. As his letter to the commandant indicates, he was using the ever-faithful jeep of World War II fame more often than the helicopter, now that much of his division was in the higher elevations (TL, 1). He took deliberate steps to ensure the safety of his command. The vulnerability of the MSR prompted Smith and Field Harris, commanding the First Marine Aircraft Wing, to check out the feasibility of locating an airfield that could accommodate two-engine planes. Such an airstrip would be a forward base of operations where supplies could be stockpiled, injured men could be evacuated, and replacements delivered, independent of the MSR. The site at Hagaru-ri met all their requirements, and construction began on 19 November.

Smith also created a large supply dump at the railhead of Chinhung-ni, from which supplies were trucked northward to Koto-ri, Hagaru-ri, and Yudam-ni. A supply regulating station was established at Hagaru-ri to control traffic between Hagaru-ri and Chinhung-ni. These measures played a major role in the ability of the division to survive the Chinese onslaught. It is a tribute to Smith's leadership that he put in place this safety net of communications and supply.

Division orders for 17 November directed a continuation of the advance to the Manchurian border. RCT 1 was to move north and west to Huksu-ri, on the western boundary of the Tenth Corps. RCT 7 was to protect the left flank between Hagaru-ri and Yudam-ni, and the MSR from Koto-ri through Hagaru-ri.

The Seventh Marines was ordered to give up its "King" (K) Battery, Fourth Battalion, Eleventh Marines and turn it over to the Fifth Marines, which would pass through the Seventh at Hagaru-ri on its way to Sinhung-ni on the east side of the Chosin reservoir. RCT 5 was to leave one battalion at Koto-ri for MSR security. Recon Company was sent to the left flank of the division to act as a screening force and to maintain the security of the higher elevations overlooking the MSR. The Eleventh Marines had been parceled out to the infantry regiments, except for its Fourth Battalion, which was in the vicinity of Majon-dong, prepared to move north on orders from division. A sort of flying artillery was provided by the courageous airmen of Marine Aircraft Group Thirty-three. Many survivors of the Chosin reservoir campaign owe their lives to the pilots of the dark blue F4U Corsairs, who came to their aid time after time.

It was Smith's intention to consolidate his division as much as his orders from Tenth Corps allowed. The First Marines had one battalion, at Huksi-ri, without a truck-road access. Wrote Smith, "I do not intend to put Puller out on a limb where he cannot be supplied. Also I would like to close him up behind the regiments moving towards the Chosin Reservoir" (KL, 84). Smith was very happy to hear from Almond that the Third Infantry Division was going to take over Puller's duties at the southwestern edge of the corps's boundary. The airstrip at Hagaru-ri was progressing slowly, because of the frozen ground. The mountainous area to the west of the division was beginning to reveal some of its secrets. Aircraft were reporting alarming numbers of enemy soldiers to the southwest, west, and northwest of Hagaru-ri. Civilians were reporting similar sightings. The fighting on most of the fronts was sporadic, but almost constant contact was maintained with Chinese forces.

Almond ordered Smith to move RCT 5 to the east side of the Chosin reservoir en route to the border on 23 November. Smith later wrote, "I did not want to push Murray too far or get Litzenberg out on a limb at Yudam-ni until I could close Puller in rear of them. I therefore did not press Murray to advance rapidly and I directed Litzenberg to occupy for the time being a suitable blocking position west of Hagaru-ri and not over the mountain pass [Toktong Pass]. I hoped there might be some change in the orders on the conservative side. This change did not materialize and I had to direct Litzenberg to go on to Yudam-ni" (KL, 87).

General Lowe accompanied General Craig on visits to the Fifth and Seventh RCTS' command posts on 17 November. Lowe was well received by the troops. Whenever Lowe visited an operations post, "he arrived with his jeep Task Force composed of his aide-de-camp, Capt. A. Hume, USA and Sgt. V. Diala, USA, a Filipino gunner, along with treasured 'goodies' such as fresh milk, fresh vegetable, and coffee that he stockpiled every time he went to Japan."[13]

Smith attended a Thanksgiving dinner on 23 November at Tenth Corps. The table was laid out complete with place cards, linen, and silver. Admiral Struble and Generals Barr, Ruffner, Harris, Biederlinden, and Smith were present. Smith explained in his daily log that he would have preferred to remain at division headquarters and enjoy the cooked turkey sent compliments of Admiral Doyle (KL, 87).

November 24 was an active day in the division. Craig had gone to Hagaru-ri to locate a suitable location for a new command post. The Eighth Army had jumped off for its attack to the border, accompanied by an optimistic announcement from MacArthur that it was the southern arm of a pincer of which the First Marine Division would be the northern arm. The division was ordered by Tenth Corps to cut across Korea to the north of Eighth Army, severing road and rail connections from Huichon Kanggye, reportedly an assembly area for the North Korean troops. Smith wrote that "our line of communication will be very tenuous" (KL, 88). His greatest concern remained his vulnerable left flank. According to Sexton, there was a "tremendous gap on the left flank of about eighty (80) miles, and apparently it was going to increase as the Division continued its advance."[14] It was an invitation to the disaster that followed.

MacArthur's modified orders to the First Marine Division made some changes necessary. Smith had to seek permission from General Almond to bring the RCT 5 to Hagaru-ri and Yudam-ni in support of RCT 7. Almond informed Smith that elements of the Seventh Division would relieve the Fifth Marines. Smith later recalled, "The 3rd Infantry Division was to take over the protection of the MSR to Hagaru-ri. This never transpired and to the end of the operation I had to retain one battalion of the 1st Marines at Chinhung-ni at the foot of the mountain and another battalion of the 1st Marines at Koto-ri at the top of the mountain. Otherwise there would have been no protection for this vital part of the MSR."[15]

RCT 5 had dispatched a platoon from the Third Battalion, reinforced with two tanks, to the eastern side of the Chosin reservoir. It was to patrol northward to determine enemy strength and the condition of the Chosin Dam, between the Fusen reservoir and the Chosin reservoir. The patrol encountered an estimated 100–150 Chinese; otherwise no other enemy activity was noted. The dam appeared to be in good condition. The advance of RCT 5 was cautiously controlled in order to build up supplies at Hagaru-ri before pushing farther. Also, Smith wanted "to reduce the dispersion of the division by moving RCT-1 to the MSR behind RCT-5 and 7 before pushing the advance further. Later developments justified this caution" (A-M, 627).

Almond ordered the Seventh Division to provide whatever units it had available to relieve RCT 5 on the eastern side of the Chosin reservoir. "This would concentrate all of the 1st Marine Division for the push west to Kanggye and would transfer the mission of protecting the right or east flank of this attack to another force—a new regimental task force from the 7th Division."[16] Litzenberg's RCT 7 was holding in a blocking position at Yudam-ni and waiting for RCT 5 to arrive, pass through its lines, and continue the westward attack. The Seventh Marines had been in continuous and heavy combat since landing at Wonsan, so Smith ordered it to hold while the Fifth led the advance.

Early in November, Smith was advised that the British Forty-first Independent Commando, Royal Marines was anxious to serve with the First Marine Division. Smith said that he would be glad to have the commandos assigned to the division; he visualized using them on his open left flank, where he then had Recon Company. On 23 November, Smith ordered the Forty-first Commando, composed of fourteen officers and 221 enlisted men, to commence operations west of the MSR between Koto-ri and Hagaru-ri, coordinating its activities with RCTS 1 and 7.

In the middle of this hectic period, a situation developed that would place an added burden of command upon Smith's shoulders: General Craig's father was seriously ill, and Smith agreed that Craig should go home on emergency leave.

The day that Craig left, RCT 5 passed through RCT 7 and made progress westerly. The evening of 27 November 1950 is probably the most memorable date of the campaign for veterans of the Chosin: "Throughout the night all of our units were the focus of an enemy attack aimed at their destruction. . . . As dawn broke, all separate Marine and Army units were surrounded—cut off to the rear and from each other."[17] When Smith flew into Hagaru-ri to establish the new command post, his helicopter came under fire. The Fifth and Seventh Marines had been hit hard, and the road between Yudam-ni and Hagaru-ri was effectively blocked, with several bridges blown. Puller, farther to the south, was making an all-out effort to reopen the road between Koto-ri and Hagaru-ri. Litzenberg's efforts to break the road blocks from Yudam-ni had ended in failure.

Smith's command had been broken into several parcels along the MSR and was holding all-around defensive perimeters at four distinct locations—Yudam-ni, the Toktong Pass, Hagaru-ri, and Koto-ri. To the west, the Eighth Army front was rapidly crumbling. Smith received no orders from Tenth Corps to discontinue the advance to the west, but "under the circumstances I felt that it was rash to have Murray to attempt to push on and I directed him to consolidate on the positions he then held west of Yudam-ni" (KL, 91).[18] Division staff personnel and some of their equipment and records had, fortunately, arrived at Hagaru-ri by truck convoy before the roads were cut. Other vehicles and equipment for the new command post were dispatched by truck convoy on 28 November from Hamhung. The convoy joined a larger one on its way to Koto-ri. Smith's personal van was one of the vehicles.

The main supply route that connected the fragmented elements of Tenth Corps to the coast was of special significance. If the First Marine Division and portions of the Seventh Division were to fight their way out of the trap, the only exit was the single MSR. From Chinhung-ni south to the coastal town of Hungnam, the road was open; from Chinhung-ni northward to Yudam-ni, however, it had been overrun at several points. Puller organized a large convoy from a varied group of vehicles and units collected at Koto-ri to smash through to Hagaru-ri, which was surrounded and in need of every bit of help it could get. The convoy was composed of "Baker" (B) Company (commanded by Capt. Charles Peckham) from the Thirty-first Infantry; "George" (G) Company, First Marines; a company of tanks from the First Tank Battalion; elements of the First Marine Division forward command post battalion; and the Forty-first Commando (under the command of Lt. Col. Douglas B. Drysdale), which had been awaiting assignment in Koto-ri. Puller had placed Drysdale in charge of the column, but very few of his subordinates were aware of that.

Captain Peckham was ordered by Puller to lead the convoy to Hagaru-ri. About four miles north of Koto-ri, the column came under intense small-arms and mortar fire that set several vehicles on fire. There was much confusion, because of the diverse nature of the units in the convoy and because radio communications had been knocked out. Colonel Drysdale, impatient with delays, with a "Tally ho!" moved off in his jeep to Peckham. The Forty-first Commando drew all the tanks and most of the rest of the column along until it was stalled again by a burning truck. Unable to advance, several of the vehicles turned around and headed for Koto-ri. The men deployed on either side of the road.

When Smith was finally able to contact Drysdale, he ordered the column through to Hagaru-ri regardless of the cost. Drysdale organized those vehicles that could not bypass the burning trucks into a column and sent them back to Koto-ri with a tank escort; they came under heavy fire and sustained heavy losses along the way. The balance of the tanks and infantry fought on toward Hagaru-ri. That evening the decimated column arrived at Hagaru-ri with George Company of the First Marines and 150 Royal Marines. Colonel Drysdale had lost half of his force![19]

Smith lavished praise on the Royal Marines. "The 41st Commando participated in the defense of Hagaru-ri and the breakout therefrom to the coast. At all times the performance of this unit was outstanding. It was primarily a reconnaissance unit, but it proved its worth in pitched battle both in attack and the defense. The members of the Marine Commando were fully accepted by the Marines of the 1st Marine Division" (A-M, 633).

On Wednesday, 29 November Smith ordered RCT 5 to return to Yudam-ni, where the Fifth and Seventh Marines created a formidable defense posture. Litzenberg sent a battalion against the roadblocks south of Yudam-ni, but it got nowhere. Smith ordered him to use all of RCT 7 to smash through the next day. Smith knew that a strong force would be necessary as well to break through from Hagaru-ri to Koto-ri. That force would not be available to him until the Fifth and Seventh Marines arrived. Hagaru-ri was under continual attack all day and into the evening. The main Chinese thrust was from the south, where the Chinese controlled the MSR. Later in the evening the attacks were heavier from the east.

The Chinese forces included units from two Chinese field armies, the Third and the Fourth. They were filled with veterans from the fight against the Chinese Nationalists and the Japanese, the best trained, best equipped soldiers in the Chinese Communist army. Peng Dehuai, commander of the Fourth Field Army, was an outstanding tactician; reputedly he never suffered a military defeat.

The general plan of the Chinese included a delaying mission north of Hamhung to the Chosin and Fusen reservoirs, while larger forces would be brought up to launch a counteroffensive. The 124th Division was the first to make contact with RCT 7, in the Hamhung–Hagaru-ri area. The 125th and the 126th Divisions also participated in the initial blocking role. The 124th, 125th, and the 126th Divisions (with about eleven thousand men each) crossed the Yalu River on 20 October 1950, on foot (A-M, 696–97). When the massive counteroffensive struck, the following Chinese Communists' order of battle was established by the interrogation of prisoners:

Forty-second Army (Corps)
    124th Division, Sudong, Chinhung-ni, Koto-ri, 2–12 November
    126th Division, Fusen Reservoir, Hagaru-ri, 10–15 November
Twentieth Army (Corps)
    Fifty-eighth Division, Yudam-ni, 27 November
    Fifty-ninth Division, Yudam-ni, 27 November
    Sixtieth Division, Yudam-ni, 26–27 November
    Eighty-ninth Division, Yudam-ni, 22–27 November
Twenty-seventh Army (Corps)
    Seventy-ninth Division, Yudam-ni, 27 November. (A-M, 705–6)

The situation of the First Marine Division and its attached units on the evening of 29 November was as follows. The Fifth and Seventh Marines, with three battalions of artillery from the Eleventh Marines, were at Yudam-ni. The total force was 8,214, with about two hundred at Toktong Pass, between Hagaru-ri and Yudam-ni. Farther south, at Hagaru-ri, four thousand troops of various units (including army elements and the remnants of the Forty-first Commando) were fighting for their lives within the perimeter. North of Hagaru-ri, on the east side of the Chosin reservoir, over 2,500 army troops from the RCT 31 had faced an overwhelming Chinese attack, and their fate is still unknown. Over 3,500 troops remained at Koto-ri; south of Koto-ri to Hamhung were nine thousand troops. The total of UN troops astride the MSR between Yudam-ni and Hungnam on the coast was about thirty thousand.

> Within the Eighth Army zone, the defeat of the II Rok [*sic*]Corps on their right flank caused the remainder of Eighth Army to withdraw. It rapidly became a retreat. In an envelopment, the holding force is required to hold until the enveloping force can carry home its attack. In this case, the holding force (8th Army) began its withdrawal on 25 November and by the time the enveloping force (1st Marine Division) attacked on 27 November, the 8th Army was in full retreat. Therefore, the attack by the 1st Marine Division on 27 November could have no effect on the fortunes of the 8th Army and the Division itself was to become involved in a fight for its life against a Chinese Army group separate and distinct from the CCF following up the retreat of the 8th Army. (A-M, 731–32)

Smith wrote in his diary, "The situation was ominous. The Division felt that the enemy would put up a determined defense west of Yudam-ni. It was our hope that we would meet the enemy in strength at Yudam-ni before the division became still further extended along the road to Mup'yong-ni. In this we were not disappointed. Although we had not anticipated a massive counteroffensive such as was launched by the CCF, we had taken sufficient precautions to be able to withstand the attack when it was launched" (A-M, 745–46).

Efforts to obtain accurate intelligence had failed. "When we moved up to the Chosin reservoir in November, we had a feeling [the Chinese] would come into the war. General Smith said, 'Holcomb [intelligence officer of the First Marine Division], go talk to MacArthur's staff. See if they know anything.' But in Tokyo they wouldn't tell me anything. I never got to see MacArthur. [Maj. Gen. Charles A.] Willoughby, the G-2 [intelligence officer], said they certainly would let us know if they got any firm indication that the Chinese would come into the war."[20]

Late in the day on 29 November, Almond declared that the whole scheme of maneuver had been altered and gave Smith permission to withdraw RCT 5 and

RCT 7 to a staging area at Hagaru-ri. He also informed Smith that army units east of the Chosin reservoir were now attached to the First Marine Division; Almond requested that Smith extricate these army units, now under his command.

"Before we were ordered to start the winter offensive," stated Colonel Bowser, "I had said to my plans officer, 'What I'm thinking about now is Napoleon's retreat from Moscow; you go draw up a plan for a winter defensive line.' Anybody in his right senses would have let the Chinese and the North Koreans impale themselves on our line all winter, instead of moving forward."[21] Common sense at higher command did not prevail.

10

DISASTER AT THE CHOSIN

In the fading days of November 1950, Chinese Communist forces entered the war openly and in force. The Communists' manpower resources were almost limitless, and their army was filled with veterans from the fight against the Japanese in World War II and against the Chinese Nationalists during the postwar period. The Eighth Army was reeling from the magnitude of the enemy opposition where it had least expected it. Army units at the Chosin reservoir were cut off from Hagaru-ri, and the infantry regiments of the First Marine Division, from Koto-ri to Yudam-ni, were heavily pressed by Chinese and North Korean troops. The situation was serious.

At a secret meeting with MacArthur at the American embassy in Tokyo on 29 November, General Almond said that Tenth Corps could continue attacks to the northwest and help the Eighth Army by cutting the Chinese lines of communication. This was two days after the Chinese offensive that had stopped the advance of the First Marine Division. The day before the meeting in Tokyo, Almond visited the Thirty-first RCT's forward headquarters, where he gave orders to continue the advance. He awarded Silver Stars to Lt. Col. Donald C. Faith, commander of the First Battalion, Thirty-second Infantry, and two members of his staff. Then he ordered Colonel Faith to continue the attack northward. Almond refused to understand the reality of what was happening to his command; his orders bordered on tactical incompetence. His disregard for his men sealed the fate of Col. Allan D. MacLean's Thirty-first RCT, on the eastern side of the Chosin reservoir.[1]

O. P. Smith, at his undermanned command post in Hagaru-ri, realized that his first priority was to consolidate his command as soon as possible. While the

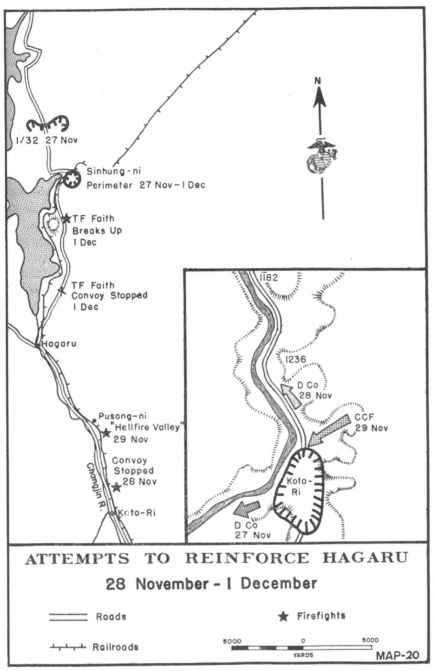

1/32 27 Nov

Sinhung-ni
Perimeter 27 Nov – 1 Dec

★ TF Faith
Breaks Up
1 Dec

TF Faith
Convoy Stopped
1 Dec

Hagaru

Pusong-ni
★ "Hellfire Valley"
29 Nov

Convoy
Stopped
★ 28 Nov

Changjin R.

Koto-Ri

N

1182

1236

D Co
28 Nov

CCF
29 Nov

Koto-
Ri

D Co
27 Nov

ATTEMPTS TO REINFORCE HAGARU
28 November – 1 December

═══ Roads   ★ Firefights

┼┼┼ Railroads

5000   0   5000
YARDS

MAP-20

Hagaru-ri, Korea. *Courtesy* MCHC.

Fifth and Seventh Marines were desperately fighting the Chinese, the First Marines was busy defending Chinhung-ni, Koto-ri, and Hagaru-ri, with only one battalion each. Hagaru-ri, lightly held and vulnerable, was the linchpin that held the operation together. The lifesaving airfield at Hagaru-ri, still being improved when the Chinese attacks came, ensured that this small town at the foot of the Chosin reservoir would become an important staging area. At that moment, it was the most important piece of real estate in Korea, and General Smith intended to defend it at all costs.

A junction with the Eighth Army was out of the question. Survival of the division depended upon the two marine regiments reaching Hagaru-ri, fourteen miles away. The long, circuitous climb through the mountains to Toktong Pass was destined to be a rugged fight all the way.[2] In order to ensure passage along the MSR, it was necessary for the marines to clear the enemy from the hills along both flanks and hold them while the convoys slowly cleared the defile. After passage of the column, the troops holding the ridges became part of the rearguard at the end of the train, while troops ahead of them rotated to the flanks in a continuous cycle of small units. This simple tactic contributed immeasurably to the successful movement of Smith's command.[3]

Smith's daily log indicates that on 30 November two army battalions from RCT 31, on the eastern side of the Chosin reservoir, that had been cut off from each other by enemy roadblocks had made a juncture and had fallen back to Sinhung-ni, where they consolidated their forces.

The story of RCT 31, covering the right flank of the First Marine Division, is a heroic saga of courage in the face of overwhelming odds. For four days and five nights, this understrength command stood its ground, slowing the Chinese advance long enough for Smith to bring the Fifth and Seventh Marines southward into the Hagaru-ri perimeter. With two-thirds of its infantry strength plus army and British elements at Hagaru-ri, the First Marine Division was strong enough to stand off anything the Chinese army was capable of mounting against it. It should never be forgotten that in those critical days at the end of November and the first days of December, the encircled troops guarding the airfield and the CP of the First Marine Division did not have to contend with the Chinese divisions that were busy attacking from the eastern side of the Chosin reservoir. The Thirty-first was bled to death, buying time with its sacrifice. Recognition of its valor and determination does not detract from the magnificent performance of the First Marine Division. Indeed, recognition of the deeds of their army brothers can only increase the stature of the marines who survived Chosin.

General Smith's narrative of the Seventh Infantry Division experience at the eastern edge of the Chosin reservoir covers several pages in his Korean diary. The narrative in the pages that follow reflects the way Smith viewed the events in 1951.

Maj. Gen. David G. Barr, commander of the Seventh Infantry Division, had had to scramble to find enough units for the regiment-sized task force he was ordered to assemble for operations on the eastern side of the Chosin reservoir. The Fifth Marines was being pulled out so that it could spearhead an attack to the west. The lead unit of the Thirty-first RCT had been Lieutenant Colonel Faith's First Battalion of the Thirty-second Infantry, about nine hundred men. The balance of the Thirty-second Infantry and elements of the Thirty-first Infantry had been scheduled to arrive within thirty-six hours. The Chinese had hit the understrength regiment before all of the units could get to the staging area. The last of the Fifth Marines had pulled out only hours before the heavy Chinese attack took place.[4]

At 2218 on 29 November, Smith received from Tenth Corps orders that read as follows: "Part 1: Effective at once all elements 7th Inf Div in Koto-ri ... Hagaru-ri ... Chosin Reservoir area are attached to 1st Marine Division. Part 2: 1st MarDiv redeploy one RCT without delay from Yudam-ni area to Hagaru-ri area, gain contact with elements 7thInfDiv east of Chosin Reservoir; coordinate all forces in and north of Hagaru-ri in a perimeter defense based on Hagaru-ri; open and secure Hagaru-ri–Koto-ri MSR. Part 3: X Corps coordinates movement to Koto-ri of elms [elements of] 7th InfDiv now south [of] Koto-ri" (A-M, 888–89).

The next day, 30 November, Smith was officially ordered to withdraw any elements of the First Marine Division located north of Hagaru-ri. He had already prepared for such a move and now told Murray and Litzenberg to coordinate their movements and fall back from the area west of Yudam-ni. Smith was well aware that he could not do much except provide air support to the army forces until the Fifth and Seventh arrived at Hagaru-ri. When that took place, "if it is still necessary, I will have to use one of them to rescue the Army battalions on the east side of the Chosin Reservoir" (KL, 95).

The night of 27–28 November, RCT 31 was located at Sinhung-ni, about a mile east of the reservoir at the Pungnyuri Inlet, with approximately 2,500 men, with another three to four hundred troops a couple of miles farther north. Part of the advanced command post of Tenth Corps represented another 267 army troops on the Hagaru-ri perimeter. Most of the units assigned to RCT 31 were still northbound somewhere on the MSR, in scattered small groups. They were as well prepared for the rigors of combat in the much colder elevations around the Chosin reservoir as any of the American forces then in Korea; however, they had very little tentage and very few stoves.

RCT 31 was hit hard on the night of 27–28 November. The Chinese had been reinforced by one or two armored vehicles, which overran the artillery positions in the Sinhung-ni area and to the north, inflicting heavy casualties on the army units. Faith's battalion had been planning an attack against the dam complex at the end of the reservoir. According to Capt. Edward P. Stamford, usmc, a forward air controller attached to the battalion, a large number of casualties were inflicted by the enemy, but the attack was beaten off by daylight of 28 November. Stamford called in a strike against enemy concentrations later in the day; it took a heavy toll of the Chinese.

Colonel MacLean, commander of RCT 31, arrived at Faith's CP on 28 November. He decided that the next day 1/32 (First Battalion, Thirty-second Infantry Regiment) would fight its way south toward the positions held by the Third Battalion of the Thirty-first Infantry near Sinhung-ni. (Colonel MacLean was killed on 28 November, and the unit has been called "Task Force Faith" ever since.) Under constant heavy fire from the higher elevations to the north, Faith fought his way to the Third Battalion of the Thirty-first Infantry, bringing out all of his vehicles with him. He took command of battered RCT 31 at that time, but even when the two battalions joined forces, the situation was desperate. Third Battalion had lost its air controller and was without air support until Stamford arrived. Near midnight on 29 November, the Chinese mounted an attack, which increased in intensity until dawn of 30 November.

On 30 November, Brig. Gen. Henry I. Hodes, assistant commander of the Seventh Infantry Division, established an advance CP a few miles north of Hagaru-ri on the road leading around the east side of the reservoir. Hodes attempted to open up a secure route to the beleaguered RCT 31 but met with such heavy resistance that the effort had to be abandoned. The relief column, composed of Capt. Robert E. Drake's Thirty-first Tank Company and an infantry force, left Hudong-ni and advanced northward toward Hill 1221. After four hours of intense combat near Hill 1221, the tanks were withdrawn. The enemy still held their positions. The tanks had been stopped one mile from where Task Force Faith was halted.[5]

General Hodes reported to Smith on 30 November that the isolated battalions were unable to break out on their own. They had accumulated over four hundred casualties by that time. Smith explained to Hodes that it was impossible for the Hagaru-ri garrison to extract Task Force Faith, but ample air support would be provided to the latter. Now that the task force was under his command, Smith realized, instructions from him were necessary; he directed Hodes to draw up a dispatch in his (Smith's) name to Colonel Faith. The dispatch told Faith that he was now under the command of the First Marine Division and that he should make every effort to move south to Hagaru-ri as soon as possible. The dispatch also stated that unlimited air support was available to his air controller, Captain Stamford. Faith was authorized to destroy whatever equipment he felt would impede his movements, and, finally, he was directed to "do nothing which would jeopardize the safety of the wounded" (a-m, 896–97).[6]

General Barr flew to Smith's command post on 30 November. Smith loaned Barr his helicopter so that he could confer with Colonel Faith. When Barr returned, he and Smith agreed that the task force could improve its position with additional air support. Barr was still at Hagaru-ri when General Almond arrived. Task Force Faith was the subject of much of their conversation, which ended with Almond directing Smith and Barr to draw up a plan and timetable for extricating the trapped units. Almond also proclaimed that if Faith failed to attack, he should be relieved of his command. Barr objected and defended Faith as an excellent officer in whom he had great confidence. Almond requested that the plan be delivered to his headquarters that evening when Barr left Hagaru-ri. As soon as Almond left, Smith and Barr agreed that the plan was superfluous until the two marine regiments arrived from Yudam-ni.[7]

Daylight hours of 30 November brought some relief to the weary soldiers of Task Force Faith. Enemy activity lessened, thanks to the air support provided by gallant pilots who answered every call for assistance from Captain Stamford and his Tactical Air Control party. However, as soon as the shadows lengthened and the threat of planes overhead disappeared, the Chinese attacked with renewed vigor, using heavy mortars. The possibility of being overrun was real! Faith had made preparations to fight southward toward Hagaru-ri during the early daylight hours of 1 December. He sent a message to Smith advising him of his intention and requesting air support. By 1000 aircraft were on station overhead, and the troops on the ground were ready to move out. Faith's battalion (1/32) was at the head of the convoy, 3/31 was the flank guard, and the 157th Field Artillery acted as rearguard.

Part of the preparation for the breakout attempt involved an air strike, but some of the napalm bombs fell short, killing and injuring many Americans. The tragic error caused havoc among the troops assembled for the breakout. Most survivors believe that demoralization was irreversible from that point on. Eventually the column forced its way some distance (four or five miles) past Sindae-ri, two and a half miles north of Sasu-ri, where the road turned away from the reservoir. The column received heavy machine-gun fire from the hills to the north, as well as from Hill 1221 to the south.

By the time darkness settled over the area, troops had knocked out a roadblock, allowing the convoy to continue past Hill 1221 to the second blown bridge. At this point Colonel Faith was mortally wounded, and the column ground to a halt, with several trucks out of gas. Captain Stamford found an intact railroad bridge nearby, which allowed the convoy to continue for another mile or so, where it became surrounded by large numbers of enemy soldiers, who threw grenades into the trucks. At this point all organized resistance ceased; it was every man for himself.[8]

In the meantime, a new task force was being organized around Lt. Col. Berry K. Anderson, senior army officer in the Hagaru-ri perimeter. (It should be noted that some veterans of RCT 31 dispute whether the following action actually took place, but it is mentioned in three very reliable sources.) The force was the equivalent of a rifle company, reinforced by tanks and air support. Anderson planned to jump off between 0930 and 1100 on 2 December and reach out to assist Task Force Faith into Hagaru-ri. The force was reduced at the last minute to only two platoons and tanks, but it jumped off as planned, with specific instructions from General Smith. As the general later recalled, "Task Force Anderson was ordered not to become so heavily engaged that it might be cut off. After reaching a point about 4000 yards north of Hagaru-ri, the task force came under heavy attack from the flanks and rear and the tail of the column was momentarily cut off. After picking up some 10 [of] Task Force Faith's wounded in the vicinity of the road block, Task Force Anderson was ordered to return to Hagaru-ri. The column turned around and successfully reached the perimeter of Hagaru-ri" (A-M, 901–2).[9]

Task Force Faith was no longer functioning as a military unit. It had been overrun by superior numbers, and the numbing cold and lack of adequate medical supplies and ammunition had taken a heavy toll. Individual soldiers felt abandoned, and indeed they had been poorly served by higher command. Some effort was made by Almond to get more supplies air-dropped to Task Force Faith, which was short of everything, especially ammunition, gasoline, food, water, medical supplies, and spare parts. On 28 November, sixteen tons of supplies had been dropped. Almond had unrealistically requested four hundred tons of supplies, but it was impossible to meet the demand. However, in the first few days of December, 250 tons were dropped to the remaining survivors by the Far East Combat Cargo Command.[10]

Many of the survivors from Task Force Faith found their way to the marine perimeter at Hagaru-ri. At the southern end of the Chosin reservoir, Lt. Col. Olin L. Beall, USMC, commanding officer of First Motor Transport Battalion, searched the perimeter and went out on the ice, where he rescued over three hundred soldiers, using jeeps and improvised sleds to carry the weak and wounded men. (Colonel Beall was later awarded the Distinguished Service Cross for his rescue efforts.) Other survivors found their own way into the perimeter, some coming through minefields. All of the marine units that manned the perimeter close to the reservoir were involved in helping the soldiers into their lines and safety. Army forces at Hagaru-ri also mounted rescue operations. One was led by Lt. Hodge S. Escue, S-3 (operations officer) of the Thirty-first Infantry; he rescued several truckloads of wounded soldiers. (It is possible that some of those he saved were included in the number of men reportedly rescued by Colonel Beall.)[11]

General Smith directed Colonel Anderson to furnish jeeps and men to assist in the rescue of troops making their way into the lines and also to organize the army troops already within the perimeter. The army command-post element from Hudong-ni was present in the Hagaru-ri compound, and it facilitated the reorganization of its own personnel. A report from the division surgeon, Capt. Eugene R. Hering, USN, about the large number of wounded men being evacuated caused Smith some concern. Hering was suspicious that some of the army troops were getting aboard flights out of the war zone by faking injuries; Col. George A. Rasula has written to the author that some of his marine friends from Yudam-ni told him that they saw some marines fake injuries also. Smith would later state, "If . . . on 2 December, malingerers succeeded in getting aboard planes it was our fault. The Air Force had sent up an 'Evacuation Officer' to supervise the loading of planes. The doctors assumed that he was responsible for seeing that only casualties got on the planes. The Evacuation Officer had no such responsibility. The following day the situation was under control as far as malingerers were concerned" (A-M, 904).[12]

RCT 31 had had approximately 2,500 officers and men. Of these men, 1,050 were evacuated; the rest were missing and assumed lost. Casualties, including wounded, had been 80 percent. The task force had lost all of its vehicles and equipment. Colonel Anderson organized a composite provisional battalion of about 380 men. It would fight its way to Hungnam with the First Marine Division.

As soon as elements of RCT 31, the men suffering from the cold, started arriving in Hagaru-ri, marines maintained warming tents and a galley to prepare food around the clock for their benefit. At that time priority was given to airlifting in tentage, foodstuffs, and kitchen supplies for the survivors. The army had four galleys of its own functioning. When the Fifth and Seventh Marines eventually made it to the Hagaru-ri perimeter, the army galleys were directed to assist in feeding the large influx of marines.[13]

During the forty-five years since Smith wrote his Korean narrative, more information has become available regarding the performance and fate of the RCT 31. The loss of all records and most of the officers and noncoms had contributed to a lack of appreciation for the contribution that the unit made. This lack of appreciation has been addressed by several members of the "Chosin Few," a fraternal organization of veterans from the Chosin reservoir campaign. It is not the intention here to delve deeply into the subject, but certain facts should be pointed out, because they directly relate to O. P. Smith's performance as commanding general of the First Marine Division.

When Smith assembled what he called his "aide-memoire," he was not aware of the significant role played by the army units east of Chosin. As a matter of a fact, he was probably influenced by Colonel Beall (of the First Motor Transport

Battalion, who had been responsible for the rescue of hundreds of survivors from RCT 31). Ironically, in 1953 Colonel Beall submitted a scathing report against the army in the Chosin campaign, which calls into question his powers of observation and his integrity.[14] A retired marine officer later described Colonel Beall: "I had known him earlier and he used to tell stories that we all agreed that he would have had to have lived a thousand years to have done all the things he claimed to have done. He was a braggart who apparently had done a great many of the things he claimed."[15]

It is now clear that RCT 31's actions spared the First Marine Division the heavy casualties that the Chinese would have inflicted if the army units had not delayed their attack. It is possible that RCT 31 saved the division from destruction.

Maj. Patrick C. Roe, USMC (Ret.), a Korean War veteran from the Seventh Marines, has researched Chinese records for new information on the Chosin reservoir story and has shed upon it some new light. As Colonel Rasula has written, "It was during the next few years [that] Pat's [Major Roe's] research into Chinese documents revealed that RCT 31 units east of the reservoir were attacked by two full CCF divisions, and a regiment of a third CCF division, reaffirming the belief that the primary objective of the CCF was the most direct route to Hagaru-ri where they would then have cut off the 5th and 7th Marines before they arrived from Yudam-ni."[16]

A Korean War veteran from the Fifty-seventh Field Artillery Battalion, Col. Edward L. Magill, Judge Advocate General Corps, has written an eloquent article about the "Soldiers of Changjin" (Chosin). An excerpt follows:

The condition of the units at the time the breakout began on 12/1 [1 December] has never been properly weighed. . . . The soldiers were suffering from hunger, dehydration, lack of sleep, long exposure to severe cold, and the physiological effects of prolonged combat. Most of the units' officers and NCO's had been killed or incapacitated. . . . For the most part, these soldiers had performed splendidly for the first 110 hours of battle, despite all odds. Yet, they have been unfairly evaluated based on the events that took place during the next seven to nine hours. . . .

It has always angered me that Generals Almond and Barr did nothing to secure recognition for the soldiers who fought and died on the east side of the Chosin Reservoir. As you probably know, the troops who failed to reach Hagaru-ri never received any unit recognition. Inexplicably, they have never been honored for their unit's outstanding efforts. For the most part, Baker Battery's officers, NCO's and men died by their guns. . . . They never considered surrendering for a moment. They just fought like elite artillerymen to the bitter end. For that, they did not even receive a salute.[17]

Col. George A. Rasula, assistant operations officer of the Thirty-first, concludes a recent letter, "The Army units east of Chosin were poorly served by every command to which it was linked."[18]

The above statements are stinging accusations of Almond and Barr and, indirectly, of General Smith. Could Smith have done more to assist the survivors? At the time, his command was in danger of being overrun; his staff was not functioning at its normal capacity, because most of its personnel were still en route to Hagaru-ri; his assistant division commander was away on emergency leave; and he had just become responsible for the extraction of the army units east of Chosin, even though he had never had any input about their mission, which had got them into their desperate situation in the first place. Smith's position was a thankless one, but he did try to do the right things at a time when all that could be done was to increase air supply and air support. "How" (H) Battery of Eleventh Marines did give some artillery support, from 1 through 3 December.[19]

An ugly element of interservice rivalry was also present in 1950. Eric Hammel, an eminent military historian, has written:

> Marines evidenced a growing hostility to the army men in their midst. It was unfair for them to do so, but there was not a member of the 1st Marine Division who did not feel that his plight in some way reflected a lack of concern on the part of the army [officers] who ran X Corps. Since the Corps staff was not available to bear the Marines' rage[,] . . . the full burden fell upon the survivors of Task Force Faith and several smaller elements of the 31st Infantry which had been north of Hagaru-ri. Those were the last soldiers who should have drawn such hostility, for they were men who had survived eight days of constant combat with the Chinese. Moreover, theirs were small companies with no organic supporting arms taking on jobs that would have troubled larger, rested, better-equipped units. It was an unfortunate turn of emotions, and it lingers yet.[20]

Lack of communication equipment proved to be one of the most fatal consequences. Army infantry units could not communicate with army or marine tanks. Army radios were incompatible with marine radios. "Task Force Faith was annihilated largely because higher headquarters remained ignorant of its actual combat requirements. . . . The communications breakdown in Task Force Faith bordered on criminal negligence."[21]

In bringing the discussion of the tragic chain of events on the east side of the Chosin reservoir to a close, it is important for the survivors of RCT 31 to know that their ordeal is, at last, appreciated. They should be proud, satisfied that they did all that mortal men could do under such wretched circumstances.

The marines under General Smith's command should thank God that their army brothers steadfastly stood between them and the Chinese for four days and five nights; they deserve to be recognized for what they did.

On the west side of the Chosin reservoir, the strength of the marines at Yudam-ni on 27 November was as follows:

Fifth Marines	3,449
Seventh Marines	2,571
Three battalions of the Eleventh Marines	1,946
Attached miscellaneous units	140
Total	8,106 (A-M, 779)

As soon as the First Battalion of the Fifth Marines arrived at Yudam-ni from the eastern side of the reservoir, the MSR was closed behind it. It would remain closed until the next day, when the blockages were removed by a combined force of the Fifth and Seventh Marines on its way south.

On 28 November, Smith initiated steps to meet the serious situation that the division was now facing. The strongholds at Yudam-ni, Hagaru-ri, and Koto-ri were isolated from each other and from the rest of Tenth Corps. The subsequent movements of every unit under Smith's command were initiated as a result of sound staff work at the CP, which maintained a solid grasp of the ever-changing situation. Smith directed individual units to complete assignments that were but segments of a larger, complex plan of operations. The plans were constantly completed, modified, and amplified in accordance with Smith's approval. Very little was left to chance.

Smith believed in detailed planning. His ideas were executed by his staff, especially Colonel Bowser. Smith was not one to tell his staff how to do things; however, he did insist that it translate his wishes into precise, clear orders. He was known throughout the Marine Corps as a commander who gave a lot of latitude to his subordinates. He wanted the goals reached; he did not particularly care about the methods used, but he never failed to follow through to see that his orders were carried out. He did not make an issue of his authority, but he had a low tolerance for individuals who were "not up to the job." He expected and received maximum performance from his subordinates.[22]

Smith noted that the Chinese seemed to be incapable of sustained operations. At Yudam-ni on 28 November they had attacked viciously, yet they had remained quiescent the next day. Similar operational characteristics were observed at Toktong Pass, Hagaru-ri, and Koto-ri. Smith attributed their lack of staying power to their poor logistical system and to heavy losses from the battles and from the severe weather conditions encountered in the mountains (A-M, 797).

On 28 November Smith had no knowledge of Tenth Corps's plans for the situation. The evening of 28–29 November brought division-sized attacks against the defenders of Hagaru-ri and Koto-ri. Hagaru-ri suffered five hundred casualties, dangerously reducing the garrison's ability to maintain the perimeter. The attacks against Hagaru-ri and Koto-ri continued, with heavy losses to the enemy, mainly from marine air support. Task Force Drysdale began arriving at Hagaru-ri by late afternoon of 29 November. Those units that were unable to break through the roadblocks returned to Koto-ri that night.

The situation at Hagaru-ri was more serious than at Yudam-ni or Koto-ri. The garrison was thinning hourly from combat losses, and the enemy continued to attack. By 28 November, when Smith ordered Puller to send Task Force Drysdale north, the garrison was composed of 3,378 officers and men. Smith specifically ordered the task force to continue even though it had had sustained frightful losses in storming the formidable roadblocks. "The casualties of Task Force Drysdale were heavy, but, nevertheless, by its partial success the Task Force made a significant contribution to the holding of Hagaru-ri which was vital to the Division. To the slender infantry garrison of Hagaru-ri were added a tank company [army] of about 100 men and some 300 seasoned infantrymen" (A-M, 868).

The key defense feature of Hagaru-ri was East Hill, a steep, rocky ledge at the northeast corner of the perimeter. Late in the evening of 28 November, during a light snowfall, it was repeatedly attacked. The hill was defended by army engineers from the Tenth Engineer Battalions and an army signal battalion. They held the commanding terrain feature against heavy odds, even though they were abandoned by the ROK troops attached to them. When the army units were relieved, they counted four hundred enemy dead in front of them.[23]

The 30th of November was a busy day at the division command post. Generals Hodes, Barr, and Almond all descended on the CP to discuss the Task Force Faith situation with Smith. However, Almond's visit was significant for another reason also: "He [Almond] authorized me to burn or destroy equipment or supplies, stating that I would be re-supplied by air drop as I withdrew. I told him that my movements would be governed by my ability to evacuate the wounded, that I would have to fight my way back and could not afford to discard equipment and that, therefore, I intended to bring out the bulk of my equipment" (KL, 94).

The life-saving airstrip at Hagaru-ri was only 40 percent complete, but there was room for two C-47s to land. On 1 December they removed sixty wounded men on their first flights.[24]

The Far East Combat Cargo Command of the U.S. Air Force played a significant role in the withdrawal from the Chosin. Airdrops of desperately needed supplies to isolated units maintained the ability of the ground troops to resist heavy enemy pressure. Frequently the airdrops drifted into enemy hands, and some disintegrated upon impact; however, the 20 to 30 percent of the material that was salvageable made the difference between life and death in many instances. Smith praised the airdrops: "Without the extra ammunition, many more of the friendly troops would have become casualties and fewer of the enemy would have been killed. Supply by air was available and was used to the maximum. There can be no doubt that the supplies received by this method proved to be the margin necessary to adequately sustain the operations of the Division during this period" (A-M, 1010).[25]

The man responsible for the remarkable performance of the Far East Combat Cargo Command was air force major general William H. Tunner. He had commanded some of the largest cargo airlifts in aviation history, the first being the airlift across the Himalayas in support of the Chinese Nationalists during World War II. Tunner had also been in charge of the Berlin Airlift of 1948. The airlift effort to supply the ground troops in Korea during the crucial winter operations of 1950 was in good hands.[26]

The situation faced by the Fifth and Seventh Marines at Yudam-ni was serious, and there was no chance of relief until the regiments reached Hagaru-ri. By 30 November they had accumulated over 450 casualties. Litzenberg and Murray formulated a plan for the withdrawal southward. The plan was sent by helicopter to Smith at Hagaru-ri, where he immediately approved it. Smith would recall that "an ADC [assistant division commander] would have come handy at this point" (KL, 94).

Murray later commented upon the command situation: "Litzenberg [commanding the Seventh Marines] and I got together and decided that we were going to cooperate. Many people have asked why he [Smith] didn't just assume command up there. I can't answer that question definitely. After all, there was a Division Headquarters over the hill from us, and we were still part of that Division, so we had a common head.... We planned together what we were going to do to come out, and everything worked fine."[27]

The plan called for the Seventh Marines to lead the way down the MSR from Yudam-ni, with the Fifth Marines covering the rear. Artillery and supply trains were positioned at the center of the column, with the wounded on board the trucks and ambulances. The able-bodied men and walking wounded marched in columns along the road.

The remarkable story of Fox Company, Second Battalion, Seventh Marines is one of courage and determination. About six miles out of Yudam-ni, the MSR went through the narrow defile of Toktong Pass. It was perhaps the most strategic location on the entire MSR at that time. Fox Company, under Capt.

William B. Barber, had been dropped off during the movement northward. He selected an excellent position that commanded the roadway and had a 360-degree field of fire. He sent out patrols during the daylight hours and set up listening posts during the long nights. The men were put on a 50 percent alert. Radio communication was available with the Seventh RCT CP at Yudam-ni and the First Marines CP at Hagaru-ri. Fox Company had two forward observers, one for artillery and one for air support. Heavy enemy attacks hit the outpost on 28 November from all four sides. The perimeter was broken at one point, but it was reestablished later in the day, with heavy losses to the enemy. About 450 enemy dead lay in the snow around the outpost.

Airdrops were necessary if Fox Company was to maintain itself. Some of the drops landed in the hands of the Chinese, but enough was collected to sustain the company until the ordeal was over. Litzenberg wanted to call Fox Company into his perimeter once he got to Yudam-ni, but it was unable to break out from its isolated position, so it remained in place. That was a fortunate turn of events, because the stronghold proved to be invaluable to the column on its return trip down the MSR a few days later. If Fox Company had not been in place, it would have been a costly operation for the column to secure the position so that its logistical train could safely pass below. The Chinese then found out how costly the position could be to themselves.

Twice, helicopters had to fly into the perimeter of Fox Company under heavy fire to drop off radio batteries. Radios were the company's only link with the outside world. Air and artillery support helped make it possible for the small force to survive on the hill until relieved, even though the costs were becoming high. Requests for assistance came into the CP at Hagaru-ri from the army units on the east side of the reservoir and from Fox Company. Hagaru-ri itself was hanging on by a thread and could not meet the demands. According to Smith, "Toktong Pass was the key terrain feature between Yudam-ni and Hagaru-ri. F Co[.] . . . held its position for five days and nights against attacks of the Chinese in estimated regimental strength. . . . .Captain Barber . . . was awarded the Medal of Honor for his leadership" (A-M, 811).

Four inches of snow fell in the mountains the night of 30 November–1 December, making the already difficult road surfaces even more treacherous. In the morning the Fifth and Seventh Marines started to move southward from Yudam-ni.

There were elements of five Chinese divisions in the Chosin reservoir area, the Fifty-ninth, Sixtieth, Seventieth, Eightieth, and the Eighty-ninth. The Fifth and Seventh slugged it out for every inch of the MSR, with most of the action taking place on the adjacent ridges. Lt. Col. Raymond G. Davis forced his First

Battalion, Seventh Marines across country to relieve Fox Company at Toktong Pass. Davis could not make it before nightfall but did reach the stronghold by midday on the 2d of December. (Davis was to receive the Medal of Honor for his relief of the besieged company.)

On 3 December, Smith sent the Forty-first Commando and the army's Thirty-first Tank Company north on the MSR to see if they could relieve some of the pressure the two-regiment column was experiencing on the way from Yudam-ni. The Royal Marines and army tankers cleared the perimeter north of Hagaru-ri of enemy forces, making it easier for the Fifth and Seventh Marines to make contact with the Hagaru-ri garrison. The commandos and tankers were withdrawn into the perimeter at nightfall. About 1935 an advance element of the Seventh Marines arrived at Hagaru-ri. Smith described the scene: "The entry of the 1st Bn [Battalion] 7th Marines into the Hagaru-ri perimeter was quite an emotional experience for both those in the column and those who met the column at the road block on the perimeter. First came the troops covering the head of the column, then came a long column of walking wounded, and then came jeeps and trucks loaded with casualties. In some cases casualties had been strapped on the hoods of jeeps. . . . I was considerably relieved to have RCTS 5 and 7 rejoin us at Hagaru-ri. I considered that the critical part of the operation had been completed. Even with two depleted RCTs I felt confident we could fight our way out to Koto-ri where we would gain additional strength. I am sure my confidence was shared by all hands" (A-M, 943, 950).

By the time the last element of the column arrived at Hagaru-ri on 4 December, all of the casualties accumulated from operations at Hagaru-ri and the surrounding areas, including the wounded survivors of Task Force Faith, had been evacuated—by aircraft from all of the U.S. services and several nations, notably the Greek air force. Doctors estimated that up to 1,200 casualties would have to be evacuated upon their arrival at Hagaru-ri, but as it turned out, there were many more than anticipated. The following table lists the number of casualties airlifted by C-47 aircraft from the Hagaru-ri airstrip:

Casualties
    Brought in by Fifth and Seventh Marines

2 December	900
3 December	700
4 December	1,000
5 December	1,400
6 December	60

  Total (Suffered at Hagaru-ri) 4,060 (A-M, 997–98)

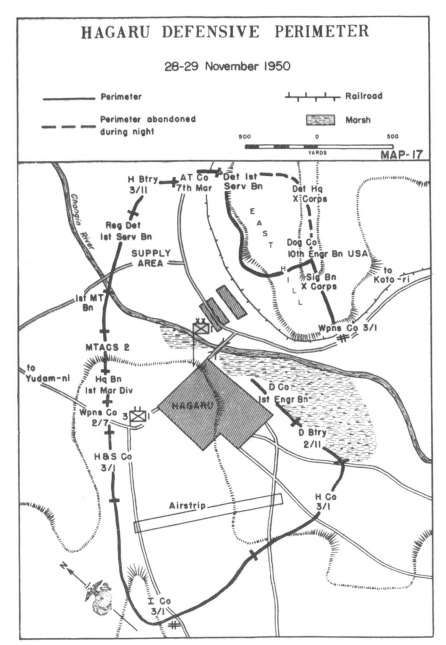

HAGARU DEFENSIVE PERIMETER

28-29 November 1950

—————— Perimeter	┴┬┴┬┴┬┴ Railroad
— — — — Perimeter abandoned during night	▭ Marsh

500   0   500
YARDS

MAP-17

Changjin River

H Btry 3/11
AT Co 7th Mar
Det 1st Serv Bn
Det Hq X Corps

E A S T

Reg Det 1st Serv Bn

SUPPLY AREA

Dog Co 10th Engr Bn USA

1st MT Bn

H I L L

Sig Bn X Corps

to Koto-ri

MTACS 2

Wpns Co 3/1

to Yudam-ni

Hq Bn 1st Mar Div

D Co 1st Engr Bn

Wpns Co 2/7

3 ⊠ 1

HAGARU

D Btry 2/11

H&S Co 3/1

Airstrip

H Co 3/1

N

I Co 3/1

Hagaru-ri, Korea, and the eastern side of the Chosin Reservoir. *Courtesy MCHC.*

Once the Fifth and Seventh Marines were within the Hagaru-ri perimeter, preparations for the attack to the south could begin in earnest. While the planning was under way, thousands of men were desperately in need of rest and warm food. This slight delay while the wounded men were evacuated was a time of replenishment, for body and soul.

General Almond arrived at Hagaru-ri on 4 December, obviously pleased with the performance of the First Marine Division. He awarded Distinguished Service Crosses to Smith, Murray, Litzenberg, and Beall. Smith noted that Almond appeared to be weeping during the ceremony; he could not determine if it was because of the bitter cold or if it was an emotional release.[28]

The command post at Hagaru-ri was not fully staffed, but by 28 November it had enough personnel and equipment to carry out its functions. Smith stayed at a Japanese-style house located at the northern outskirts of the town, against a stand of pine trees, about three hundred yards from the front lines. With a limited staff and a twenty-four-hour operation under way, staff officers were placed under severe strain. Smith was aware that "decisions do not come easily to minds which have been drugged by loss of sleep."[29]

General Tunner visited the CP on 5 December, and Smith took this opportunity to thank him for the tremendous effort of his command. Tunner mentioned that he had caught up with all of the casualties and that he could begin flying out any and all of the troops remaining and as much equipment as possible. Smith told him that he had just flown in five hundred replacements, and the division was going to fight its way out (A-M, 974).

The cargo planes continued to land at Hagaru-ri with supplies; since they had already taken the wounded, Smith decided that they could now take out the dead. He would later recall, "We flew out 138 bodies from Hagaru-ri. We didn't want to bury them in that God-forsaken place. We had a good cemetery in Hungnam. . . . When we got to Koto-ri we had a very limited strip there; we couldn't fly out the dead, so we buried 113 there. [The dead that were buried at Yudam-ni and Koto-ri were eventually returned by the North Koreans as part of the truce terms.] . . . I've got to hand it to the North Koreans—they did an excellent job of digging up those bodies and put them in bags and sent them to Panmunjon" (OH, 239).

Smith had an interesting visit on 5 December from an old acquaintance, Baron Lewe von Aduard, a member of the United Nations Commission for the Unification of Korea. Von Aduard had been a Royal Dutch Marine attached to the Dutch embassy in Washington when Smith was commanding officer of Marine Corps Schools. Von Aduard was interested in determining whether or not the Chinese soldiers were volunteers, as China claimed. Smith told him that they were not volunteers and that his opinion could be confirmed by the

Chinese prisoners at Hungnam. Smith was pleased with the visit and with the
letter that arrived after the visit:

My dear General Smith,

Yesterday, upon leaving, I felt somewhat awkward. I compared my story
of a hopelessly confused and divided world, trying to avoid a global war,
with your calm and clearcut statement, outlining your task of getting your
men out of the reservoir area.

Well General, . . . you cleared up a lot of thoughts in my mind, and I hope
that the same fresh and courageous "marine-wind" will blow through many
heads in Washington, and in [U. N. Headquarters] Lake Success and in other
capitals.

The world owes you and the Marines under your gallant leadership a great
debt. I hope we find the courage to live up to the standards which you have set,
and which you have shown me yesterday, in hard battle. (A-M, 975–76)

During the interlude at Hagaru-ri, letters of congratulation began to arrive.
General Almond's timely note read as follows: "The Tenth Corps admires your
courage and that of your officers and men in the fighting from Yudam-ni to
Hagaru-ri to Koto-ri. Please inform the commanders of your regiments, Puller,
Litzenberg, and Murray, of my high confidence in their fighting qualities and
the leadership now being exhibited. This Corps is doing all in its power to supply your Division, evacuate your wounded, and hold open the route of withdrawal. I am confident of your success in the present operation" (A-M, 976).

The news correspondents had not been aware of the potential story at the Chosin
reservoir until the Yudam-ni breakout by the Fifth and Seventh RCTs. When they
finally understood what was taking place, it became one of the most heavily reported stories of the Korean War. On 5 December, several correspondents, including Charlie Moore of UP, Macbeth of the Associated Press, Edward L. Keyes Beach
from *Time*, and Marguerite Higgins of the *New York Herald-Tribune* arrived to
report on developing events. The presence of Miss Higgins at such an exposed
position prompted General Smith to issue instructions to get her out of Hagaru-
ri, regardless of her pleading to stay and "go out with the troops" (A-M, 977–78).

Marguerite Higgins found a chilly reception whenever she appeared at the
center of activity during the breakout from the Chosin reservoir area. She came
in by plane on 7 December and was met by Puller, who immediately assigned
an officer to her with precise orders to see that she was put on the last plane out
of the area. Miss Higgins appealed to General Smith for help in the matter. She
told him that she wanted to walk out with the men, because it was a terrific
story and she thought that she had a right to tell it. Smith told her, "There are a

lot of good Marines who are getting frostbite, and if you march down with these Marines you probably will get frostbitten, and then somebody is going to have to take care of you. I am sure these Marines will see that you are taken care of and we haven't got men for that kind of business" (OH, 241).

On 9 December General Shepherd visited Smith with the intention of staying overnight, but Smith insisted that he leave on the last flight out of Koto-ri. He did so, with Marguerite Higgins as a fellow passenger. The plane was hit by ground fire but got safely airborne.[30]

Higgins later wrote a book about her experiences in Korea, noting that "General Smith had a strong seizure of chivalry that afternoon and insisted that the walkout was too dangerous."[31] As Captain Sexton recalled decades later, "Smith firmly directed Colonel Puller to see that she was personally escorted to the next plane and flown out of the area. This mission was accomplished with firmness, amid loud protests and profanities from the female passenger."[32]

Artillery preparations foretold the breakout from Hagaru-ri. The artillery emplacements at Hagaru-ri could shoot approximately halfway to Koto-ri, while other batteries at Koto-ri could reach northward an equal distance. It was the intention of the artillerymen to use up all of the ammunition that had been stockpiled at Hagaru-ri so that they would not have to carry it out. Essentially, the artillery from Koto-ri and Hagaru-ri covered both sides of the road with a blanket of steel.[33]

Smith had expressed a desire to drive out with the column from Hagaru-ri to Koto-ri. According to Stormy Sexton, the staff members talked him out of such an act. He would be more valuable to the division if he flew to Koto-ri, where he could influence events affecting the breakout. Smith agreed to the logic and decided to stay at Hagaru-ri until he was assured that the attack to the south was successful; then he would fly out by helicopter.[34]

Smith was later asked how he felt at the time of the breakout. "I felt pretty optimistic.... It never occurred to me at any time that we wouldn't get out, and I don't think it occurred to any man in the Division.... The only time I had cause for great concern was when Litzenberg and Murray were fighting out from Yudam-ni, and I got a call from Litzenberg along midnight somewhere, and he said, SITUATION GRAVE. I didn't like that at all. But it was followed within an hour or two by a message stating that they had come through and everything was all right" (OH, 244).

The arduous march to the coast from Hagaru-ri began at first light of 6 December, with the Seventh Marines in the lead. It was an orderly operation, but it required heavy fighting all the way past Koto-ri. Highlights of the order for the movement were that all members of the column were to do their share

Major General Smith attends memorial services at the division cemetery in Hungnam, December 15, 1950. *Courtesy of MCUA.*

Celebration of Christmas 1950 by some members of the First Marine Division, Masan, Korea. *Standing, from left:* unknown, unknown, Lt. Col. Raymond L. Murray, unknown, Col. Homer L. Litzenberg, Col. Lewis B. Puller, unknown, unknown, Col. Alpha L. Bowser, Major General Smith, Brig. Gen. Edward A. Craig, unknown and Col. Gregon A. Williams. The men kneeling are unknown. *Courtesy of MCUA.*

in protecting the vehicles; all personnel except drivers, relief drivers, radio operators, and casualties were to walk; vehicles breaking down were to be pushed to the side of the road and destroyed; and routine flank protection of the convoy during halts would be maintained.

Before the march began, Smith ordered that post-exchange supplies be issued to the troops free of charge. A portion of that issuance was thousands of Tootsie Rolls. On the long, cold trek southward, many men became sick from eating frozen C rations, but the fortunate men who were sustained by Tootsie Rolls had no such stomach problems (A-M, 1018).

For the column to proceed toward Koto-ri safely, it was necessary to secure the high ground on both sides of the road. The Second Battalion, Fifth Marines secured the eastern ridges south of Hagaru-ri. Remnants of the army's Thirty-first and Thirty-second Infantry Regiments secured parts of the left flank of the rearguard.[35]

The Seventh Marines, augmented by three hundred artillerymen from the Eleventh Marines, had to smash its way through nine roadblocks between Hagaru-ri and Koto-ri. The First Marine Aircraft Wing maintained sixteen planes on station and ready to assist the Seventh Marines, with eight other aircraft prepared to help the Fifth RCT at Hagaru-ri. The Fifth RCT needed the help, because the enemy pressed a heavy attack against Hagaru-ri, and the town's defenses were not as strong as they had been before the column started its movement south.[36]

Colonel Bowser would later say that he "had hoped that the very strength of the column, organized as a 'flying wedge' with regiments intact front and rear and the trains enclosed, and having been given all possible help by air and the preliminary fires of the artillery, would discourage CCF from pressing along the ridges against the column. . . . This proved not to be and the 7th Regiment's movement had developed into a road-block clearing and out-fighting operation, as the advance continued. . . . In the light of this experience the plan for a further advance from Koto-ri southward was radically different. Five main objectives were specified which when taken in conjunction with the advance of 1/1 [First Battalion, First Marines] toward Koto-ri from the south would give the column commanding positions along the high ground on both flanks of the road."[37]

Smith moved the operational command post to Koto-ri by plane and helicopter on 6 December, after he was assured that the column could break through the enemy roadblocks. Puller's First Marines had erected a large hospital tent to house the division CP. Since most of the staff members were leaving Hagaru-ri by truck convoy, the CP would be lightly manned until the convoy arrived.[38]

The phrase most associated with the First Marine Division in Korea is "Retreat hell, we're just attacking in a different direction." First used by Robert K. Martin in a news broadcast on 7 December 1950, it became a rallying cry for the marines and captured the attention of the whole world. Smith laughed when he heard about the communiqué, disclaimed the comment, and expressed his reservations about the cuss word. "But," he would concede, "it did the job."[39]

On 8 December, Captain Capraro, the division public information officer, was called into General Smith's tent at Koto-ri. Smith had just received a note from President Truman about the appropriateness of the press release. According to Capraro, Smith was gracious and courtly, as usual. They talked casually about many things, then Smith suggested that after the war the two of them should get together on his porch and discuss things (Capraro was in civilian life a reporter on the *San Francisco Chronicle*). Smith never asked another question, and Capraro's fitness report, signed by Smith, would state that he "is very capable of using his own judgment." The origin of the release remains a mystery, and the myth continues.[40]

In the meantime, at 0700 the Third Battalion of the Seventh Marines reached the safety of Koto-ri, but it was immediately ordered to return to the north in order to help hold the MSR open for the Fifth RCT. By 1700, all elements of RCT 7, including the army's provisional battalion, had cleared the Koto-ri perimeter. Murray's Fifth RCT had as difficult a time at the rear of the column as Litzenberg's Seventh did at the point. At midnight of 7 December, after fighting off heavy attacks all the way from Hagaru-ri, the Fifth reached Koto-ri. The advance from Hagaru-ri to Koto-ri produced another five hundred casualties.

As soon as press reports of the conditions facing the division arrived in the United States, there was fear that it would be lost. The Eighth Army had been badly mauled and would need time to regroup. From a distance, the chances of the division did not look good. A comment by Gen. Walter Bedell Smith, then director of the Central Intelligence Agency, was typical of the feelings in Washington: "Only diplomacy can save MacArthur's right flank [First Marine Division]."[41]

Before the airstrip at Koto-ri was lengthened, World War II–vintage Grumman TBM aircraft flew out over two hundred casualties. The strip was lengthened an additional four thousand feet—at great cost, because the Chinese had to be driven from the area. They still fired on every plane that took off from Koto-ri, but C-47s were able to remove all of the casualties by late in the day of 7 December.

Maj. Gerald J. Clinton, Sr., was a member of the Thirty-first Infantry Regiment on his way to join army forces east of the Chosin reservoir when the Chinese attacked. He was unable to join his comrades, so he acted as a liaison officer for Chesty Puller at Koto-ri. Clinton observed an incident at the Koto-ri airstrip after the Royal Marines arrived there from their ordeal on the MSR. The airstrip was constantly being fired upon by enemy forces in the hills overlooking the field. Puller was tired of being shot at by the snipers but had little success in eliminating them with a company of marines that had just returned from the hillside. Drysdale observed the situation and asked Puller if he would like the Royal Marines to "give it a go." Puller said yes. The British fixed bayonets, went up the hill, and cleaned out the Chinese in a short period of time. Everyone who was watching thought it was a great performance. "Chesty Puller about cried."[42]

Air support to the moving column was crucial to its survival. Navy and marine aircraft normally covered the strip from the edge of the MSR out to approximately three miles. Targets of opportunity beyond three miles were handled by air force B-26s.[43] One innovation, used here for the first time in combat, is described by Colonel Bowser, G-3 of the First Marine Division, who helped implement the concept: "About three days before the movement started, the air controllers of the air support section were flown to Yonpo to equip a C-54 provided by the 1st Marine Air Wing, with communication facilities capable of controlling aircraft and receiving requests from the ground units, thus giving a continuous method for control of support planes. This C-54 was flying at 10,000 feet altitude. This was the first time it was ever done and the results were excellent."[44]

The descent down the mountain in the winter conditions was filled with peril even without the added element of the Chinese, who constantly pressed the column from all sides. The next significant benchmark on the MSR was Chinhung-ni, about ten miles distant from Koto-ri. A couple of miles south of Koto-ri, the mountainous terrain falls off precipitously, all the way to Chinhung-ni, where the First Battalion of the First Marines was being relieved by Task Force Dog from the army's Third Infantry Division.

Smith's plan was fairly simple and basic. The Fifth and Seventh Marines would hold the commanding elevations halfway along the MSR to Chinhung-ni, while Puller's First Battalion was to attack northward from Chinhung-ni once it was relieved, so as to hold open the corridor up to the halfway point. The Third Battalion, First Marines and the army Second Battalion, Thirty-first Infantry were already at Koto-ri. They would hold the Koto-ri perimeter until the last of the 1,400 vehicles of the train left. "Once the commanding ground was seized, it was our intention to push the trains down the mountain. As the trains cleared, infantry would leave the high ground and move down the road. The last vehicles in the column were the tanks" (KL, 109).

There was one major problem ahead of the column: a blown bridge one-third of the way to Chinhung-ni, where four large ducts carried water to the turbines of a power plant below. The pipes were encased in a heavy concrete apron on the uphill side of the road. The destroyed bridge had been a single-lane concrete structure over the pipes. There was a sharp drop-off, leaving no possibility of bypassing the bridge site. Foot travel was possible on the uphill side of the break, but if the column was to get off the mountain with its vehicular train, the only way was to repair the bridge.

The division did have a stroke of luck. Almond had visualized the possibility of a Tenth Corps command post in the mountains and had sent a group of engineers to Koto-ri to erect the buildings. Included in this group of engineers was a Treadway bridge unit. The First Marine division engineer, Lt. Col. John H. Partridge, consulted with the army engineers, and together they formulated a plan of action. Four heavy-duty Brockway B666 six-ton bridge-erector trucks in 1st Lt. George C. Ward's platoon of the Fifty-eighth Treadway Bridge Company were at Koto-ri. Lieutenant Ward had had extensive experience in the installation of Treadway bridges in Italy during World War II and as an instructor in army schools after the war.

Preparations were made to airdrop the needed sections of bridging at Koto-ri, where they could be retrieved and carried to the site on Ward's trucks. Four sections of bridging were needed to span the gap; eight sections were dropped, in the hope that at least half of them would be undamaged. Colonel Partridge coordinated his moves involving the bridge sections and other equipment with Colonel Bowser. When the essential engineer units were assembled, they led the way out of Koto-ri on 8 December. They were stopped by a brisk firefight at the head of the column. Enemy mortar rounds and small-arms fire began falling around the precious Brockway trucks, and Colonel Litzenberg advised the engineers to pull them out of the line of fire until the enemy could be cleared away.

The next day, 9 December, the road was secure enough so that the engineer section could proceed to the bridge site, where another firefight took place. At 1230, after a short delay, work started on the bridge. Three hours later, a sturdy Brockway truck slowly positioned the final section of the bridge into place. The plywood center sections of the bridge were quickly installed, allowing the first elements to start crossing the bridge at 1800. The first portions of the train to cross the bridge consisted of large tractors pulling earth-moving pans. One of these pans broke through the plywood centers, blocking the bridge and rendering it unusable for the remainder of the column.

The Brockway trucks were in advance of the column and could not be called back to effect repairs. Partridge studied the situation for a moment, measured a number of the vehicles for width, and decided that if he were to move one side of the Treadway bridge inward, the span would accommodate all of the vehicles that remained north of the gap. He made the repair with a bulldozer. Subsequently, all vehicles crossed the bridge without further incident. When the last of the rearguard and tanks crossed the bridge on 11 December, the span was blown by the engineers who had built it.[45]

As Bowser recalled, "General Smith remained at Koto-ri until we were sure that our attack plan was succeeding, that the bridge was operable, and all [was] going okay. At that point, having established a new 'forward rear' CP for the Division at the railhead at Chinhung-ni, we closed the Division CP Koto-ri, overflew the 'rear' CP at the railhead, and opened the Division 'rear' at Hungnam, using the railhead as our CP. Col. Ed Snedeker, the deputy chief of staff, took charge at Hungnam so we could move out of Koto-ri."[46]

The last three elements of the rearguard were made up of Second Battalion, First Marines, the tank column and the division reconnaissance company. As they approached the bridge site, Puller made the decision to remove the infantry from the heights overlooking the bridges. He assumed that the tanks in the line could take care of themselves—whereas in fact only the first and last tank in the line had freedom of movement or the ability to maneuver. No infantry protection was given to the tanks except by portions of Recon Company.

The seventh tank from the rear broke down and blocked the MSR; the halted column was immediately fired on from the high ground. Several of the tanks were overrun. Recon Company sustained fourteen casualties, while the tankers suffered heavily from the lack of infantry cover. It was decided to abandon the stranded tanks and destroy them with aircraft gunfire. This constituted the major loss of vehicles or equipment during the breakout from Yudam-ni. "It is apparent now," Smith would later observe, "that had an adequate infantry rear guard been provided and had the 2nd Battalion First Marines remained on Objective D [the overlooking heights] until the column had passed, the pressure on the tank column might have been avoided and at least 6 of the 7 abandoned tanks might well have been brought out. It is also difficult to understand why the 1st Battalion 1st Marines moved on to the road ahead of the tank column instead of following it. It is accepted that tanks require infantry protection against close in attack, which was particularly necessary in this case" (A-M, 1088). Smith also later commented on Puller's failure: "Finally, elements of the Recon Company were the last out. They should not have been. Lewie's infantry should have been the last out" (OH, 254).

When the rear of the column left Chinhung-ni, it reached the part of the MSR that had been secured by the Third Infantry Division. It was now clear sailing for the men who had been through so much and survived the ordeal. Tents were ready to receive them as they unloaded from the trucks that met the column below Chinhung-ni. All elements of the column were in their staging areas by 11 December. The First Marine Division was ordered to embark at Hungnam for transport to Pusan. By the time the last of the trains arrived at the large staging area at Hungnam, some elements of the division were already boarding the transports.

On the evening of the 11th, Smith attended a birthday party for General Almond at his quarters in Hungnam. Several high-ranking officers were present, including Generals Soule, Shepherd, and Barr. At the dinner, General Ruffner gave a short eulogy for General Almond, saying "that never in the history of the Army had a Corps in such a short period of time done so much" (KL, 114).

General Lowe came to Smith's CP for a visit. He enjoyed his visits with the division staff operations branch, especially Colonel Bowser. As a matter of a fact, Lowe made a point of dropping in to the operations CP of the various units he visited, so that he could get a "feel" of what was happening. His visits at the First Marine Division CP were an opportunity for him to talk freely. He was upset about the way the marine division had been handled by Tenth Corps and wrote the President that the marines should not be placed under army command again in Korea (KL, 115).

On a personal note, Smith's family had obviously been concerned about his safety and waited anxiously for information. After the successful advance to Hungnam, Smith's daughter, Virginia, wrote a beautiful letter that must have warmed her father's heart: "We are so grateful for the safe return of you and your men we can hardly contain ourselves. Mother has been wonderful through it all. . . . She keeps saying how she would just like to have one little talk with you about it all. There is certainly enough being written about the 'epic' as it is called. I keep thinking of what one writer said about the 'calm brilliance of the Marine leadership.' If that isn't a description of my Dad I don't know what is! . . . You were described as 'hollow eyed, haggard and as grimy as any corporal' when you came in and I felt guilty laying my head on my pillow that night."[47]

Stormy Sexton recently sent this author a letter that his wife received from Esther Smith. The accompanying note from Stormy said in part, "The letter graphically illustrates that Mrs. Smith possessed the identical characteristics of her husband." The letter read, in part:

December 4, 1950
    Dear Mrs. Sexton, . . . For sometime I have wanted to write to you, but it seems that it has taken the present uncertain and unhappy conditions to force me to sit down and write.
    I know nothing more than you do I'm sure, as my only source of information is the radio and the newspapers. My last letter from Gen. Smith was dated the 27th, just a day or so before this last retreat started. . . . There is not

a doubt in my mind but that they will be able to get through to the coast again. So let's just keep our chins up and hope and pray.

Virginia and her little daughter, Gail, are here with me. We are renting a small house and are very comfortable. . . . I hope that the time is passing pleasantly for you. Who knows but what we might all be together again in the not too distant future. I hope so.

Most affectionately.

[Signed] Esther K. Smith[48]

The escape of the First Marine Division was not the result of luck or desperation. Smith described the situation in a letter to the noted army historian S. L. A. Marshall as follows: "There was no doubt about the determination of the individuals, but to my mind, the decisive factor was that every resource which the division possessed or could obtain on request was used to assist and support the individual Marine in extricating himself from a dangerous and critical situation. There was a plan, and, with minor exceptions, that plan was carried out."[49] Marshall in turn described Smith's performance: "Final disaster had been averted . . . because of the steadiness and wisdom of a great Marine Commander, Major General Oliver P. Smith. Fighting all the way out, but timing his moves so that his troops could rest between battles, Smith brought his division and remnants of the 7th Division back to the zone held by the 3rd Division."[50]

MacArthur's report of 31 January 1951 to the United Nations reads in part:

In this epic action, the First Marine Division and attached elements of the Seventh Division, marched and fought over 60 miles in bitter cold along a narrow, tortuous, ice-covered road against opposition of from six to eight Chinese Communist Force divisions which suffered staggering losses. Success was due in no small part to the unprecedented extent and effectiveness of air support. The basic element, however, was the high quality of soldierly courage displayed by the personnel of the ground units who maintained their integrity in the face of continuous attacks by numerically superior forces, consistently held their positions until their wounded had been evacuated, and doggedly refused to abandon supplies and equipment to the enemy.[51]

Colonel Bowser sums up his thoughts on the operation in this way: "I felt then, and I feel now, that one of the major contributions to the success of the Chosin Campaign was the presence of the division CP, with the division commander in residence, along with a fully operating division staff. All of the units in the division were fully aware that we were not somewhere in that mythical 'rear' but were in the midst of the division, and in most cases, but unfortunately not all, able to influence the action. Our initial move of the division CP from Hungnam to Hagaru-ri was more timely than we had ever dreamed it would be."[52]

It is important to understand that the differences between Smith and Almond never became as rancorous as has been reported in some writings about the Korean War. Several years later, Smith looked back on the period and wrote, "My impression of the Army in the first few months of the war was that the commanders alternated between soaring optimism and black pessimism. Although General Almond and I did not always see eye to eye, I will say this for him; when we had come out of the Chosin reservoir area and the Eighth Army had retreated below the Han River, he was still full of fight and advancing plans for taking the offensive."[53]

Smith should have the last word about the performance of his division. "The performance of officers and men in this operation was magnificent. Rarely have all hands in a division participated so intimately in the combat phases of an operation. Every marine can be justly proud of his participation. In Korea, Tokyo and Washington there is full appreciation of the remarkable feat of the division. With the knowledge of the determination, professional competence, heroism, devotion to duty, and self-sacrifice displayed by officers and men of this division, my feeling is one of humble pride. No division commander has ever been privileged to command a finer body of men."[54]

11

In Central Korea

The battle-weary First Marine Division left Hungnam at 1030 on 15 December 1950, bound for Pusan. Hot coffee and warm food on board the ships was a welcome contrast to the frozen rations that had sustained the marines during the long march out of the Chosin reservoir.[1] The performance of the division during the Inchon-Seoul campaign had added new laurels to its colorful history; in fact the withdrawal from the Chosin remains unique. Most likely, the exhausted men did not think much about what they had accomplished, but they had established a standard of excellence that will be remembered as long as soldierly courage and resolution are admired.

The First Marine Division of 1950, with its various attached army units, under the inspiring leadership of Gen. Oliver P. Smith, ranks as one of the finest military formations in American history. Its raw courage at Chosin was supplemented by a professionalism that pervaded from the commanding general to the squad leaders. The division fought as a land army, away from its maritime roots, and it defeated massive enemy forces in one of the most hostile environments on earth. The Chosin reservoir campaign was the crowning achievement of Smith's military career.

Smith stepped ashore at Pusan twenty-four hours after the transport USS *Bayfield* weighed anchor at Hungnam. He immediately went by station wagon to Masan, thirty miles to the west. Brig. Gen. Eddie Craig had already spoken to Smith about the crowded conditions at Pusan and had suggested Masan as a rehabilitation center. It had ample areas for training, and its location adjacent to the Sea of Japan and the Korean Strait was satisfying to the maritime traditions of the marines. They were glad to be near blue water, regardless of where it was.

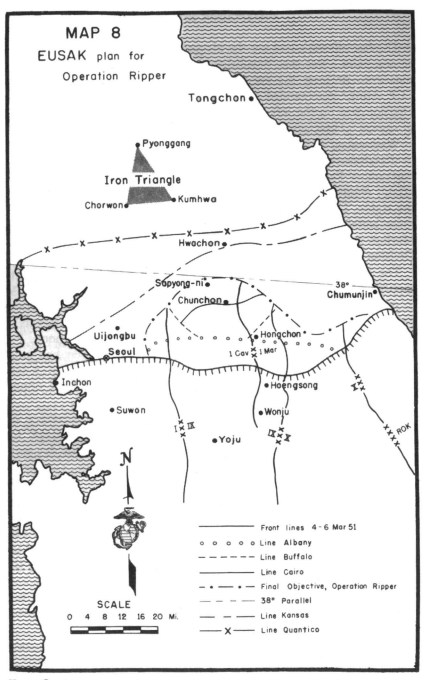

MAP 8

EUSAK plan for Operation Ripper

Tongchon

Pyonggang

Iron Triangle

Chorwon   Kumhwa

Hwachon

Sopyong-ni

Chunchon   38°

Chumunjin

Uijongbu

Seoul   Hongchon

1 Cav 1 Mar

Inchon   Hoengsong

Suwon   Wonju

Yoju   ROK

SCALE
0   4   8   12   16   20 Mi.

Front lines 4 - 6 Mar 51
o o o o o o Line Albany
— — — — — Line Buffalo
———————— Line Cairo
—•—•—•— Final Objective, Operation Ripper
— — — — 38° Parallel
— — — — Line Kansas
—X—X—X— Line Quantico

Korea. *Courtesy* MCHC.

An advance party had previously been sent to the Pusan-Masan area to make preparations. Chesty Puller, accompanied by now-Major Capraro, was scouting the area for a suitable campsite when he came upon a marine military policeman, who recognized Puller and gave him a sharp salute. Chesty bellowed to the MP, "Hey, old man! Where is there a good site for a f—— bivouac?" The MP pointed to a dish-shaped patch of farmland where beans were grown. This became the famous "bean patch," where the infantry regiments of the First Marine Division bivouacked.[2]

Craig had located a set of old Japanese barracks near the Bay of Masan and established the division CP at that point. The day after his arrival, Smith conferred with his unit commanders. There was a desperate need of supplies and equipment, but most of all the men needed rest and ample nourishment. Large numbers of replacements needed to be integrated, and training was necessary to maintain the efficiency of the division. "We have cleaned up on all of our casualties. We still need clothing and individual equipment. Our losses in trucks have not been too bad. We will have difficulty in getting new tanks and vehicles. The spare parts [situation is] also acute. What I want to impress on the unit commanders is that we must get our men in hand, do everything we can for them, but do not let them begin to feel sorry for themselves" (KL, 117).

A short time after the establishment of the division CP at Masan, a young Lt. (later Lt. Col.) Robert L. Dahlberg was "volunteered" to move some of the gear of a fighter squadron back to Masan on an LST. He selected a flat section of terrain to which to offload the gear, where it would be easy to reload for the transfer to the airfield, seven miles to the east.

> Two days later, as I was driving a forklift, . . . a jeep drove up, flying more flags than one could carry. Out jumped this General, who asked if I was in charge. As I was wearing a red baseball cap (with a gold bar), I wondered if it was proper to salute, but I did and it was returned without adverse comment.
>
> "I'm General Smith, and I would like to know when you will get all of this gear out of here—you've parked it right in the middle of the airstrip for my OY's" [observation aircraft]. Naturally I gave him a prompt "tomorrow" promise, and he got back in his jeep. As he pulled away, I leapt back on the forklift and being a little flustered, drove it right into an old foxhole! The jeep slowed, General O. P. Smith just shook his head and then went on.[3]

Security is important under any wartime circumstances, but the presence of thousands of guerrillas in the mountainous areas forty miles west of Masan provided a powerful incentive. Smith established the following measures: All roadways were to be patrolled. Civilians were to be questioned about enemy activity, but Marines were not allowed to enter private homes, except for important official business. Each patrol was to return at the end of the day and to report by telephone directly to division headquarters (A-M, 1244).

On 18 December the division was notified that it was now attached to the Eighth Army. In some ways this administrative move made it easier to obtain badly needed supplies. Smith forwarded a long letter to Lt. Gen. Walton H. Walker, commander of Eighth Army, outlining his command's supply needs:

> Parts of the Division have been in almost continuous action since 2 August 1950. . . . There was considerable material loss and damage as a result of enemy action, extreme cold, and primitive roads. During this period the equipment on hand has received varying degrees of maintenance characterized by an erratic or non-existent supply of spare parts. Expendable supplies replacement has varied from minor quantities to none. Requisitions to fill deficiencies are being submitted as rapidly as they can be prepared. . . . It is requested that deliveries of supplies and equipment be expedited to the maximum extent practicable in order that this division can be restored to its original degree of combat efficiency without delay. (A-M, 1248–49)

It is interesting that there was a considerable shortage of M-1 carbines. The infantrymen had found them unreliable in the extreme cold experienced at the Chosin reservoir and had discarded them in favor of the heavier but more reliable M-1 rifle.

By the end of the first week at Masan, the division was well on its way to being resupplied to its original level. The navy responded to the need of the men for fresh meat, and Eighth Army also provided improved rations; Smith said that his marines had turkey "coming out of their ears." By 21 December, beer rations arrived at Masan; it soon became available at the post exchange. Perhaps this liquid item did as much to boost morale as did the turkey. According to Sexton, "The men were getting good chow. . . . The menu for a week would very well read as follows: turkey twice a week, with steak, beef or ham during an average week."[4]

New tanks were provided from army stockpiles at Pusan. Spare parts for individual weapons were scarce, but the army ordnance people worked closely with marine ordnance to help bring the table-of-equipment level of the division back to normal. The two ordnance organizations remanufactured thousands of weapons to like-new condition and distributed them.[5]

Sexton would recall, "Drawing motor transport from the Army was a little more difficult to achieve. . . . They cooperated as much as possible, but one point that came to light in the requisition for new trucks and jeeps . . . was the fact that the units, when they came down from the reservoir had been so scrupulous to let not a single vehicle pass that was possibly movable, get away from them. Consequently the division came out of the reservoir with practically all the organic transportation which it had gone up with."[6] Smith later lamented that "sometimes it pays to lose your equipment."[7]

Smith spent much of his time at Masan on public-information matters. His natural reticence kept him away from the press as much as possible, but when he did agree to an interview, he was very good at it. One idea that he had already rejected before leaving Hungnam was an insistence by Keyes Beach, a prominent journalist and former combat correspondent, that Smith allow Colonel Murray to write the story of the Chosin reservoir campaign.

> I opposed the idea, as I felt the story should be told by the three regimental commanders. . . . I talked to him [Keyes Beach] frankly, setting forth my views and urged that he write the article, which he was well qualified to do. He admitted he could write the article . . . but that was not what the editors of *Colliers* wanted. I thought the matter would be dropped, but, later, I had reason to believe that [Edward L. Keyes]Beach had informed Murray that I had approved the idea. . . . I wrote General Silverthorn, Assistant Commandant of the Marine Corps, asking him to intercede with *Colliers,* which he did. In 1954, Beach wrote a book entitled *Tokyo and Points East* in which he covered the Chosin Reservoir Operation and gave a very good account . . . of the part played the 5th Marines, commanded by Colonel Murray. Colonel Murray did a magnificent job and was deserving of all the praise one could heap upon him. At Masan, my concern was to prevent any misunderstanding on the part of the other regimental commanders, who also did magnificent jobs. (A-M, 1266–67)

When Lt. Gen. Walton H. Walker was killed in an accident on 23 December, Lt. Gen. Frank Milburn, commanding general of First Corps, assumed temporary command of Eighth Army until Lt. Gen. Matthew B. Ridgway arrived in Korea. Ridgway's leadership would have a profound and positive effect upon the men in his command. He revived a dispirited Eighth Army and earned the lasting respect of Oliver P. Smith and the First Marine Division. Matthew Ridgway was one of America's great captains.

By 24 December, the division had been directed to prepare for a move by rail and truck to Wonju, about 130 miles north of Masan. Since the division had not integrated all of its replacements and was still critically short of spare parts, Smith directed the regiments to submit lists of their deficiencies to him within two days. Once the information was received, he assembled the data and turned it over to Eighth Army.

I also made a strong recommendation that the Division not be committed until it was re-equipped and until replacements were received. I sent this dispatch to CG, 8th Army for the information of Commander Naval Forces Far East in the hope that the latter might head off a precipitate employment of the Division. This was prompted by the fact that the young staff officer who requested the logistical data talked in terms of taking no tentage and only the weapons we now had in our possession. . . . These weapons had been used in a hard campaign and there was need of rebarreling, . . . renewal of parts, etc. Given the necessary spare parts, we had the qualified technicians and repair facilities to accomplish the task, but it could not be done overnight.

I had seen Army units handled in this manner, specifically units of the 7th Infantry Division which had been rushed to the Chosin Reservoir area without tentage and with inadequate winter clothing[,] with disastrous results. I wanted the Army Commander himself to know that we were ready and willing to fight but that we felt we had a right to expect that we would be allowed to reach a reasonable degree of combat readiness before [being] committed. On this date the Army was faced with no dire emergency. Its retreat had been so rapid that the Chinese had had difficulty in regaining contact and in the process had overextended their own supply lines. (A-M, 1259–60)

In January 1951 Smith learned that members of the Eighth Army staff were thinking in terms of moving the First Marine Division to Suwon, near the Inchon-Seoul battleground of the past fall. Smith thought that the Eighth Army had a defeatist attitude. Some staff officers were talking in terms of evacuating Korea. When General Ridgway arrived, he ordered the staff to give him a plan for an attack instead of evacuation. Smith wrote, "General Ridgway, by display of a high degree of personal leadership, changed the Army thinking, stopped the withdrawal of the Army, and moved forward again. This took about a month to accomplish" (A-M, 1261–62).

Ridgway later wrote about his thoughts while he was en route to Korea: "As Deputy Chief of Staff for Operations [in Washington], the map of Korea had become as familiar to me as the lines in my hand. I knew our strengths, and our weakness. I knew personally all the top commanders in Eighth Army, except General Oliver Smith of the 1st Marine Division, and from what I knew of him, I knew I could depend on him implicitly."[8]

One of the first things that Ridgway did was to order a staff study of the "desirable location of major elements of the Eighth Army for the period February 20 to August 31, 1951." The study urged that nothing be done for the winter and that the army withdraw to the Pusan area in the summer months. Ridgway could not approve such a plan, because it surrendered the initiative to the enemy—he was interested in carrying the fight *to* the enemy. It should be noted that the defeatist attitude that permeated parts of the higher command in Korea at that time was not subscribed to by the Tenth Corps or other commands that had strong leadership.[9]

Ridgway was painfully aware that he could not get any more reinforcements (even replacements were difficult to obtain) from the United States or the other United Nations members. Therefore, he carefully planned his advances by distinct stages, with goals obtainable by the forces available to him. He was also acutely concerned about interservice rivalry, and he made an effort to develop an appreciation and understanding of what each service was doing.[10]

Smith's first meeting with Ridgway took place at Tenth Corps headquarters at Kyongju, forty-five miles from Masan, near the eastern coast. The First Marine Division was placed under Tenth Corps control on 28 December. Smith later wrote, "General Ridgway . . . gave us a talk expressing his complete confidence regarding the outcome in Korea. He stressed the necessity for reconnaissance and maintaining contact. In the case of [enemy] breakthroughs at night he wanted it understood that the breakthroughs would be contained during the night and the enemy mopped up on the following day. He wanted less looking backward toward the MSR, stating that when parachutists landed their MSR was always cut" (A-M, 1270).

At the same conference Smith learned that his division might be scheduled to stage to the Pohang area for potential employment farther north. Even though Smith was slightly skeptical of some of the time and space requirements of the proposal, he praised General Almond's unfailing spirit. "Certainly, no one could accuse . . . the Corps Commander of defeatism" (A-M, 1271).

The very next day, 31 December, Smith was notified that the division was once again detached from Tenth Corps and placed in the Eighth Army reserve. Plans were under way to move the division to the Pohang-Kyongju-Yongchon axis, where it would take up a blocking position against further penetration from the north. General Craig and a small staff made a detailed reconnaissance of the area and confirmed the assumption that the division should maintain a strong hold on the coastal region of Pohang (KL, 126–27).

Smith was concerned about the mobility of his administrative headquarters when it was attached to the division command post, in view of its large number of personnel and volume of documents and records. "Its movement with the Division CP reduced our mobility, and, with the rapidly changing situation in Korea, there was a danger of losing valuable records in sudden movements which were often ordered. Throughout the subsequent campaigns of the Division during my tenure of the command the Administrative Headquarters remained at Masan and functioned very satisfactorily. Contact with the forward CP was maintained by daily courier planes" (A-M, 1315).

Col. S. L. A. Marshall visited Smith on 2 January 1951 at Masan. Marshall was head of the Operations Research Office of Johns Hopkins University, which was employed by the Far East Command for a variety of studies. Marshall had been gathering information about the U.S. Second Division at Kunu-ri, data that he later incorporated into the book *The River and the Gauntlet.* His current project was a study of the "CCF in the attack." His reception was sincere and helpful. Smith told him, "Colonel Marshall, we heard you were coming. We know about your work in the past. I have already called up my regimental commanders and told them that all personnel are to give you absolute cooperation. This Division has nothing to hide. If you have any trouble anywhere along the line, come back and tell me; but I don't believe you will have any difficulty."[11] Marshall's stenographer compiled over a hundred thousand words of notes in the week and a half the team visited the division. "On 12 January, when he had finished, Colonel Marshall came in to say good-bye. He was highly pleased with the cooporation he had received. He told me he felt the notes he had taken were really the property of the Marine Corps and that a book should be written about the operation. He was willing to write the book but felt that the Marine Corps should sponsor it" (A-M, 1272).

The report submitted by Marshall, "A Study Based on the Operations of the First Marine Division in the Koto-ri, Hagaru-ri, Yudam-ni Area, 20 November–10 December, 1950," was immediately classified "secret" and given only limited distribution. Smith was able to obtain a few copies for the commandant of the Marine Corps and selected officers on his staff (A-M, 1272). Marshall published the study in one of his later books, *Battle at Best,* in 1963. His tribute to the First Marine Division and Smith's leadership was notable: "No other operation in the American book of war quite compares with this show by the 1st Marine Division in the perfection of tactical concepts precisely executed, in accuracy of estimate of situation by leadership at all levels, and in promptness of utilization of all supporting forces."[12]

When Marshall told Smith that he would be willing to write the Chosin reservoir story, Smith immediately wrote to his old friend Silverthorn, recommending that an accommodation be made between the Marine Corps and

Marshall. He had no reservations about having such a highly qualified military historian writing about the Chosin reservoir campaign (A-M, 1273–74).Two months later, on 21 March, Maj. Andrew Geer appeared at Smith's CP with a letter of authorization from Headquarters Marine Corps to collect material for a book about the Chosin reservoir campaign. One detects a certain amount of disappointment in Smith's comment: "Apparently Headquarters, Marine Corps has given up the idea of employing Colonel Marshall to write a book. Geer advised me that Headquarters, Marine Corps is not sure whether or not Colonel Marshall's book would be objective" (KL, 172).

The first week of January saw the release of Colonel Drysdale and his hardy band of Royal Marines from Smith's command. Smith attended a cocktail party at Drysdale's quarters; it lasted until Drysdale had to leave for Pusan. His unit was to be evacuated by ship to Japan, where it would refit for combat. A strong bond had been built between the English and American sea soldiers.

On 8 January, Smith went to Taegu, about forty-five miles north of Masan, to discuss the future deployment of the division with Ridgway. After a difficult treetop helicopter ride, Smith was able to talk privately with him. Ridgway told Smith that he had been looking for an area where he could use the First Marine Division offensively. He was planning to send an RCT to Andong (eighty-five miles north of Masan), where it would be attached to the Tenth Corps, and to send the remainder of the division to the Pohang area, where he felt the greatest threat existed. Ridgway suggested that Smith talk it over with his staff to see how its members felt about the proposed employment.

Following his visit with Smith, Ridgway convened a conference with his corps commanders. After the meeting, during lunch at Ridgway's mess, Almond informed Smith that if Ridgway approved, the First Marine Division would revert back to Tenth Corps. General Smith, always the good soldier, did not comment (A-M, 1276).[13]

> After lunch I again saw General Ridgway. He asked me what I thought of the proposed employment of the Division. I told him frankly that I did not like it as it split up the division. I told him that we had had previous experience involving dispersion of the division; that we had been put out on a limb; that we had gotten ourselves off that limb; but that, as a result of this experience, there had been a loss of confidence in the high command which had permeated down to the privates. General Ridgway stated that he knew nothing of the events I referred to, but he assured me that as soon as the situation was stabilized in the X Corps zone of action he would return the detached RCT to me. He stated he sympathized with my desire to keep the Division

intact; that when he had been a division commander he [had] felt the same way. (A-M, 1278)

Four hours after Smith returned to Masan, he received the following message from Ridgway: "Subsequent your departure, alternate plan occurred to me on which I would like your views soonest. It follows: 1st Marine Division, under Army control, move without delay to general area outlined to you personally today, to take over the responsibility at date and hour to be announced later for protection of MSR between Andong (50 air miles northwest of Pohang), Kyongju (15 air miles southwest of Pohang), both inclusive, and prevent hostile penetration in force south of Andong-Yongdok road." Smith concurred with the alternate plan. The great Pohang guerrilla hunt was about to take place! On 9 January, Ridgway followed up on his desire to visit the division. Smith met his L-17 airplane near Masan and drove him to the CP, where he met the division staff and regimental commanders. "He [General Ridgway] gave the officers a short talk, during which he emphasized the necessity for reconnaissance, and regaining and maintaining contact. He stated that he felt that the present day Army was too dependent on trucks. He envisaged limited offensive action by the Army. The impression he made on the officers was excellent" (A-M, 1279).

Smith lost no time in implementing his new role. He assigned Puller's RCT 1 to protect the MSR from Kyongju and Uisong, and he sent the remainder of the division to Pohang. The bivouac area vacated by the First Marines was in need of more policing than those of the other regiments. Smith noted that it required constant pressure on the regiments to ensure that their areas were clean, especially with regard to tin cans (A-M, 1312).

Smith and Sexton left Masan by helicopter on 16 January en route to Pohang via Pusan, a place that Smith wanted to observe in light of persistent rumors of a "last stand" at the perimeter. The First Marine Division, less Puller's RCT 1, was already set up south of Pohang, near the airfield. Smith thought that it was the best bivouac location the division had had so far in Korea, and he set up quarters with General Craig in an army wall tent with a wood floor (KL, 135).

The First Marine Division was assigned the following missions by Eighth Army: protect the MSR leading from Pohang through Kyongju to Andong and prevent any enemy penetration south of the leading west from Andong about forty miles to Yongdok, on the coast. Smith then assigned his subordinate units to carry out the directive. RCT 1 was to patrol an area ten miles east and west of the MSR, maintaining one battalion in the vicinity of Andong and another in the vicinity of Uisong. RCT 5 was assigned an area fifteen to twenty miles astride the Yongchon-Pohang highway, maintaining one battalion at Yongchon and the other near the Pohang airstrip. RCT 7 was to patrol an area extending north of Yongchon and west of Pohang, maintaining a strong presence at the Pohang airstrip area. The Eleventh Marines was to patrol a strip about seven miles wide along the east coast from Pohang to ten miles north of Yongdok. The tank battalion would patrol the roads southwest of Pohang for about twenty miles. VMO 6 was to support the various units of the division on an "as needed" basis (A-M, 1334–35).

The division was conducting counter-guerrilla operations in an extremely difficult mountain region. The area had always been infested with Korean brigands, who had evaded the Korean constabulary and the Japanese occupation forces during World War II. Communist forces had infiltrated the area for the express purpose of disrupting communications and attacking lightly defended rear installations. The marines now aggressively patrolled the roadways with motorized units and used foot patrols on the forested and mountainous terrain. Their massive firepower forced the guerrillas away from the populated regions and farther into the steep highlands, where their supply situation became more and more tenuous.[14]

On 17 January Smith received an alarming message from Puller requesting additional ammunition and trucks in case he had to evacuate the area. Puller also requested a change in his mission so that he could deploy his Third Battalion on more favorable ground near Andong. Reports from intelligence and POWs indicated the presence of twelve to sixteen thousand North Korean troops. The division staff did not believe that such large numbers had filtered through the sixty thousand American and ROK troops north of Andong, but Smith immediately dispatched Craig to evaluate the situation. Craig returned with a recommmendation that another battalion from the First Marines be moved to Andong in order to secure the airfield. A battalion from the Fifth Marines took over the duties of the displaced battalion.

The next day Smith flew to Puller's CP.

I wanted to be sure that Colonel Puller, whose headquarters was still at Yongchon, was perfectly clear as to his mission, as there had been several changes therein since his departure from Masan. . . . Colonel Puller was not very happy about his mission. He felt it was a move to detach his regiment from Division and turn it over to the X Corps. He was apprehensive about being put out on a limb. The basic difficulty was that he had no confidence in the staying power of the Army units deployed north of Andong. . . . As far as Division was concerned, we felt that the 60,000 American and ROK troops north of Andong would not fade against the opposition they were facing, and, in any event, RCT-1 was strong enough to protect its own withdrawal if it came to that. (A-M, 1407)

Ridgway flew into Smith's CP to let him know that he had discounted the possibility of amphibious landings along the eastern coast. In regard to defense efforts around the Andong area, he approved Smith's request that Puller coordinate all marine, army, and ROK elements in the vicinity. Ridgway also informed Smith that the United Nations troops in the area were fully capable of crushing the North Korean troops that had previously threatened their communications on the east coast. Smith sent Craig to explain to Puller the new situation with regard to the latter's authority to coordinate efforts. "With Puller it is necessary that he thoroughly understand instructions. Once he understands them they will be carried out explicitly" (KL, 137).

The division spent January and February 1951 chasing elements of the North Korean Tenth Division all over the Pohang area. Prisoners indicated that their mission was to capture or destroy the city of Taegu, an important communication center for the Eighth Army.[15]

Years after his retirement, Smith spoke about the Pohang operation:

The 10th NK Division . . . had filtered through the Army lines and was running loose up by Pohang. . . . We worked up there until February. . . . We started patrolling. It was intensive patrolling. We would drive those North Korean devils crazy. The 1st Marines would drive them over to the 7th Marines' area and they would chase them over to the 5th Marines. The North Korean Commander had a nervous breakdown. . . . We just made life miserable for them. Finally, General Ridgway wanted to know when he could use me again. I told him, "Probably when we cut these people down to small units. If you take me out, you have to bring someone in to continue the process," which he did.[16]

The division covered over a thousand square miles while pursuing the guerrillas.[17] The benefits of this unique style of combat were invaluable, as Stormy Sexton observed: "For the most [part], it was excellent training for the new replacements; it gave them the opportunity of getting a conditioning, and an experience of the hardest type of warfare, mountainous warfare, and fast moving situations."[18]

Brig. Gen. Thomas J. Cushman, deputy commander of the First Marine Aircraft Wing, visited Smith with the encouraging news that the division would be supported by up to six squadrons of marine aircraft. The downside of the news was that calls for support would have to go through the air force's joint operations center, which frequently resulted in delays and poor execution. For the remainder of Smith's tour in Korea, he would fight unsuccessfully for the use of marine air controlled by marine forward control groups. The superior system that had been developed after long experience by the Marine Corps was being denied him by a bureaucratic system dominated by the air force. The conflict with the air force continued when Maj. Gen. Gerald C. Thomas assumed command of the division after Smith. Thomas was also unsuccessful.[19]

On 24 January, Smith arranged for a simple ceremony for the promotion of Chesty Puller to brigadier general. In recognition of the promotion, Smith organized "Task Force Puller" at Andong; it included RCT 1 and elements of the ROK forces in the Andong area. Two other richly deserved promotions were celebrated on the same day: Lt. Col. Raymond L. Murray to full colonel, and Brig. Gen. Edward A. Craig to major general (KL, 139). Craig was scheduled to leave for the United States, and Puller was to replace him as assistant division commander. The very able division chief of staff, Col. Gregon A. Williams, was replaced by Col. Edward W. Snedeker. Col. Francis M. McAlister took command of the First Marines.

In the meantime, the pattern of aggressive patrolling continued. On 1 February, Smith flew to Ridgway's advance CP at Suwon, which was also the CP of First Corps. They reviewed possible assignments for the First Marine Division. Ridgway admitted that he had not planned very far ahead, because of political considerations, and asked Smith to submit his own recommendations for the division's future employment. After conferring with his staff, Smith outlined a preference for tying the operation of the division to blue-water access. The document is an overview of the awesome potential and versatility of a fully equipped Marine division.

2 February 1951

LIEUTENANT GENERAL M. B. RIDGWAY, USA
COMMANDING GENERAL, 8TH U.S. ARMY
My dear General Ridgway:

Since talking to you yesterday I have given considerable thought to your tentative proposals for the future employment of the 1st Marine Division. I have also discussed the matter with my staff.

In our opinion the following factors appear to favor employing the division on the east coast of Korea, an employment which you suggested;

(1) If, at a later date, it is desired to employ the division amphibiously, mounting out could be accomplished with a minimum strain logistically. Facilities

are available for mounting out at Pohang, Hajo-dong [near Yongdok], Samch'ok, and possibly Kangnung. The 1st Marine Division is the only division in Korea which is fully equipped and trained to carry out amphibious operations.

(2) The division with its organic Anglico [air and naval gunfire liaison company] is capable of exploiting to the fullest the capabilities of naval gunfire and carrier support. There should be considerable opportunity to employ naval gunfire support on the east coast.

(3) The strain on the road and rail facilities [on the] Yong'chon, Andong, Wonju axis could be relieved by the substitution of a South Korean division as the relieving force for an American division in that area and the relief of a South Korean division on the east coast by the 1st Marine Division. American divisions are, unfortunately, much heavier than the South Korean divisions. The 1st Marine Division, operating on the east coast, could be supplied by LSTs and lighterage from AK [cargo] type vessels. Our Shore Party has the capability of developing port facilities for the support of the division.

I want to assure you that whatever may be decided upon, the 1st Marine Division will give you its best.

Sincerely,
Oliver P. Smith, Major General
U.S. Marine Corps[20]

A week later Ridgway called Smith to Taegu, where, as Smith later recalled, he

stated that he appreciated the logic of the reasons I had given for keeping the Division near the coast. He stated further, however, that there was one basic difficulty in such employment, namely, the 1st Marine Division was the most powerful division in Korea and he wanted to find employment where that power could be exploited. What he really wanted us to do was to relieve the 24th Division in the Han River corridor northwest of Woju. He felt that if the Chinese launched a major attack, the Han River corridor was the logical avenue of advance. He wanted to have a powerful division across this avenue of advance. (A-M, 1461–62)

A powerful Chinese Communist counteroffensive was well under way northeast of Wonju while Smith and Ridgway were still considering the relief of the Twenty-fourth Division. This thrust by the Chinese was in response to the heavy pressure exerted by Eighth Army after it had regained the initiative over the past few weeks. The First Marine Division received warning orders on 12 February that it should be prepared to move to Chungju, seventy-five miles northwest of

Andong. The ROK Second Division would take over the Pohang assignment. The sudden change of plans was dictated by reverses suffered by the Tenth Corps north of Wonju. An excellent road linked Chungju with Wonju. The division could play a major role in stemming the advance of the Chinese. The First Marine Aircraft Wing was already "working over" the Chinese with numerous sorties that helped slow their advance.

Marching orders for the division came on 13 February; it was to move by RCTs and was to report directly to Eighth Army on the progress of the march. Operational control of the division would later pass to Ninth Corps. (Ninth Corps was composed of the Twenty-fourth Infantry Division, the First Cavalry Division, the ROK Sixth Division, and the British Commonwealth Twenty-seventh Brigade.)

The ubiquitous Gen. Frank E. Lowe continued to be a frequent visitor to the First Marine Division CP. When he showed up, it was usually as "Task Force Lowe," composed of the general and his aide, Capt. A. Hume, and drivers for his van and jeep. The jeep was a standard army-issue model that Lowe had modified to incorporate some of his own ideas, which included a leather kneepad on the dashboard, armor plating under the seats and gas tank, and a stirrup for Lowe's right foot outside on the passenger side. Smith described one of his visits when they were in central Korea:

> When General Lowe arrived at Pohang, he brought with him a considerable supply of fresh rations and other useful items. . . . He explained his philosophy to me, which was derived from his World War I experience. He stated that during World War I if anyone went to Paris he was expected to bring back something for the troops. In the present case he was in Tokyo and wanted to bring us something. . . . General Lowe's status as a special representative of President Truman in Korea carried quite a bit of weight in Tokyo and the Quartermaster people thought it advisable to cater to his wishes. He talked them into giving him a refrigeration ship, fresh rations, milk, and various other items. He brought this loot to Pohang. . . . We were able to make distribution of the fresh beef and veal to the regiments without great difficulty. (A-M, 1402)

During one of General Lowe's visits to the CP, he was showing visitors, of which there was a steady stream, around the lines when he drove too close to an embankment. He flipped over in his jeep. No one was injured, mainly because of the sturdy .50-caliber machine-gun mount, which prevented the jeep from crushing him to death.

Smith moved the division CP from Pohang to Chungju on 19 February. Ridgway wanted to attack from Wonju toward Hoengsong by noon of February 21st. Smith suggested to Gen. Bryant E. Moore, commanding general of Ninth Corps, that the attack be delayed for another twenty-four hours, but Moore told him that Ridgway wanted to trap as many as possible of the North Korean forces that had already broken through Tenth Corps (KL, 150). When the First Marine Division had operated under Tenth Corps control, it had experienced a certain autonomy and independence that it would not have under Ninth Corps. It was functioning now as simply another land division, under rigid army control.[21]

"Operation Killer" marked the end of allied withdrawals in Korea. It was initiated to hold the Han River south of Seoul and attack eastward at the same time, so as to retake areas lost to the Chinese. At the early stages of Operation Killer there was no plan to cross the thirty-eighth parallel.[22]

The scheme of attack called for the First Marine Division to attack north-easterly through the Wonju Basin in an attempt to cut off enemy troops that had penetrated as far as Hoengsong. The division was expected to regain control of the roads running to the east, by seizing the higher elevations south of the town. On the eve of Operation Killer, Ninth Corps headquarters stressed the importance of not allowing any hostile forces to become bypassed: "Maintenance of lateral contact between all units is of prime importance."[23]

Ridgway and Moore paid Smith a visit on 23 February to discuss engineering and supply problems. By that time, RCT 1 was overlooking the town of Hoensong. Early spring floods had destroyed a large pontoon bridge at Chungju, and the water and mud were as much enemies as the Chinese and North Korean troops. On this same day, Smith had a welcome visit from an old acquaintance, Brig. Gen. E. D. Post. Post had served as chief of staff of the Tenth Army on Okinawa, when Smith was the assistant chief of staff. He was now assistant commander of the First Cavalry Division.

On 24 February Smith received a call from the chief of staff of Ninth Corps. Moore, the commanding general, had died of an apparent heart attack brought on by his helicopter's becoming entangled in a telephone wire. He had fallen from the helicopter into the river and had been picked up and given a dry change of clothes in a nearby van. There he had died quietly while sitting in a chair. Smith, the senior division commander in the corps, immediately flew the twenty-five miles to Yoju, where the tactical command post of Ninth Corps was, and assumed command.[24] Ridgway did not hesitate to confirm Smith as a temporary successor to Moore. He told the Ninth Corps staff members that "General Smith is to be taken into their hearts . . . and, by definite action, made to feel that he belongs there."[25] Smith's broad military experience, coupled with his proven competence in difficult situations, ensured his acceptance at Ninth Corps. His reserved demeanor and warm courtesy was completely void of ostentation. It is probably safe to say that the army staff found it easy to take him into their hearts, as Ridgway had directed (KL, 155).[26]

Smith knew that the army would not allow a marine to remain in command of an army corps. An army officer could receive his third star by holding a corps command for six months; according to the Marine Corps promotion system in effect at that time, Smith could expect his third star only in two or three years. His replacement was Maj. Gen. William H. Hoge, whom Smith called "a very good general officer." Smith turned Ninth Corps over to Hoge in a simple ceremony on 5 March and returned to Wonju and the First Marine Division CP (OH, 24–65).[27]

While Smith commanded the Ninth Corps, he attended a meeting of corps commanders where Ridgway announced "Operation Ripper," a plan of attack designed to maintain momentum against the enemy forces. The First Marine Division was to attack straight ahead to Hongchon and then veer northeasterly, astride a main road. The attack date was 7 March (KL, 158–60).[28] On 9 March the division advanced, against sporadic opposition. Its left flank was securely held by the First Cavalry Division, but the Second Infantry Division on the right flank failed to keep up. Therefore, Smith temporarily slowed the marine advance until the Second Division could come abreast in the line.

Loss of control of marine air support was a constant source of irritation. The quality of support had improved somewhat since the beginning of the campaign in central Korea, but it was not as responsive as the original system developed by the marines. Smith complained, "What we would like is to have one of the Marine squadrons maintain planes on station. This the Air Force does not want to do" (KL, 169).

The change in support had come about, as noted, at the time of the Pohang guerrilla operation. The air force had established a joint operation center (JOC) with the purpose of receiving and managing all requests for close air support and any other missions requiring air participation. The missions were then evaluated and assigned to available aircraft in whatever zone the request originated. The First Marine Aircraft Wing constituted one of the largest groups of aircraft available. The ground marines complained that the JOC system meant longer waits for aircraft, potential distortion of requests from the ground controller, and sometimes the failure of any support aircraft to show up at all. Those army units that had used marine close air support joined the marine division in protesting the new status quo. The timing of close air support is crucial, frequently a matter of life and death to the infantryman; the air force seemed indifferent to that fact.[29]

Smith flew on 17 March to Wonju, where he joined Ridgway and Hoge for a visit from General MacArthur, who had said that he wanted to visit as many command posts and troops as three hours would allow, without getting out of his jeep. Smith rode in the jeep with MacArthur and Ridgway. They first visited Smith's advance division CP, continued to the Seventh Marines (Litzenberg) across the Hanchon River, and then went on until MacArthur saw a frontline unit (one of Litzenberg's battalions). Five hours later the troupe returned to Wonju, without a relief stop. When they finally halted, as Smith would later recall, Ridgway bawled him out: "'Why in the hell didn't you suggest that we stop?' I said 'You're the senior. I figured it was up to you.' At Wonju the General got out of his jeep and marched over to his plane. Then everybody else just disappeared to the johns" (KL, 169–70).

The advance north continued, against token resistance. By 15 March, Smith's command post was moved to Changbong-ni, halfway between Hoengsong and Hongchon. The front was relatively quiet, and steady progress was being made. On 20 March, Colonel Bowser complained to Smith that the corps G-3 was harassing him for lack of speed in the advance. The Eighth Army had always stressed the importance of keeping "buttoned up," so the division was conscientiously combing every square foot of the terrain. This type of methodical advance took time even when resistance was light. The division's units were becoming worn down by the laborious covering of such a vast amount of terrain, but there was not a spot on its front where the enemy could hide.[30]

One result of the thorough combing of the front was that the marines picked up over seven hundred butterfly bombs, air-dropped land mines, in the Hongchon area. Smith noted the seriousness of this development: "These [butterfly bombs] should not have been dropped" (KL, 172). It seems that the air force had dropped them erroneously. As Colonel Sexton describes the situation, "There was a feverish haste, with directives coming from 8th Army, apologies from the Air Force, and tying up all available personnel within the 1st Marine Division, to locate these butterfly bombs and dispose of them before the troops incurred any great casualties from them."[31]

Puller's promotion to assistant division commander placed him in that rarefied air of higher command that he had scoffed at for his whole career. Smith respected his devotion to duty and to the Corps: "Beneath his rough exterior, Lewis was a gentleman. He was profane, but he was not vulgar. He was well read as far as military history is concerned."[32] Sexton would remember the following story about Puller that occurred when the division was part of the Eighth Army:

After . . . Puller became Assistant Division Commander, an interesting incident took place. . . . Army Command had been having difficulty in transporting supplies from the port of Pusan up to Seoul by rail. Approximately fifty percent of the supplies loaded at the southern port were being lost prior to their arrival. Consequently, a meeting of representatives from all major commands was convened to discuss remedial action. General Smith directed General Puller to represent the 1st Marine Division at the meeting. When he returned from the all day meeting, General Smith asked how the meeting had gone. "Chesty" said that the General conducting the meeting stated: "We have tried everything that we can think of to overcome the en route loss of supplies." The problem was discussed for a long time, and then Chesty stated that he had inquired: "Has anything been done to relieve the s.o.b. who is in charge?" General Smith then inquired: "What happened then, Lewis?" The reply was; "The meeting broke up."[33]

By 23 March all units of the division were on the "Cairo" phase line, which was ten miles north of Hongchon and less than ten miles from the thirty-eighth parallel. Ridgway called a conference of all commanders on 27 March. There was a general feeling that no one knew what was going to take place next. Far East Command in Tokyo had more or less given the problem to Ridgway, telling him to do as he wanted. Long-range goals had not been set. The UN forces were now at the objective originally set for Operation Ripper. Smith wrote that Ridgway "will continue the advance unless he is directed otherwise. He would only consider withdrawal if the Soviets intervene" (KL, 175).

A new plan was developed by which the First Cavalry Division was relieved by the First Marine Division north of Chunchon. The First Cavalry Division then went into reserve in the west to provide for a defense in depth against a possible enemy counterattack, which in fact took place on 22 April.[34]

Lowe visited the division CP on 8 April 1951 for the last time. He had developed a warm relationship with Colonel Bowser, the resourceful division G-3, who would recall, "General Lowe and I became good friends. When he left our Division, he 'willed' his special jeep to me—.50 caliber machine gun mount, armor plated underbelly, with more comfortable seats. My two drivers were in 'hog heaven.'"[35] One of Lowe's last reports to the president contained a glowing endorsement: "The First Marine Division under the command of O. P. Smith is the most efficient and courageous combat unit I have ever seen or heard of."[36] There was an element of irony in the fact that Truman's personal representative in Korea had become a strong advocate of the Marine Corps's finest.

Gen. Douglas MacArthur was relieved of his command by President Truman on 11 April. At the same time, Lowe was asked to return home, his mission terminated by his old friend the president. Lowe was a tired and discouraged man when he returned to the United States. He felt responsible for MacArthur's firing; he would carry that burden to his grave. Lowe remained loyal to Truman

Above: Major General Thomas (*right*) arrives at Division Command Post north of Chunchon, Korea, to relieve Major General Smith as commanding officer of the First Marine Division. *Courtesy of MCUA.*

Left: Maj. Gen. Frank E. Lowe was President Truman's personal representative in Korea. He was an admirer of the First Marine Division. The inscription reads: "To Major Martin J. Sexton, USMC, From the shores of Inchon Bay to the wastes of Hagaru-ri. Affectionately, Frank E. Lowe, Maj. Gen. USAR. Korea—Sept. 50—Apr. 51." *Author's private collection.*

Maj. Gen. Oliver Prince Smith is awarded the Distinguished Service Medal with five stars by Adm. Arthur W. Radford, Commander in Chief, U.S. Pacific Fleet, while Lt. Gen. Lemuel C. Shepherd looks on. The ceremony took place when Smith stopped at Pearl Harbor before heading to the States. *Author's private collection.*

but maintained that neither the president nor MacArthur had been well served by the White House staff.

MacArthur's relief caused a partisan uproar. Smith was later asked by MacArthur's biographer, D. Clayton James, how he would rate MacArthur's handling of the Korean situation. "For Inchon it was outstanding. Certainly for that Yalu operation, I can't go along with greatness. . . . He had qualities of greatness, no doubt about that. When he came out of the Philippines on a submarine and had to abandon his command, which was a terrible blow to him, he went to Australia thinking that he would have an outfit there that he could build up and take back with him. He found nothing there and nothing coming, but he never gave up. He kept on going and did come back to the Philippines. I think you have to give him credit for that."[37]

Lt. Gen. James A. Van Fleet replaced Ridgway as commanding general of Eighth Army, and Ridgway went to Japan to replace MacArthur at Far East Command. Hoge and Van Fleet visited Smith every day until he turned over the First Marine Division to Maj. Gen. Gerald C. Thomas.

There was a lot of activity at the front; the enemy was building up for an offensive. The First Marine Division was anchored on the "Quantico" phase line, against a leg of the Hwachon reservoir that protruded to the south. On 23 April, Hoge ordered Smith to pull back to the "Kansas" line, about five miles south of the reservoir. At that time the marines were positioned farther north than any other units of the Eighth Army. The ROK Sixth Division, on the marines' left, had simply vanished as a force, leaving that flank uncovered while the Chinese offensive continued unabated.

On 24 April, the British brigade tried to fill the gap left by the ROK division, but it was pushed back and had to regroup. In the meantime, Smith moved elements of the First Marines to the left flank, while an RCT from the First Cavalry Division moved toward the First Marines on the left flank. On 24 April Puller moved the division CP to Masan. The division was moving to the "Kansas" phase line.[38]

Wednesday, 25 April, was Smith's last day with the First Marine Division. His relief, Major General Thomas, was already at the division command post, insisting on an early turnover. The front was very active, and Smith was not comfortable handing over the division earlier than expected. Thomas responded, "The table of organization only calls for one major general in a division. Either you turn over to me, or I'm going to leave."[39] A formal turnover ceremony had been planned, but in view of the serious nature of the enemy's offensive, Smith did not feel that a band would be appropriate. He simply lined up the staff officers and introduced General Thomas to them (OH, 297–98).

The division that Smith handed over to Thomas was probably the finest military formation ever fielded by American arms. Smith was admired and respected by all levels of his command. Capt. William B. Hopkins's tribute is typical: "As one of the survivors, I am forever grateful that Oliver P. Smith commanded UN troops at Chosin. He embodied all of the features required by [the sixth century B.C. Chinese theoretician] Sun-tzu: 'By command I mean the general's qualities of wisdom, sincerity, humanity, courage and strictness.'"[40]

Thomas was to experience the same kind of problems with Almond that had plagued Smith when he served under Almond at Tenth Corps. He also had, as noted, the same problems as Smith in regard to the control of air support by the air force. Thomas's blustery manner may have blown more wind at the subject, but, again as noted, he was no more successful in effecting a change than Smith. As a matter of fact, the matter has never been reconciled.

Smith later wrote the following tribute to the marines who served in central Korea with him: "The unit commanders and staff of the Division deserve great credit for the manner in which they planned and conducted the operations which resulted in blunting the Chinese counteroffensive in our area. In my opinion, it

Major General Smith is greeted by his family when he arrives at the Alameda Naval Air Station, California. *From left:* daughter Virginia McHenry, granddaughter Gail McHenry, daughter Dorothy Wolf, Esther Smith, and General Smith, May 1, 1951. *Courtesy of* MCUA.

was the most professional job performed by the Division while it was under my command."[41]

After Smith handed over the command, he left Chunchon for Pusan, where President Rhee presented him with the Korean Order of Military Merit with Silver Star. Field Harris then accompanied him to Japan, where Smith went shopping for gifts for his family. He visited Admiral Joy and General Ridgway before flying to Pearl Harbor, where he was a personal houseguest of Lemuel Shepherd. Adm. Arthur H. Radford, the commander in chief of the Pacific Fleet, awarded Smith the Navy Distinguished Service Medal, at a luncheon filled with military dignitaries. After the luncheon, anxious to get home, Smith and Sexton boarded a flight for San Francisco. He was met at the Alameda airport by Esther, his daughters Dorothy and Virginia, and his granddaughter Gail. Gen. Graves B. Erskine and the mayor of Oakland were also there to meet the general's plane, with a band and a large contingent of reporters.

The gentle warrior had returned to the tranquility of his family and his home.

12

Post-Korea

Gen. Oliver P. Smith left Korea to serve as Commanding General, Marine Corps Base at Camp Pendleton, California. He applied himself to the demands of his position, but the Korean War continued to dominate his time and thoughts. He completed his monumental narrative of the war, an "aide-memoire" composed from his own recollections, his daily Korea log, after-action reports of the First Marine Division, and detailed letters that he wrote to his family. This unique 1,474-page document reflects Smith's meticulous treatment of situations of which he was a part. His intellectual power is evident to anyone who reads it.[1]

The principal function of Camp Pendleton was training replacements for Korea, but a big part of Smith's time was taken up by public-relations work. He was very much in demand as a speaker, even though he did not enjoy being in the limelight. He wrote his own speeches, which were primarily about his experiences in Korea.

While Smith was at Camp Pendleton, two movies were made about the marines in Korea. Warner Brothers wanted to produce a drama depicting a small group of marines during the withdrawal from the Chosin reservoir. Smith let the producers know that he, personally, wanted no part in making the film and did not want his name mentioned in the script. He did, however, assign a young lieutenant to the production staff as an advisor. He also allowed portions of the base to be used for filming.

Smith later described the way the filmmakers reproduced the MSR in Korea: "They did a remarkable job . . . of reproducing the road. They took a canyon between U.S. 101 and headquarters[,] . . . and they bulldozed a road out of the side of the canyon, and then sprinkled gypsum all over the whole area. . . . It looked like snow. . . . For the Hagaru-ri airstrip, they just took our little airstrip at Pendleton and scattered gypsum all over the place; they had a wind machine that blew the 'snow' all around, and that was very realistic" (OH, 305). The movie, *Retreat Hell,* starring Frank Lovejoy, was released in the fall of 1951.

In 1952 another movie was produced with the assistance of the marines at Camp Pendleton. Capt. John M. Terry, a Korea veteran, was a training officer at Pendleton when he was notified that he was to report to the commanding general:

> He [General Smith] greeted me warmly and directed me to take a seat close beside his desk. I noted that his desk was almost completely devoid of any material except for a rather thick package that resembled a telephone directory. Of course he had a pipe in his hand.
>
> We discussed the Korean Campaign, in general, and although I had not made the Chosin Reservoir trek with him, he seemed genuinely interested in my area of operations which included the 1st Marine Division's move to the west, where my battalion straddled the Panmunjon Road. Finally, he pushed the package, I had noted earlier, forward and directed me to pick it up; it was not a telephone directory.
>
> The package I held in my hand was a movie manuscript, entitled *Battle Zone,* and the text centered on Marine Combat Cameramen in Korea. I hastily commented to the General that I knew virtually nothing about cameramen and/or their effort in combat; all I knew was what I saw in the newspapers and magazines. . . . He then gave me one of his famous smiles of benevolence and said, "Well, Captain Terry, that's all the more reason I think you are the man for the job." Almost speechless, I finally muttered, "What job, Sir?" "I'm assigning you as Technical Advisor to that movie and I'm sure you will do just fine. Some of it will be shot here on Base and some of it will be shot in or near Hollywood. Some actual Marines will be used in some shots and many will be actors or extras. I just want you to be certain that those actors look like Marines and that those Marines that are used, continue to look like Marines. The details of who to contact and coordinate with on those units available here at Camp Pendleton will be handed to you on your way out." He paused and lit his pipe, waiting (I think) for my reaction. All I could come up with was, "Sir, I'll do the best job I can. . . . By the way, when do I leave?" His reply . . . [was] "Right away . . . this afternoon!" He rose and escorted me out.[2]

Captain Terry went on to describe how he talked the two main actors in the movie, John Hodiak and Steven McNalley, into getting regulation haircuts. Terry had difficulty getting some of the civilian extras to obtain similar haircuts. As a matter of fact, when he was overruled by the producers, he insisted in having the fact authenticated in writing. "My dreams of wearing my dress blues to an Academy Award Ceremony had just ended. . . . I suppose, in one sense of the word, that I failed the General . . . in that assignment, but I never got any flak about it."[3]

Exactly one year to the day after the Chinese attacked the First Marine Division in Korea, members of the tenth draft rotation were welcomed home at San Diego. Cpl. Paul G. Martin was one of the returning marines. He described the situation as follows: "I was the last of the Inchon-Chosin Marines from Recon Company entering San Diego. I did not expect much fanfare but it was fine after all. We got a fireboat reception coming to dock and many bands played. The Commanding General of MCRD [Marine Corps Recruit Depot] San Diego, General Clement, greeted us. . . . 'I introduce you to a Marine from the Chosin Reservoir, General O. P. Smith.' The Marines on deck continued cheering for over five minutes. Who was greeting whom?"[4]

Training facilities for the Marine Corps on the West Coast were expanded during Smith's tenure at Camp Pendleton by the acquisition of a cold-weather training center outside of Bridgeport, California, and a desert training area known as Twenty-Nine Palms, also in California. The marines had not been prepared for the extremes of weather that had confronted them in Korea; therefore the commandant, General Cates, had ordered that any marines destined for Korea would receive cold-weather training. The high Sierras near Bridgeport were ideal for acclimating the men. The base became known as Pickle Meadows.[5]

A prisoner uprising took place at the Camp Pendleton brig while Smith was there. It seems that prisoners refused to work and threatened their guards. A riot started, with the prisoners throwing rocks at the guards and trying to start fires in the compound. Smith was temporarily in the base hospital at that time, so his deputy commander, Col. Joseph C. Burger, took steps to control the situation.

The Korean War was quite unpopular in the same way as the Vietnam War is [in 1973] with certain individuals. Camp Pendleton had a very small brig at that time. Because of the excessive number of men destined for duty in Korea who went over the hill and deserted, the number of disciplinary cases at Camp Pendleton was considerable, and there was not enough money . . . to build a brig sufficiently large to accommodate this number of people. . . . We established a temporary setup . . . made up of tents and two old temporary barracks. One night we had quite an uprising of the prisoners there, but . . . I called up the Fleet Marine Force and asked them to provide me with a company to settle this uprising. . . . So on arrival of the Fleet Marine Force company things quieted down in very short order.[6]

When Chesty Puller was awarded his fifth Navy Cross, Smith ordered a small review for the occasion and had the distinction of presenting the decoration.

> I told Lewie at the time—I didn't think he would take it seriously—"Lewie, this is your fifth Navy Cross, and they ought to do with this like they do with the Air Medal." (In those days if you got five Air Medals you got the Distinguished Flying Cross.) "You got five Navy Crosses, and they ought to give you the Medal of Honor." Well, I didn't think he'd take it seriously. But doggone it, he got people working on the Congress to try to give him the Medal of Honor. And they wrote me, and I said, "The Medal of Honor has to be given for individual acts, it can't be cumulative." The only thing they can do is to take one of the Navy Cross Citations and change it to a Medal of Honor citation. And frankly, the one I gave him in Korea could not be changed, it wasn't worth more than the Navy Cross. (OH, 307–8)[7]

On 3 March 1952, Smith wrote a long letter to Lemuel C. Shepherd, the new commandant of the Marine Corps, recommending that the First Marine Division and its attached units be awarded the Presidential Unit Citation (or PUC) for their actions at the Chosin reservoir. The eight-page document was a concise description of the withdrawal to the port of Hungnam, and it listed those units that Smith felt were entitled to the award, along with some that were not. Of the twenty-three units *not* on the list, nineteen were marine; only four of them were army. Smith stated that such a request should normally have been initiated by the army's Tenth Corps but that "no recommendation has been forth coming from that source."[8]

The document went through eleven endorsers: General Shepherd as commandant and eight other command echelons, including the Department of the Army, which attached a list of army units that should be included for consideration in the PUC. The endorsement by the Navy Department's Office of Decorations and Awards, dated 14 April 1953, established the standard that all units had to meet in order to be included on the list: "Only those units were included which made a direct contribution to the successful breakout of the 1st Marine Division from the Chosin Reservoir Area."[9]

This endorsement has caused a great deal of hard feeling among the surviving members of the Thirty-first RCT, which fought on the eastern side of the Chosin reservoir. They believe that they were poorly served by General Smith in that he recommended that the Thirty-first RCT as a whole should *not* be included, as the Army Department proposed.[10] Smith had designated the provisional battalion of army survivors attached to RCT 7 as the "Provisional Battalion, USA (Dets [detachments] of 31st and 32d RCTs, USA)." Smith made no attempt to elaborate on his decisions regarding the PUC.[11]

More is known today about the makeup of the Chinese forces that attacked Tenth Corps and the situation on the eastern side of the Chosin reservoir than was available to Smith in 1952. An assessment of that action is needed to answer the question of why General Smith did not recommend recognition for the entire Thirty-first RCT. In 1950 there was, as we have noted, in the First Marine Division a pervasive lack of confidence in the army high command—some of it justified, some of it merely the same old army/marine rivalry. This attitude was mentioned by every army and marine veteran that the author has talked with, and it was probably reinforced by what Smith and others observed firsthand as remnants of the Thirty-first RCT started to arrive at the perimeter at Hagaru-ri. It is unfortunate, but *at that time,* as we have seen, the marines viewed the survivors in a derogatory way. One of the reasons may have been that they were fighting for their own lives to escape a trap that the army's higher command was responsible for. Smith was not briefed by Almond or any other staff officer in regard to the Thirty-first RCT, except perhaps when Generals Almond, Barr, and Hodes were at Hagaru-ri after responsibility for the RCT had been passed to the First Marine Division. Also, to a certain extent Smith undoubtedly was influenced by Colonel Beall's negative view of the army, mentioned in an earlier chapter. Smith observed some survivors entering the marines' lines without weapons and with poor accountability for their wounded comrades. It would have been easy to misjudge the survivors of the Thirty-first RCT, at that time and place, in the absence of adequate information.

The test that General Smith (like the Navy Department) applied for inclusion on the PUC was whether or not a unit made a direct contribution to the breakout. We know now that the Thirty-first RCT's actions probably ensured that the Fifth and Seventh Marines successfully reach Hagaru-ri. However, Smith did not have that information available to him; trying to be as fair as his standard would allow, he substituted the disputed "Provisional Bn., USA (Det. 31st and 32d RCTs, USA)," for the Thirty-first RCT. By Smith's standard, objectively and unemotionally applied, he was correct in limiting the citation to the provisional battalion, because it was this unit that he saw make a direct contribution to the breakout. Smith does not state that he sought or received information from outside sources. Some veterans of the Thirty-first RCT claim that additional information about the performance of the Thirty-first RCT was provided to Secretary of the Army

Lieutenant General Oliver P. Smith and his wife, Esther, attend the Marine Corps birthday party, Norfolk, Va., November 10, 1953. *Courtesy of* MCUA.

Frank Pace on 31 May 1951 by General Ridgway: "The 31st RCT withstood repeated attacks of more than two CCF divisions of over 20,000 before being overwhelmed by a numerically superior enemy."[12] It is unlikely that Smith was aware of this somewhat privileged information. If some official in the army chain of command was aware of the performance of the Thirty-first RCT, why did not that person take a stand in support of the traumatized survivors of RCT 31 when the PUC endorsements were being circulated?

It is evident that the Thirty-first RCT was worthy and deserving of the PUC, an opinion supported by many knowledgeable people, such as Lt. Gen. Alpha L. Bowser, G-3 of the First Marine Division.[13] Those individuals who were deprived of its recognition are justified in feeling forgotten and bitter, but their anger should not be focused on General Smith. He was a fair and compassionate leader who went out of his way to avoid controversy, and when he dealt with other services he was respectful, fair, and truthful. That is a matter of record.

To resume the narrative—Smith received orders to relieve Gen. Graves Erskine as commanding general of Fleet Marine Force Atlantic on 27 May 1953. The post would be the last duty station for Smith. Before Smith left Camp

Pendleton, Shepherd asked if there was anything he wanted and if he had any "bees in his bonnet." Smith replied, as he would later recall, "'Well, the only thing is I'd like to make three stars [lieutenant general] when my turn comes.' I guess he figured my turn would come in 1953" (OH, 314–15).

Smith reported to Adm. Lynde D. McCormick, Commander in Chief, Atlantic and U.S. Atlantic Fleet on 22 June 1953 at the naval base in Norfolk, Virginia, while General Erskine was still on the job, bargaining for a promotion and a position at the Pentagon. Smith was not pleased: "They didn't get around to giving me my three stars until the 23rd of July, and Erskine was detached on the 1st of July. That kind of annoyed me a little bit, it seemed to me they could have been more speedy than that. . . . Vice Admiral [Frank G.] Fahrion who was my opposite number and commanded the Amphibious Forces said, 'What goes on with those people? From the standpoint of prestige you should have had three stars the day you relieved Erskine'" (OH, 320).

After World War II, the Marine Corps operating forces were separated into the FMF Atlantic and the FMF Pacific, each with a peacetime-strength division and air wing plus support and service units as they were needed. Fleet Marine Force Atlantic (FMFLant) was a "type" command, similar to those in the navy responsible for the training and maintenance of cruisers and submarines on each coast. Its military components were the Second Marine Division at Camp Lejeune, North Carolina, and the Second Marine Aircraft Wing at nearby Cherry Point.[14]

The strategic priorities of the United States during the Cold War years were Europe and the Middle East, with a casual concern with South American nations around the Caribbean Sea. Battalions of marines were constantly rotated through the Mediterranean, where they frequently conducted training operations with forces from Greece, Turkey, and Italy. FMFLant also had a strong connection to the North Atlantic Treaty Organization, NATO. One of the first things Smith did was travel to Europe to become familiar with NATO operations and to meet with some of the commanders in the region. He traveled to London and Germany, as well as Paris, where he attended an important meeting with Gen. Alfred Greunther, chief of staff of Supreme Headquarters Allied Powers Europe (SHAPE). After the conference broke up, Smith delivered a lecture to students of the NATO Defense College in the same building where he had attended the École de Guerre in 1934 (OH, 323).

By September 1954, "Chesty" Puller was commanding general of the Second Marine Division. Smith and Puller had parallel careers in the Marine Corps, and their paths crossed frequently over the years. Although Smith was known within the Corps as an intellectual and an accomplished military history expert, a class of officer that "Chesty" detested, they got along well. Smith never hesitated to criticize Puller (as he had on several occasions in Korea) when he thought it was justified, and temperamentally they were complete opposites, but they remained on friendly terms. When in September 1954 Puller suffered a cerebral hemorrhage, Smith was duly concerned.

> I talked to Snedeker afterwards on how it hit him; they were in the mess and he [Puller] started to walk out . . . and ran into a wall, he couldn't see. . . . Well, Lewie protested it was not a cerebral hemorrhage, it was heat exhaustion; he had spent the day inspecting 600 rifles and that was it. However, he got the doctors to change the diagnosis a bit over a period of time. He first got them to change it to vascular thrombosis, which was not quite so serious as cerebral thrombosis. . . . After a while they changed it again to hypertension, benign, which was quite a drop. . . . In the meantime, Lewie had gone to the examining board at Lejeune for his annual physical and he twisted their arms, and they pronounced him fit for all duties at sea and in the field. But he went up to Bethesda [Naval Medical Center, outside Washington, D.C., where they did not go along with his annual-physical results]. . . . He eventually was retired and was very bitter. When he got his three stars commission he wouldn't have any officer give it to him; he had a sergeant major pin the three stars on his shoulder. (OH, 325–26)

Afterward Chesty said, "I hate like hell to go."[15]

Smith's own retirement from the Marine Corps was handled poorly by General Shepherd, who exhibited a careless indifference throughout the whole affair. It was a situation that disturbed Smith.

> I was due for retirement on November 1st, 1955—my birthday was October 26th, and I would have been retired, therefore, on November 1st, 1955. Well, General Shepherd had asked me sometime in the spring what my plans were, and I said, "I'd like to finish out my time on this job." I realized that they had this two year limit, but I didn't figure it was stretching the regulations too much to hold on to me until November. After all, he held on to Brute [Victor H.] Krulak for four years as CGFMFPac. But he didn't say much about it. But suddenly I got a letter from him and orders detaching me from FMFLant on September 1st and ordering me to Headquarters Marine Corps for board duty. . . . In his letter he [Shepherd] said I would have been there for 31 months, so that was that. That was really cockeyed: I'd come there in July of '53 and in November of '55 it would have been 27 months. . . . I wanted no part of being relieved and going up to Washington for two months and then to California. . . . The Navy didn't quite understand what was going on. (OH, 329–30)

Smith's staff gave him a farewell dinner celebration on 29 August. Brig. Gen. Gordon D. Gayle, who had served with Smith on Peleliu, was present: "I attended his retirement ceremony at Norfolk, and was surprised to learn that he seemed bitter at his retirement. Bitterness was inconsistent with all that I knew of him. I could only speculate that after a lifetime of dedicated and loyal service to the Corps, we are all somewhat resentful of being told that the Corps has no further use for us."[16]

One of the many farewells to Smith at his retirement celebration was a cassette recording made by Edward E. Craig. It was a wonderful tribute from a fine officer. Some excerpts from the transcript follow:

> I know this is a great moment in your life[,] O. P. Retirement from active duty is something we all look forward to during our career in the Corps and if ever a military man deserved a long and happy one, it is you. Of course I include in this the wonderful lady who has stood by you and shared with you the many trials and tribulations of service life from Guam to Norfolk—your wife Esther. You are both beloved by all who know you.
>
> I am fortunate in being one who was privileged to be close to you during a most critical period in your distinguished career, and saw at first hand your great qualities of leadership . . . in Korea. . . . Thanks to you the Division . . . under your command carried out an operation that is recorded in history as one of the most heroic and outstandingly successful in military annals.
>
> Without your planning and leadership thousands of lives would have been sacrificed and the division defeated in detail. This is but one instance. Your friends like to remember many others that go to make up a distinguished career that has carried you through three major wars and many lesser campaigns.
>
> Good luck and God Bless. . . . This is Eddie Craig speaking.[17]

Lt. Gen. George F. Good, a Naval Academy graduate, had worked directly under Smith as chief of staff at Marine Corps Schools. When asked to reflect on those officers who had impressed him during his thirty-five years of service, Good would answer: "General O. P. Smith, whom I feel was the tops of all the general officers I have ever seen—intellectually, personally, in any aspect of his character and personality. . . . He was highly capable, and I felt that he was the man in the Marine Corps that I most admired." When asked if Smith was a forceful leader, General Good replied,

> If you think of a forceful person as one who beats his chest and shouts loudly and utters tirades, no, he is not that type of person at all. However, he was a very forceful person. But aside from the fact that it was contrary to his personality

Pinning on four stars at General Smith's retirement ceremonies. *Foreground, from left,* Esther Smith, General Smith, and Admiral Wright, September 1, 1955. *Courtesy of* MCUA.

to shout and scream and make a fuss about things, he didn't have to. The people that I know who worked for him and with him—because he did inspire people to work with him—listened for any expression of opinion that he gave and took it to themselves as a directive. No, he is not the chest beating type at all. That I do not feel is necessarily the most forceful personality. Now I do feel that the Marine Corps's future lies in quality. I think that on the occasion[s] where we substituted size for quality we have gone astray. I think that we must stress personal leadership, which I feel has not been stressed as much as it should, but again that ties right in with quality, and if the Marine Corps establishes a high level of quality, we can do anything. And I don't think that we have to fight other services. I think our future lies in having the capability to do the job that is given us better than anybody else, and I think if we have that capability we need not bother about the other services.[18]

Three days after the retirement dinner, Smith was promoted to four-star general, at a simple change-of-command ceremony. Adm. Jerauld Wright, commander in chief of the Atlantic Command and the U.S. Atlantic Fleet, attended the ceremony and pinned the stars on one of Smith's shoulders. Mrs. Smith attempted to do the same on the other shoulder but ran into difficulty because she was much shorter than Smith's six-foot, one-inch height, so Admiral Wright assisted her. When the celebrations were completed, Smith and his wife left immediately for California. General Shepherd had insisted that Smith vacate his quarters on the same day he was relieved of command (OH, 331).

The *New York Times* for Thursday, 1 September 1955, contained the following editorial:

THE MAN WHO DIDN'T RETREAT Gen. Oliver P. Smith, United States Marine Corps, retires today at Norfolk, Va., from his last command—Fleet Marine Force, Atlantic—after thirty eight years of service. Ordinarily the retirement of a general officer attracts little attention. But General Smith is no ordinary general. Scholarly and soft spoken, he looks like a college professor. But he has never lacked the flash of fire; among a corps noted for its fighting men he was eminent.

He saw bloody fields in World War II—Cape Gloucester; Peleliu; Okinawa—but his name did not become famous until the Korean fighting.

The sudden Chinese Communist attack with overwhelming numbers and the safe withdrawal of the division to Hungnam and the sea—epitomized the leadership which General Smith possesses to so high a degree—. . . .

But the world expects its military leaders to possess physical courage. Much rarer is the quality of moral courage, possessed by Oliver Smith to an unusual degree. It is generally agreed that his leadership saved the First Division at Chosin; it is not generally known that one reason that the division could be saved was that General Smith disobeyed orders. The orders were to continue to advance; the general knew the division was sticking its head into a noose; he ignored the order and consolidated his positions.

Oliver Smith, a Marine's general, richly deserves the honors to be done him this day. The country, proud of his part in her history, will wish him well in retirement.[19]

Admiral Wright wrote O. P. Smith's last fitness report: "I know of no officer in the U.S. Marine Corps who has contributed more to the splendid reputation of that service than Lt. Gen. Smith. His splendid personality, able leadership and sound judgment has won him the admiration and respect of senior and juniors in all services. His retirement is viewed with regret by the entire Atlantic Navy and Marine Corps Command. The Marine Corps and Naval Service has gained much by his many years of faithful and loyal service to our country."[20]

O. P. Smith entered retirement without fanfare. Now he would be able to sit on his back porch and visit with friends, content in the knowledge that he had given his country the best that he was capable of giving.

13

GEN. OLIVER PRINCE SMITH, USMC (RET.)

Oliver Prince Smith served the Marine Corps and his country for thirty-eight years. His command of the First Marine Division in Korea was the crowning achievement of his military career. The Inchon-Seoul campaign, Chosin reservoir campaign, and the central Korea guerrilla hunt all stand as testaments to his ability to inspire and lead men in battle.

Yet Smith's most enduring legacy may be the man himself. He was a warrior possessing the mind and soul of a philosopher. He does not fit the mold of a Chesty Puller and all that Puller represents in boldness and colorful public relations. Smith's legacy is one of unadorned excellence. Alpha L. Bowser, who knew Smith better than most marines did, has described him: "He [General Smith] was admired and respected by every Marine of every rank who ever served with and for him. He was the personification of a true gentleman and leader, in every sense, and our Corps was graced by his presence."[1]

Smith's leadership qualities reflected his character, the critical component of military leadership. His calm air reflected confidence in his own abilities. He was not a posturer; indeed, he deplored such conduct. But even though he was self-effacing and unassuming, no subordinate of his ever had a problem understanding who was in charge. Men in his command soon understood that General Smith "knew what he was doing" at all times. His thoroughness in evaluating alternatives was a hallmark of his leadership style.

When Smith retired from the Marine Corps, he and his wife purchased a home in the Los Altos Hills, overlooking the Stanford University campus to the north and the Santa Cruz Mountains in the west. He described his retirement in a letter to Gen. Robert O. Bare, USMC (Ret.): "My problems are no longer big

problems, and I have ample time to solve such problems as do present themselves. I have a half acre plot and I can see about six months work ahead getting
the garden organized. Esther is thoroughly enjoying settling in her own home.
Here, again, we are taking our time; there is no rush to get settled. So far I am
enjoying retired life. The *Navy Times* and the *Marine Corps Gazette* keep me
abreast of what you fellows who are carrying the ball are doing."[2]

For the rest of his years, Smith cultivated his roses and continued to review
manuscripts, articles, and expressions of points of view from a wide assortment
of writers, historians, and researchers. He made contributions to almost every
book written about the Korean War while he was living.

S. L. A. Marshall maintained a cordial relationship with Smith, and they
exchanged letters and information over several years. Another author who asked
Smith for guidance was Burke Davis, author of Chesty Puller's biography. Davis
was having trouble with some of Puller's recollections, especially about the
Peleliu campaign, and he confided in Smith:

> What I am after, and tried to express to General [John T.] Selden [who was
> opposed to the biography] today, is to protect General Puller as well as oth-
> ers from the defects of his recollections. My aim is not to try to build up a
> sensational book, but simply to tell the story of his life without doing vio-
> lence to fact. I have realized the legendary qualities surrounding many cases
> we have already handled—and for long seen that the Peleliu operation might
> be the most difficult of all to put into proper focus.
>
> My hope is that you'll be willing to write a commentary to me on the
> Peleliu narrative by Puller. . . . I will then take the versions [by] you and
> General Selden to him, as well as the record, and see if we cannot agree on
> some more objective view, using at least middle ground. I am much con-
> cerned over General Selden's feeling that the book should not be written.[3]

Smith responded with a four-page commentary on the document: "I confess
that I was surprised at some of Lewie's recollections, because I must have attended the same conferences he did and my recollection does not jibe with his."[4]

A few days later, Burke Davis queried Smith again: "There will be a need for
someone with a cool mind and a background of historical scholarship, who is
yet intimate with the modern Marine Corps and Lewis Puller, to give the manuscript of this biography a critical pre-publication reading. We have wondered if
you would be willing to undertake that." In the same letter, Burke suggested
that Smith should be engaged in the writing of his own memoirs.[5]

Smith's reply:

While I appreciate your confidence in my ability to objectively review the proposed biography of Lewie Puller, I would like to beg off. I feel I have been too close to Lewie to be objective. Also, I would probably get involved in trying to reconcile Lewie's recollections of Cape Gloucester, Peleliu, Korea, Camp Pendleton, and Camp Lejeune with my own, and I would not see the forest for the trees. After all, Lewie's recollections are his, not mine, and it is Lewie's biography. All I hope is that Lewie will view the past objectively, and not give vent to any bitterness he may feel.

With reference to your suggestion regarding personal memoirs, I have never considered writing any. I have furnished considerable material to the Historical Division at the Headquarters Marine Corps. I have no desire to write anything that would not be frank, honest, and objective. It would be difficult to do this without being critical. I would rather leave the criticism to some future historian.[6]

Smith's passion for history can be discerned in a statement written to Andrew Geer, the author of *The New Breed:* "I may be old fashioned, but history and biography have more attraction for me than all the films and novels ever produced."[7]

Robert Debs Heinl, Jr., wrote a letter thanking Smith for his "unstinting help" in writing *Victory at High Tide: The Inchon-Seoul Campaign* (1968) and extended best wishes for a speedy recovery of broken ribs sustained in a fall from a ladder. Smith replied, "I became overly ambitious about cleaning out the gutters around the house. When I was almost through, one leg of the ladder gave way and I took a bad fall. As a result, I spent some time in the hospital waiting for several ribs to mend."[8] Smith was seventy-four at the time.

While being interviewed for an oral history, General Smith said that the most rewarding duty of his thirty-eight years in the Marine Corps was command of the First Marine Division. The duty he had disliked the most was staff duty in Washington, D.C., in the twenties. "In the fourteen years of my retirement I've had very little contact with the Marine Corps, but I do continue to follow with interest the progress of the young officers that were under my command, and what they are doing and how they are getting along. And they have done pretty well, I think. . . . I have no complaints" (OH, 332).

The author has received numerous tributes to General Smith. They refer to his strength of character which inspired respect and confidence among his peers and subordinates. He was physically brave, but he is universally remembered as a quiet warrior who had the courage to act on his convictions. His life was dedicated to the pursuit of excellence. Here are some of the tributes, to the man and to his abilities:

Robert Sherrod: "I admired General O. P. Smith. . . . He certainly commanded the Marines in what was regarded by many as their 'finest hour.'"[9]

Gen. Raymond G. Davis, USMC (Ret.), Medal of Honor: "A tower of goodness, one of the best men I have ever known. . . . [H]e was a tower of strength."[10]

Lt. Gen. Herman Nickerson, Jr., USMC (Ret.): "No regimental commander could have had better support. General Smith and his Division staff were exemplary."[11]

Lt. Col. Edward Tom, USMC (Ret.): "General Smith was to the Corps what General Marshall was to the Army. A great combat leader, and a great gentleman of honor and dignity."[12]

Lt. Col. Richard M. Elliott, USMC (Ret.): "A very reserved yet congenial officer and gentleman. He reminded me quite often of General Robert E. Lee. He was an outstanding leader of men, and he inspired subordinates to the peak of their capabilities."[13]

Lt. Col. Peter Thomas, Royal Marines (Ret.): "Only by good generalship and the qualities of the U.S. Marines was his division saved. . . . It always surprises me that O. P. Smith never became Commandant of the USMC. He certainly deserved to."[14]

Gen. Samuel Jaskilka, USMC (Ret.): "We would be long dead if he had blindly followed the orders of Gen. Almond, and worse, if that is possible, the campaign would have gone down in history as a great debacle."[15]

Brig. Gen. F. P. Henderson, USMC (Ret.): "I admired him tremendously for his high level of integrity, professional knowledge, [and the] wonderful quiet personality you would hope for in a Commanding General. All of my contemporaries in the 1st Marine Division at the Chosin Reservoir agree that his leadership and military skills were the primary reasons it was not overwhelmed by the Chinese."[16]

Maj. Gen. Raymond L. Murray, USMC (Ret.): "I was always a great admirer of him. . . . In Korea he was a very competent Commanding General."[17]

Gen. Matthew B. Ridgway said that the foundation of an army is its officer corps, and the soul of performance was supervision of execution. He discussed leadership in the Korean War and singled out General Smith: "There was a magnificent leader, that O. P. Smith. . . . If it wasn't for his tremendous leadership, we would have lost the bulk of that division up north. His leadership was the principal reason it came out the way it did. He was a great division commander."[18]

Adm. Jerauld Wright signed Smith's fitness report as follows: "Lt. Gen. Smith is an officer of distinguished attainments. His performance of duty in every respect is outstanding. Quiet, studious, intelligent, devoted and possessing unsurpassed leadership qualities, he is, without doubt, one of the ablest generals of his time."[19]

The final tribute to Smith is reserved for *Lt. Gen. Alpha L. Bowser, USMC (Ret.):*

I would like to state that he was one of the best educated and best qualified generals of our Corps. Many of us have given our thanks that he was in command of the 1st Marine Division at some critical periods in the Division's history; namely Inchon and the Chosin Reservoir. He knew exactly what each of his General and Staff officers were supposed to do, and unlike some commanders (who shall remain unnamed), he permitted them to do it; offering gentle but firm guidance where needed. From a personal standpoint, my nine months as General Smith's G-3 . . . were one of the highlights of my 35 years in the Corps. I think that my service with Gen. Smith was one of the major factors in giving me the privilege of serving the Marine Corps as one of its General Officers for 11 years.[20]

Oliver Prince Smith's legacy is more than the sum of his accomplishments. The simple virtues, high principles, and dedication to the work at hand are also parts of his legacy, and they help define his tenure in the Marine Corps.

General Smith died on 25 December 1977, at the age of eighty-four. He was buried with his beloved wife, Esther, who had passed away in 1964, at the Golden Gates Cemetery in San Bruno, California. Surrounding the site are the graves of thousands of veterans buried there since 1941. Nearby are the graves of Adms. Chester Nimitz, Raymond Spruance, and Richmond Kelly Turner.[21] Immediately adjacent to General Smith's grave is a chapel that stands in silent testimony to the brave deeds of those who have been buried on the hilltop. Nearby the American flag floats in the gentle breeze that softly blows from the Pacific Ocean. May Gen. Oliver Prince Smith and all the brave souls who occupy this beautiful place rest in peace.

> His toils are past, his work is done;
> And he is fully blessed;
> He fought the fight, the victory won,
> And enters into rest.[22]

Appendix A

Chronology of Gen. Oliver P. Smith's Marine Corps Career

17 April 1917	Commissioned second lieutenant in the Marine Corps Reserve
14 May 1917	Reported for active duty at Mare Island, Ca.
26 June 1917–28 March 1919	Duty at Marine Barracks, Guam
3 October 1917	Temporarily promoted to first lieutenant
8 September 1918	Temporarily promoted to captain
6 May 1919–8 October 1921	Duty at Marine Barracks, Navy Yard, Mare Island, Ca.
26 April 1921	Permanent promotion to captain
13 October 1921–15 May 1924	CO, Marine Detachment, USS *Texas*
13 June 1928–10 June 1931	Duty in Garde d'Haiti, Republic of Haiti
17 September 1931–1 June 1932	Student at the Field Officer's Course, Infantry School, Fort Benning, Ga.
30 June 1932–5 September 1933	Instructor, Company Officer's Course, Marine Barracks, Quantico, Va.

6 September 1933–17 January 1934	Assistant Operations Officer, 7th Marines, Quantico, Va.
29 January 1936–2 August 1936	Attended the École Supérieure de Guerre, Paris
3 September 1935	Promoted to major
24 August 1936–1 June 1939	Instructor and F-3, Marine Corps Schools, Quantico, Va.
17 May 1938	Promoted to lieutenant colonel
9 July 1939–9 June 1940	F-3, FMF, San Diego, Ca.
10 June 1940–31 May 1941	CO, 1st Battalion, 6th Marines, San Diego, Ca.
7 July 1941–8 March 1942	CO, 1st Battalion, 6th Marines, Iceland
5 January 1942	Temporarily promoted to colonel
29 April 1942	Permanent promotion to colonel
2 May 1942–14 January 1944	HQMC, Washington, D.C., M-4 and executive officer, Division of Plans and Policies
28 January 1944–6 November 1944	First Marine Division; participation in Talasea operation, New Britain, as CO, 5th Marines, and on Peleliu as assistant division commander
13 April 1944	Promoted temporarily to brigadier general
8 November 1944–23 June 1945	Participated in the Okinawa campaign as Marine Deputy Chief of Staff, Tenth Army
2 July 1945–22 January 1946	Commandant, Marine Corps Schools, Quantico
28 January 1946–27 February 1946	CG, 1st Special Brigade, Quantico
12 March 1946–30 December 1947	Assistant Commandant, Marine Corps Schools
31 December 1947–5 April 1948	CG, Marine Barracks, and Marine Corps Schools, Quantico

12 February 1948	Permanent promotion to brigadier general
3 April 1948	Temporary promotion to major general
5 April 1948–July 1950	HQMC, Assistant Commandant of the Marine Corps
June 1950–April 1951	CG, First Marine Division in Korea
April 1951–June 1953	CG, FMFPac and CG, Camp Pendleton, Ca.
July 1953–September 1955	CG, FMF Atlantic
August 1953	Promoted to lieutenant general
September 1955	Retired with permanent rank of general

GEN. OLIVER P. SMITH'S MEDALS AND DECORATIONS

Distinguished Service Cross
Distinguished Service Medal (Navy)
Distinguished Service Medal (Army)
Silver Star Medal
Legion of Merit with combat V (Peleliu)
Legion of Merit with oak-leaf cluster (Okinawa)
Bronze Star Medal with combat V (Talasea operation)
Air Medal
Presidential Unit Citation with three stars
Navy Unit Commendation
World War I Victory Medal
Marine Corps Expeditionary Medal (Haiti 1929–31)
American Defense Service Medal with base clasp
European-African–Middle East Campaign Medal
American Campaign Medal
Asiatic-Pacific Campaign Medal with three stars
World War II Victory Medal
National Defense Medal
Korean Service Medal with five stars
UN Korean Service Medal
Haitian Distinguished Service Medal
Korean Order of Military Merit with Silver Star
Korean Presidential Unit Citation with oak-leaf cluster
Order of the Orange (Nassau)

NOTES

1. Building the Foundation

1. For Smith's early life and military career previous to 1941, I have used the following: General Smith's "Oral History Transcript," 1975, 1–90 (cited in text with the abbreviation "OH"), Marine Corps Historical Center, Washington, D.C. (hereafter MCHC); Maj. Michael F. Shisler, "General Oliver P. Smith's Life Was a Commitment to Excellence," *Marine Corps Gazette* (Nov. 1978): 42–48; R. J. Spiller, ed., *Dictionary of American Military Biography,* vol. 3 (Westport, Conn.: Greenwood Press, 1984).

2. Spiller, *Dictionary of American Military Biography,* 1020.

3. 1917 Yearbook of the University of California at Berkeley, pp. 98, 99, 416, 417, University of California Alumni Association, Berkeley, Calif.

4. O. P. Smith, "Personal Narrative for the New Britain Island Campaign," 28 Jan. 1944–4 May 1944, p. 42, Smith Personal Papers Collection, Marine Corps University Research Center, Archives Branch, Quantico, Va. (hereafter Smith Papers).

5. Smith to Quartermaster, HQMC, Washington, 27 Aug. 1917, Smith Papers.

6. Cruise reports for USS *Texas,* 1921–24, Texas Parks and Wildlife Department, Battleship Texas, Laporte, Texas.

7. Spiller, *Dictionary of American Military Biography,* 1021.

8. Omar N. Bradley and Clay Blair, *A General's Life: An Autobiography* (New York: Simon and Schuster, 1983), 54–103.

9. Robert Debs Heinl, Jr., *Soldiers of the Sea: The United States Marine Corps, 1775–1962,* 2d ed. (Baltimore: Nautical & Aviation, 1962, 1991). William D. Parker, *A Concise History of the United States Marine Corps, 1775–1969* (Washington, D.C.: HQMC, 1970), 49–50; Charles A. Fleming, Robin L. Austin, and Charles A. Braley III, *Quantico: Crossroads of the Marine Corps* (Washington, D.C.: History and Museums Division, HQMC, 1978), 60–62.

10. Parker, *Concise History,* 48–52; Fleming, Austin, and Braley, *Quantico,* 62–65.

11. Shisler, "General Oliver P. Smith's Life," 46.

12. Ibid.

13. Gen. Edward A. Craig, USMC (Ret.), to author, 6 Feb. 1989.

14. Spiller, *Dictionary of American Military Biography,* 1021.

2. ICELAND

The primary source for chapter 2 is General Smith's own narrative of his Iceland tour of duty—"Iceland Diary" (Smith Papers), a 136-page document that covers the period from 1 May 1941 to 29 April, 1942 (cited in text with the abbreviation "ID").

1. Simon Rigge, "Warfare at World's End," in *War at the Outposts* (New York: Time-Life Books, 1980), 24.

2. Ibid.

3. Col. James A. Donovan, USMC (Ret.), *Outposts in the North Atlantic: Marines in the Defense of Iceland* (Quantico, Va.: MCHC, 1996), 3–8.

4. Lt. Gen. Victor H. Krulak, USMC (Ret.), letter, *Fortitudine* (Spring 1993): 15.

5. Drew Middleton, *Our Share of the Night* (New York: Viking Press, 1946).

6. Maj. Gen. William A. Worton, USMC (Ret.), "Oral History Transcript," 1973, p. 215, Historical Division, HQMC.

7. Ibid., 220–22.

8. Worton, "Oral History Transcript," 108–9.

9. Maj. Gen. Walter A. Churchill, USMC (Ret.), to author, 12 Apr. 1995.

3. THE NEW BRITAIN CAMPAIGN

The main sources for this chapter are General Smith's "Personal Narrative for the New Britain Campaign," 28 Jan. 1944 to 4 May 1944 (pages 1–46), Smith Papers (cited in text with the abbreviation "NB") and his "Oral History Transcript."

1. Lt. Col. K. J. Clifford, USMCR, *A Developmental History of the United States Marine Corps, 1900–1970* (Quantico, Va.: MCHC, 1973), 92. An excellent description of Plans and Policies is presented in Allan R. Millett, *In Many a Strife: General Gerald C. Thomas and the U.S. Marine Corps, 1917–1956* (Annapolis, Md.: Naval Institute Press, 1993), 225–44.

2. Clifford, *Developmental History,* 92.

3. Samuel Eliot Morrison, *The Two-Ocean War: A Short History of the United States Navy in the Second World War* (Boston: Atlantic Monthly Press, 1963), 292.

4. Col. Henry Aplington II, USMC (Ret.), interview by author, Warner, N.H., 2 Aug. 1994.

5. Henry I. Shaw, Jr., and Maj. Douglas T. Kane, USMC, *History of U.S. Marine Corps Operations in World War II* (Washington: Historical Branch, G-3 Div., HQMC, 1963), 2:418.

6. Shaw and Kane, *Marine Corps Operations,* 428–29.

7. Gen. A. A. Vandegrift, USMC, and Robert B. Asprey, *Once a Marine: The Memoirs of General A. A. Vandegrift, United States Marine Corps* (New York: W. W. Norton, 1964), 246.

8. Bernard Nalty, "Into the Unknown at Cape Gloucester," *Leatherneck* (Dec. 1993): 23.

4. The Russell Islands (R&R)

The primary sources for chapter 4 are General Smith's "Oral History Transcript" (pages 120–30) and his "Personal Narrative for the Russell Islands, May 8, 1944 to August 26, 1944" (pages 41–82), Smith Papers (cited in text with the abbreviation "RI").

1. U.S. Military Academy, *Register of Graduates* (West Point, N.Y.: Association of Graduates, USMC, 1980), 314, 448.

2. John Miller, Jr., Epilogue, "Occupation of the Russells," *U.S. Army in World War II* (Washington, D.C.: Center of Military History, 1989), 352.

3. Maj. Jon T. Hoffman, USMCR, *From Makin to Bougainville: Marine Raiders in the Pacific War* (Quantico, Va.: MCHC, 1995), 24–27.

4. Bill D. Ross, *Peleliu, Tragic Triumph: The Untold Story of the Pacific War's Forgotten Battle* (New York: Random House, 1991), 86–87.

5. Ibid., 46.

6. Ibid., 88–89.

7. Norman V. Cooper, *A Fighting General: The Biography of Gen. Holland M. "Howlin' Mad" Smith* (Quantico, Va.: Marine Corps Association, 1987).

8. Vandegrift and Asprey, *Once a Marine,* 269.

5. Peleliu

The primary sources for chapter 5 are General Smith's "Oral History Transcript" (pages 139–50) and his "Personal Narrative for the Russell Islands" (pages 1–106).

1. Francis Trevelyn Miller et al., *The Complete History of World War II* (Chicago: Reader's Service Bureau, 1945), 656.

2. Col. Joseph H. Alexander, USMC (Ret.), "Peleliu 1944," *Marine Corps Gazette* (Nov. 1996): 20.

3. Brig. Gen. Gordon D. Gayle, USMC (Ret.), *Bloody Beaches: The Marines at Peleliu* (Washington, D.C.: History and Museums Division, HQMC, 1996), 5.

4. Maj. Henry J. Donigan, USMC, "Peleliu: The Forgotten Battle," *Marine Corps Gazette,* Sept. 1994, 101–2.

5. Ross, *Peleliu,* 275.

6. Robert Sherrod, *History of Marine Corps Aviation in World War II,* 2d. ed. (San Rafael, Calif.: Presidio Press, 1980), 325.

7. Ross, *Peleliu,* 332.

8. James H. Hallas, *The Devil's Anvil: The Assault on Peleliu* (Westport, Conn.: Praeger, 1994), 221.

9. J. Robert Moskin, *The U.S. Marine Corps Story* (New York: McGraw-Hill, 1977), 583.

10. Donigan, "Peleliu," 103.

11. Vandegrift and Asprey, *Once a Marine,* 278.

12. Jon Guttman, "The Three-War Hero," *Military History* (Dec. 1997): 45.

6. Okinawa

General Oliver P. Smith's diary, "The Tenth Army and Okinawa" (pages 1–136), Smith Papers, is my main source for this chapter (cited in text with the abbreviation "TA"). An excellent source for a broader examination of the battle is Benis M. Frank, *Okinawa: The Great Island Battle* (New York: Elsevier-Dutton, 1978).

1. E. B. Potter, *Nimitz* (Annapolis, Md.: Naval Institute Press, 1976), 396–97.

2. Robert Leckie, *Okinawa: The Last Battle of World War II* (New York: Viking Press, 1995), 3–4.

3. James L. Stokesbury, "Battle of Attu," *American History Illustrated* (Apr. 1979): 34.

4. Brian Garfield, *The Thousand-Mile War: World War II in Alaska and the Aleutians* (Garden City, N.Y.: Doubleday, 1969), 302.

5. David G. Wittels, "These Are the Generals: Buckner," *Saturday Evening Post,* 8 May 1943, 17.

6. Garfield, *Thousand-Mile War,* 63.

7. George C. Dyer, *The Amphibians Came to Conquer: The Story of Admiral Richmond Kelly Turner,* vol. 2 (Washington, D.C.: Department of the Navy, 1969), 976–78.

8. Jon T. Hoffman, *Once a Legend: "Red Mike" Edson of the Marine Raiders* (Novato, Calif.: Presidio Press, 1994), 315.

9. Lt. Gen. Merwin H. Silverthorn, "Oral History Transcript," 1973, p. 219, MCHC.

10. See also Roger Willock, *Unaccustomed to Fear: A Biography of the Late General Roy S. Geiger, U.S.M.C.* (Princeton, N.J.: privately published, 1968), 284–87.

11. Ibid., 287.

12. The 81st Wildcat Division Historical Committee, *History of the 81st Infantry Wildcat Division in World War II* (Washington, D.C.: Infantry Journal Press, 1947), foreword and ix.

13. Lt. Gen. Pedro A. del Valle, USMC (Ret.), *Semper Fidelis: An Autobiography* (Hawthorne, Calif.: Christian Book Club of America, 1976), 188–90.

14. Stanley Sandler, ed., *The Korean War: An Encyclopedia* (New York: Garland Publishing, Inc., 1995), 135.

15. Adm. Harry W. Hill, "Oral History Transcript," 1966, p. 711, MCHC.

16. Thomas B. Buell, *The Quiet Warrior: A Biography of Admiral Raymond A. Spruance* (Annapolis, Md.: Naval Institute Press, 1987), 387–88.

17. Smith to Gen. Harry J. Malony, USA, 30 July 1946, 5–6, Smith Papers.

18. Potter, *Nimitz,* 455; Col. Joseph H. Alexander, USMC, "Marine Tanks in the Battle of Okinawa," *Leatherneck* (Apr. 1995): 21.

19. Col. Martin "Stormy" Sexton, USMC (Ret.), to author, 8 Aug. 1996.

20. Frank, *Great Island Battle,* 173; letter, *Marine Corps Gazette* (July 1997): 9.

21. Hill, "Oral History Transcript," 715–16.

22. Keith Wheeler, *Road to Tokyo* (New York: Time-Life Books, 1979), 193.

23. Lt. Col. Owen T. Stebbins, USMC (Ret.), "A Maneuver That Might Have . . . ?" *Marine Corps Gazette* (June 1995): 71.

24. Hill, "Oral History Transcript," 727.

25. Col. Joseph H. Alexander, USMC (Ret.), *The Final Campaign: Marines in the Victory on Okinawa* (Washington, D.C.: History and Museums Division, HQMC, 1996), 51–52.

7. Post–World War II

The primary source for this chapter is General Smith's "Oral History Transcript" (177–92). Certain documents from the Smith Papers were also used. An excellent overview for this period is Allan R. Millett, *Semper Fidelis: The History of the United States Marine Corps,* rev. ed. (New York: Free Press, 1982).

1. Heinl, *Soldiers of the Sea,* 512–13.

2. Ibid., 178; Fleming, Austin, and Braley, *Quantico,* 81; *Fortitudine* (Spring 1995): 23.

3. Heinl, *Soldiers of the Sea,* 515–16.

4. Lt. Gen. Victor H. Krulak, *First to Fight: An Inside View of the U.S. Marine Corps* (Annapolis, Md.: Naval Institute Press, 1984), 30.

5. Gen. Roy Geiger to the commandant of the Marine Corps, 21 Aug. 1946, Smith Papers.

6. Clifford, *Developmental History,* 72.

7. Ibid., 74.

8. Fleming, Austin, and Braley, *Quantico,* 85.

9. Martin K. Gordon, "Smith, Oliver Prince," in *Dictionary of American Military Biography,* ed. R. J. Spiller (Westport, Conn.: Greenwood Press, 1984), 1022.

10. Presentation to General Eisenhower, 2 Feb. 1949, p. 18, Smith Papers.

11. Smith to commandant of the Marine Corps, 8 Oct. 1949, p. 4–5, Smith Papers.

12. Ralph W. Donnelly, Gabrielle M. Neufeld, Carolyn A. Tyson, *A Chronology of the United States Marine Corps, 1947–1964* (Washington, D.C.: HQMC, Historical Branch, 1965), 11.

8. Inchon and Seoul, Korea, 1950

The primary sources for this chapter and those that follow relating to General Smith's participation in the Korean War are Smith's "Aide-Memoire: Korea 1950–51," 1,474 pages (cited in text with the abbreviation "A-M"); his "Korea Log August 18, 1950–April 30, 1951," 196 pages (cited in text with the abbreviation "KL"); and his "Travel and Flight Log for 1950–1951" (cited in text with the abbreviation "TL"), all found in the Smith Papers. An excellent overview of the Korean War may be found in John Toland, *In Mortal Combat: Korea, 1950–1953* (New York: William Morrow, 1991).

1. Col. Robert Debs Heinl, Jr., *Victory at High Tide: The Inchon-Seoul Campaign* (Philadelphia: Lippincott, 1968), 10.

2. Benis M. Frank, "Lt. Gen. Craig's Father Warned Him about the Marines," *Fortitudine* (Fall 1995): 15.

3. Lt. Gen. Edward A. Craig, USMC (Ret.), "Oral History Transcript," 1968, p. 160, MCHC.

4. The First, Fifth, and Seventh Marine Regiments were designated Regimental Combat Teams (RCT) 1, 5, and 7 after being enabled to operate independently, by heavy reinforcement with artillery, tank, engineer, and other support and service units.

5. Heinl, *Victory at High Tide*, 20.

6. Ibid., 23; CincFE to Joint Chiefs of Staff, 21 July 1950, Far East Command Outgoing Message File, MacArthur Memorial, Norfolk, Va.

7. Sexton to author, 2 July 1993.

8. Sexton to author, 10 Nov. 1994.

9. Sexton to author.

10. Lt. Gen. Alpha L. Bowser, "Vignettes of an Exceptional Marine: General Oliver Prince Smith," *Marine Corps Gazette* (Dec. 1995): 54.

11. Ibid.

12. Martin Sexton, "Korea Interview," HQMC, 1951, p. 8, MCHC.

13. Sexton, "Korea Interview," 9.

14. Toland, *In Mortal Combat*, 205.

15. E. B. Potter, *Admiral Arleigh Burke* (New York: Random House, 1990), 339.

16. Bradley and Blair, *A General's Life*, 554.

17. Lt. Gen. Edward Craig, USMC (Ret.), to author, 8 Feb. 1989. General Craig wrote a detailed, single-spaced letter of several pages in reply to my request for assistance in this biography. He was ninety-two at the time. General Craig was a very warm, gracious man. It was a privilege to have corresponded with him.

18. Smith to General Craig, 8 Sept. 1950, Smith Papers.

19. Norman Kingsley to author, 8 Apr. 1994.

20. Heinl, *Victory at High Tide*, 93.

21. Smith to the MCHC, 21 Sept. 1970, Smith Papers.

22. Craig to author, 8 Feb. 1989.

23. See Clifton La Bree, "Maj. Gen. Frank E. Lowe, USAR and the Relief of Gen. MacArthur," *Military* (Aug. 1996): 6–10. The information presented here about Gen. Lowe has been collected by the author over several years. It includes interviews and correspondence with people who served with him or knew General Lowe. See also *Congressional Record* (28 Jan. 1959): 9.

24. Sexton to author, 14 Dec. 1994; see also in La Bree, "Maj. Gen. Frank E. Lowe," 7–8.

25. Cpl. Paul G. Martin, USMC (Ret.), to author, 19 Aug. 1996.

26. Heinl, *Victory at High Tide*, 199–200.

27. Ibid., 200.

28. Bevin Alexander, *How Great Generals Win* (New York: W. W. Norton, 1993), 287.

29. Lt. Gen. Alpha L. Bowser, USMC (Ret.), to author, 27 May 1994.

30. Lt. Col. Robert D. Taplett, USMC (Ret.), to author, 7 July 1994.

31. Shelby L. Stanton, *America's Tenth Legion: X Corps in Korea, 1950* (Novato, Calif.: Presidio Press, 1989), 99.

32. Ibid., 100.

33. Brig. Gen. Edwin H. Simmons, USMC (Ret.), to author, 23 Aug. 1994.

34. Heinl, *Victory at High Tide*, 212–13.

35. Maj. Gen. Raymond L. Murray, "Oral History Transcript," 1988, 204, MCHC.

36. Sexton, "Korea Interview," 28.

37. Cpl. Paul G. Martin, USMC (Ret.), to author, 15 Apr. 1995.

38. Murray, "Oral History Transcript," 223.

39. Lt. Gen. Alpha L. Bowser, USMC (Ret.), to author, 25 May 1994.

40. Sexton to author, 14 Nov. 1994.

41. Maj. Michael Capraro, USMC (Ret.), to author, 7 Apr. 1995, 4.

42. Matthew B. Ridgway, *The Korean War: How We Met the Challenge: How All-out Asian War Was Averted: Why MacArthur Was Dismissed: Why Today's War Objectives Must Be Limited* (Garden City, N.Y.: Doubleday, 1967), 42; Bradley and Blair, *A General's Life*, 567.

9. North to the Chosin

1. An excellent general overview of the Korean War is Clay Blair, *The Forgotten War: America in Korea, 1950–1953* (New York: Time Books, 1987). The best book on Chosin is Eric M. Hammel, *Chosin: Heroic Ordeal of the Korean War* (Novato, Calif.: Presidio Press, 1990).

2. Bradley and Blair, *A General's Life*, 566.

3. Ibid.

4. Ibid., 578, 581.

5. Potter, *Admiral Arleigh Burke*, 342.

6. Hammel, *Chosin*, 8.

7. Sexton, "Korea Interview," 1951, 44–45, MCHC.

8. Ann Jensen, "To the Yalu," U.S. Naval Institute *Proceedings* (Feb. 1990): 58, 61.

9. Stanton, *America's Tenth Legion*, 161.

10. Toland, *In Mortal Combat*, 273–74.

11. Hammel, *Chosin*, 6.

12. Ridgway, *The Korean War*, 67.

13. La Bree, "Maj. Gen. Frank E. Lowe," 8.

14. Sexton, "Korea Interview," 51.

15. Smith to commandant of the Marine Corps, 17 Dec. 1950, 2.

16. Roy E. Appleman, *East of Chosin: Entrapment and Breakout in Korea, 1950* (College Station: Texas A&M Univ. Press, 1987), 5.

17. Brig. Gen. James F. Lawrence, USMC (Ret.), "For Those Who Fell at Chosin," *Marine Corps Gazette* (Nov. 1997): 38.

18. J. H. Williams, "No Advance beyond the Chosin," *Military History* (Apr. 1985): 29.

19. The story of Task Force Drysdale is taken from Eric M. Hammel, "Supply Road," *Military History* (June 1992): 35–41; Sexton, "Korea Interview," 54–55.

20. James Wallace, "Bloody Chosin," *U.S. News and World Report* (25 June 1990): 40.

21. Ibid.

10. Disaster at the Chosin

1. Stanton, *America's Tenth Legion,* 231; Blair, *The Forgotten War,* 521.

2. Lynn Montross and Nicholas A. Canzona, *U.S. Marine Operations in Korea, 1950–1953,* Vol. 3, *The Chosin Reservoir Campaign* (Washington, D.C.: Historical Branch, HQMC, 1957), 180.

3. Roy E. Appleman, *Escaping the Trap: The US Army X Corps in Northeast Korea, 1950* (College Station: Texas A&M Univ. Press, 1990), 365–66.

4. Ibid, xi.

5. Ibid., 126–27.

6. How the message was sent to Colonel Faith could not be determined.

7. Col. Alpha L. Bowser, interview by Brig. Gen. S. L. A. Marshall, 2 Jan. 1951, 11.

8. The description of the napalm bombing is from Appleman, *East of Chosin,* 170–80.

9. Bowser, interview, 14; "First Marine Division G-3 Journal," entry for 1–2 Dec. 1950, Smith Papers.

10. Appleman, *East of Chosin,* 272.

11. Blair, *The Forgotten War,* 520; George A. Rasula to author, 12 June 1998.

12. George A. Rasula, to author, 12 June 1998.

13. Bowser, interview, 15.

14. Col. Olin Beall, USMC, "First Marine Division Periodic Operational Report No. 197," p. 8, MCHC.

15. Lt. Col. Raymond L. Murray, USMC (Ret.), "Oral History Transcript," 1985, p. 232, MCHC.

16. Col. George A. Rasula, "History of the Chosin Story," *Changjin, US Army Chapter of the Chosin Few* (July 1997): 11; Patrick C. Roe, *The Dragon Strikes: China and the Korean War, June–December 1950* (Novata, Calif.: Presidio Press, 2000).

17. Edward L. Magill, "East of Chosin, Field Artillery," *Chosin Few* (Jan.–Feb. 1997): 20.

18. George A. Rasula to author, 15 Jan. 1997, 1.

19. "Special Action Report of the 11th Marines, 8 October–15 December 1950," p. 7, MCHC.

20. Hammel, *Chosin,* 310–11.

21. Stanton, *America's Tenth Legion,* 250.

22. Col. Roger Willock, USMC (Ret.), interview by author, Portland, Maine, 2 Feb. 1994.

23. Stanton, *America's Tenth Legion,* 224.

24. Bowser, interview, 12.

25. Bowser, interview, 13.

26. Richard Harris, "Berlin Airlift," *American History* (June 1998): 50–55.

27. Murray, "Oral History Transcript," 236.

28. O. P. Smith, interview by D. Clayton James, 1971, p. 6, Smith Papers.

29. Sexton, interview, 81.

30. Lt. Gen. Alpha Bowser, USMC (Ret.), letter, *Marine Corps Gazette* (Mar. 1989): 30.

31. Marguerite Higgins, *War in Korea: The Report of a Woman Combat Correspondent* (Garden City, N.Y.: Doubleday, 1951), 195.

32. Sexton to author, 14 Nov. 1994.

33. Bowser, interview, 15–16; Smith, "Korea Log," 107.

34. Sexton, interview, 81.

35. Sexton, interview, 85.

36. Bowser, interview, 19.

37. Bowser, interview, 21.

38. Bowser, interview, 20–21.

39. Michael C. Capraro, "Just a Few Thoughts on the Care and Feeding of the Press in Korea," *Military History* (Apr. 1994): 24.

40. Maj. Michael C. Capraro, USMC (Ret.), interview by author, Charlottesville, Va., 14 Nov. 1994.

41. Michael F. Shisler, "General Oliver P. Smith's Life Was a Commitment to Excellence," *Marine Corps Gazette* (Nov. 1978): 43.

42. Maj. Gerald J. Clinton, USA (Ret.), interview by author, 9 July 1992, Rye, N.H.

43. Sexton, interview, 78–79.

44. Bowser, interview, 19–20.

45. Smith, "Aide-Memoire," 1095–109. This citation covers the previous six paragraphs. Capt. Gerald J. Clinton, Jr., USAR, in an engineering study paper, dated 18 November 1986, written as part of his Command and Staff School work, notes that frozen Chinese corpses were used to help fill in a crib supporting the newly constructed bridge south of Koto-ri.

46. Lt. Gen. Alpha L. Bowser, USMC (Ret.), in a letter to the *Marine Corps Gazette* (Mar. 1989): 30.

47. Virginia Benedict (General Smith's older daughter) to Smith, 11 Dec. 1950, Smith Papers.

48. Sexton to author, 5 Jan. 1996, enclosing the letter from Mrs. Smith to Mrs. Sexton.

49. Smith to Gen. S. L. A. Marshall, 1 July 1953, Smith Papers.

50. S. L. A. Marshall, *The Military History of the Korean War* (New York: Franklin Watts, 1963), 39–40.

51. Smith to Col. Wray, USMC, 15 Feb. 1973, quoting General MacArthur's report to the United Nations, Smith Papers.

52. Bowser, letter, *Marine Corps Gazette,* 30.

53. Smith to Dave Merwin, 19 Aug. 1962, Smith Papers.

54. First Marine Division memorandum, 19 Dec. 1950, distributed to all members of the division, Smith Papers.

11. In Central Korea

1. Col. Martin J. Sexton, "Korea Interview," 16 May 1951, p. 87, MCHC; Toland's *In Mortal Combat: Korea, 1950–1953* is an excellent general history of the Korean War. A more detailed account of the war may be found in Lynn Montross and Nicholas A. Canzona, *Marine Operations in Korea*, Vol. 3. Volume 4, *The East-Central Front* (Washington, D.C.: GPO, 1962), edited by Lynn Montross, Hubbard D. Kuokka, and Norman W. Hicks, covers central Korea.

2. Maj. Michael C. Capraro, USMC (Ret.), interview with author, Charlottesville, Va., 15 May 1995.

3. Lt. Col. Dahlberg, USMC, letter, *Chosin Few News Digest* (Nov.–Dec. 1995): 5.

4. Sexton, interview, 101.

5. Sexton, interview, 102.

6. Sexton, interview, 102; Montross, Kuokka, and Hicks, *Marine Operations in Korea*, 4:12.

7. Smith, interview by D. Clayton James, 25 Aug. 1971, p. 9, MacArthur Memorial. A copy of this document is found in the Smith Papers.

8. Matthew B. Ridgway, *Soldier: The Memoirs of Matthew B. Ridgway* (Garden City, N.Y.: Doubleday, 1967), 199.

9. Ridgway, *The Korean War*, 103–5.

10. Ibid., 103.

11. S. L. A. Marshall, *Battle at Best* (New York: Jove Publications, 1963), 107.

12. Ibid.

13. Sexton, interview, 103–4.

14. R. R. Keene, "The Great Pohang Guerrilla Hunt," *Leatherneck* (Jan. 1991): 48–51.

15. Sexton, interview, 104–5.

16. Smith, interview by James, 10–11.

17. Montross, Kuokka, and Hicks, *Marine Operations in Korea*, 4:257.

18. Sexton, interview, 105–6.

19. Millett, *In Many a Strife*, 300.

20. Smith to Gen. Matthew B. Ridgway, 2 Feb. 1951, 50, Smith Papers.

21. Montross, Kuokka, and Hicks, *Marine Operations in Korea*, 4:65.

22. Harry G. Summers, Jr., *Korean War Almanac* (New York: Facts on File, 1990), 156.

23. Montross, Kuokka, and Hicks, *Marine Operations in Korea*, 4:66–67; Lt. Gen. Edward W. Snedeker, USMC (Ret.), "Oral History Transcript," 1968, p. 107, MCHC.

24. Smith to Gordon Warner, 5 Sept. 1971, Smith Papers.

25. Montross, Kuokka, and Hicks, *Marine Operations in Korea*, 4:72.

26. "The X Corps asked that the 1st Marine Division be directed to attack to the east to help cut off some North Koreans. The North Koreans are pulling back rapidly and we could not get any troops in position in time to do any damage. I did not comply with the request of the X Corps."

27. Smith, interview by James, 16; Sexton, interview, 113–14.

28. Sexton, interview, 121–22.

29. Smith, interview by James, 14–15.

30. Sexton, interview, 127.

31. Sexton, interview, 130.

32. Smith to Col. Ralph West, 13 Aug. 1962, Smith Papers.

33. Sexton to author, 10 Nov. 1994.

34. Sexton, interview, 130–31.

35. Lt. Gen. Alpha L. Bowser, USMC (Ret.), to author, 1 May 1998.

36. Maj. Gen. Frank E. Lowe, USAR (Ret.), to President Harry S Truman, 30 Apr. 1951, Military History Institute, Carlisle Barracks, Penn.; La Bree, "Major General Frank E. Lowe," 10.

37. Smith, interview by James, 26–27.

38. Sexton, interview, 138–39.

39. Millett, *In Many a Strife,* 291–92.

40. William B. Hopkins, *One Bugle, No Drums: The Marines at Chosin Reservoir* (Chapel Hill, N.C.: Algonquin Books, 1986), 230.

41. Montross, Kuokka, and Hicks, *Marine Operations in Korea,* 4:118.

12. Post-Korea

1. The Smith papers include large amounts of correspondence to writers of all descriptions and nationalities who sought and received his advice. Most of the collection is filled with Smith's narratives and diaries, with correspondence the second most voluminous section.

2. Col. John M. Terry, USMC (Ret.), to author, 8 Mar. 1994.

3. Terry to author.

4. Cpl. Paul G. Martin to author, 15 Apr. 1995.

5. Gen. Bernard Trainor, USMC (Ret.), "On Going to War," *Marine Corps Gazette* (Apr. 1996): 50–51; Gerald P. Averill, *Mustang: A Combat Marine* (Novato, Calif.: Presidio Press, 1987), 259–70; Gen. Joseph C. Burger, USMC (Ret.), "Oral History Transcript," MCHC, 1973, 242.

6. Burger, "Oral History Transcript," 245.

7. Burke Davis, *Marine! The Life of Lt. Gen. Lewis B. (Chesty) Puller, USMC (Ret.)* (Boston: Little, Brown, 1962), 325–26.

8. Smith to the commandant of the Marine Corps, 3 Mar. 1952, Smith Papers. (The above letter and the ensuing eleven endorsements hereafter cited as PUC.)

9. PUC, 11th endorsement, p. 1, para. 1a.

10. George A. Rasula, USA (Ret.), to author, 15 Nov. 1997, stating that the Thirty-first RCT was poorly served by every command to which it was linked, including the First Marine Division.

11. PUC, 11th endorsement, p. 5, para. 6e.

12. Rasula to author, 3 Sept. 1998. Colonel Rasula informed me in the same letter that a committee from the Chosin Few organization has recommended that the PUC be awarded to units of the Thirty-first RCT that fought on the eastern side of the Chosin reservoir, and that it is seeking an amendment to the citation.

13. Lt. Gen. Alpha L. Bowser, USMC (Ret.), to author, 5 May 1998.

14. Edwin H. Simmons, *The United States Marines: The First Two Hundred Years* (New York: Viking Press, 1974), 176.

15. Davis, *Marine!* 340.

16. Brig. Gen. Gordon Gayle, USMC (Ret.), to author, 8 Jan. 1995.

17. Brig. Gen. Edward E. Craig, USMC (Ret.), to author, 6 Feb. 1989, accompanied by a transcript of the cassette tape General Craig sent to General Smith's retirement celebration. General Craig was ninety-two at the time of his letter.

18. Lt. Gen. George Good, "Oral History Transcript," 1974, 139–44, MCHC.

19. *New York Times*, 1 Sept. 1955.

20. USMC Officer's Fitness Report, 1 Mar. 1955 to 31 Aug. 1955, Smith Papers.

Postscript: 8 February 2000. I have just been notified by Col. Robert E. Parrott, USMC (Ret.), chairman of the Chosin Few Awards Committee, that on 14 September 1999 the secretary of the navy approved the recommendation that the Presidential Unit Citation be awarded to units that were not included on the original decoration. A lot of good people worked hard to make this event possible, and they deserve our gratitude. To the brave men who fought on the eastern shores of the Chosin, we say, "Sorry for the delay; your valor was never in question. Hold your heads high, for a grateful nation has, at last, said thank you for your sacrifice."

13. Gen. Oliver Prince Smith, usmc (Ret.)

1. Lt. Gen. Alpha L. Bowser, USMC (Ret.), "Vignette of an Exceptional Marine: General Oliver Prince Smith," *Marine Corps Gazette* (Dec. 1995): 55.

2. Smith to Robert O. Bare, 21 Dec. 1955, Smith Papers. All of the following letter citations are from this source unless noted. The list of authors that Smith assisted includes Heinl in *Victory at High Tide*; the authors of volumes 2, 3, and 4 of the official history *Marine Corps Operations in Korea*; Robert Leckie, *Strong Men Armed* and *March to Glory*; Gen. J. Lawton Collins, USA (Ret.), *War in Peace*; Andrew Geer, *The New Breed*; and numerous other authors for newspapers and magazines. Roy E. Appleman had a lengthy correspondence with Smith when writing his excellent histories of the Korean War.

3. Burke Davis to Smith, 5 Nov. 1960.

4. Smith to Davis, 11 Nov. 1960.

5. Davis to Smith, 14 Nov. 1960.

6. Smith to Davis, 20 Nov. 1960.

7. Smith to Andrew Geer, 24 Apr. 1952.

8. Smith to Robert Debs Heinl, Jr., 12 May 1968.

9. Robert Sherrod to author, 4 Mar. 1993.

10. Gen. Raymond G. Davis, USMC (Ret.), to author, 1 Jan. 1993.

11. Lt. Gen. Herman Nickerson, Jr., USMC (Ret.), to author, 24 Jan. 1993.

12. Lt. Col. Edward Tom, USMC (Ret.), to author, 9 Mar. 1994.

13. Lt. Col. Richard M. Elliott, USMC (Ret.), to author, 20 Mar. 1994.

14. Lt. Col. Peter Thomas, Royal Marines (Ret.), to author, 18 May 1994.

15. Maj. Gen. Samuel Jaskilka, USMC (Ret.), to author, 28 Jan. 1994.

16. Brig. Gen. F. P. Henderson, USMC (Ret.), to author, 5 Sept. 1996.

17. Maj. Gen. Raymond L. Murray, USMC (Ret.), to author, 13 Mar. 1995.

18. Gen. Matthew B. Ridgway, USA (Ret.), interview by Secretary of Defense staff, 16 Oct. 1969, 17.

19. USMC Officer's Fitness Report, 13 Apr. 1954 to 31 Aug. 1954, signed by Admiral Wright, Commander in Chief, Atlantic Fleet.

20. Lt. Gen. Alpha L. Bowser, USMC (Ret.), to author, 22 Nov. 1922.

21. Director, Golden Gate Cemetery, to author, 8 June 1995.

22. This poem is taken from a Currier and Ives lithograph that was used by the Union army in the Civil War to notify my great-grandparents of the death of their son, Pvt. Eli Stilson, of the Thirty-first Maine Regiment, Company G, on 30 July 1864 at Petersburg, Virginia, during the Battle of the Crater.

COMMENTS ON SOURCES, AND SELECTED BIBLIOGRAPHY

The story of Gen. Oliver Prince Smith's military career in the United States Marine Corps would have been impossible to write without the assistance of detailed diaries and notes personally written by General Smith. The author has tried to portray Smith's career from Smith's point of view and in his own words, so that the general's unique powers of observation may be appreciated by the reader.

General Smith wrote his narratives for World War II when he returned from the Pacific after the war. Personal diaries were forbidden during the war. He wrote the narratives for Okinawa, Peleliu, New Britain, and Iceland from his recollections, special action reports, and letters written to his family.

There were no restrictions on keeping diaries during the Korean War. Smith kept notes in a pocket notebook of events as they occurred or were reported to him. He then expanded them in shorthand (Smith always said that two of the most useful tools he learned at college were shorthand and typing). Later, at some convenient time, the expanded notes were typed. If any interesting development took place after the notes were typed, it was added in parentheses by hand. The daily log contained no commentary or editorializing. There was a daily record of casualties and prisoners taken at the end of each day's entry. (This was described in a letter from General Smith to Brig. Gen. S. L. A. Marshall, USAR, of 21 July 1953, in the Smith Personal Papers Collection, at the Marine Corps University Research Center, Archives Branch, at Quantico, Va.)

The expanded (shorthand) version of the notes became Smith's "Aide-Memoire: Korea 1950–51." The notebook version became the daily "log." I also used material from other sources listed in the bibliography. I consulted and utilized the following oral histories prepared by the Marine Corps Historical Center (MCHC), Washington, D.C.:

Lt. Gen. Alpha L. Bowser
Maj. Gen. Wilbur Scott Brown

Lt. Gen. Joseph C. Burger
Adm. Arleigh Burke
Gen. Clifton B. Cates
Lt. Gen. Edward A. Craig
Lt. Gen. Thomas J. Cushman
Gen. Raymond G. Davis
Lt. Gen. Pedro del Valle
Vice Adm. James Doyle
Gen. Graves B. Erskine
Lt. Gen. Lewis J. Fields
Lt. Gen. Leo D. Hermle
Lt. Gen. Robert B. Luckey
Maj. Gen. Omar T. Pfeiffer
Gen. Lemuel C. Shepherd, Jr.
Lt. Gen. Merwin H. Silverthorn
Lt. Gen. Edward W. Snedeker
Gen. Oliver P. Smith
Lt. Gen. Gerald C. Thomas
Lt. Gen. Louis Ernest Woods
Maj. Gen. William A. Worton

The Marine Corps Historical Center published a series of World War II commemorative pamphlets as part of its fiftieth anniversary. The following issues were helpful: Col. Joseph H. Alexander, USMC (Ret.), *The Final Campaign: Marines in the Victory on Okinawa* (1996); Col. James A. Donovan, USMC (Ret.), *Outpost in the North Atlantic: Marines in the Defense of Iceland* (1992); Brig. Gen. Gordon D. Gayle, USMC (Ret.), *Bloody Beaches: The Marines at Peleliu* (1996); and Bernard C. Nalty, *Cape Gloucester: The Green Inferno* (1994).

NEWSPAPERS AND PERIODICALS

New York Times
San Francisco Chronicle
Washington Post
American Heritage
American History
Army Motors
Changjin, Army Chapter Newsletter (U.S. Army Chapter of the Chosin Few)
Chosin Few News Digest
Fortitudine
Leatherneck
Marine Corps Gazette

Military
Military History
Naval History
Newsweek
Proceedings
Reader's Digest
Saturday Evening Post
Time
U.S. News and World Report

SELECTED BIBLIOGRAPHY

The published works below have been helpful. Some have been used directly in the text, and some have provided authentic background material.

Alexander, Bevin. *The First War We Lost*. New York: Hippocrene, 1986.

Alexander, Joseph H. *Storm Landings*. Annapolis, Md.: Naval Institute Press, 1997.

Appleman, Roy E. *U.S. Army in the Korean War: South to the Naktong, North to the Yalu*. Washington, D.C.: GPO, 1961.

———. *East of Chosin: Entrapment and Breakout in Korea, 1950*. College Station: Texas A&M Univ. Press, 1987.

———. *Disaster in Korea: The Chinese Confront MacArthur*. College Station: Texas A&M Univ. Press, 1989.

Averill, Gerald P. *Mustang: A Combat Marine*. Novato, Calif.: Presidio Press, 1987.

Bartlett, Merrill L., ed. *Assault from the Sea: Essays on the History of Amphibious Warfare*. Annapolis, Md.: Naval Institute Press, 1983.

———. *A Marine's Life: Lejeune 1867–1942*. Annapolis, Md.: Naval Institute Press, 1991.

Berry, Henry. *Hey Mac, Where Ya Been?* New York: St Martin's Press, 1988.

Blair, Clay. *The Forgotten War: America in Korea, 1950–1953*. New York: Time Books, 1987.

Blumenson, Martin. *Mark Clark*. New York: Jonathon Cape, 1985.

Bonn, Keith E. *When the Odds Were Even*. Novato, Calif.: Presidio Press, 1994.

Bradley, Omar N., and Clay Blair. *A General's Life: An Autobiography*. New York: Simon and Schuster, 1983.

Buell, Thomas B. *Master of Sea Power: A Biography of Admiral Ernest J. King*. Boston: Little, Brown, 1980.

———. *The Quiet Warrior: A Biography of Admiral Raymond A. Spruance*. Annapolis, Md.: Naval Institute Press, 1987.

Cagle, Malcolm W., and Frank A. Manson. *The Sea War in Korea*. Annapolis, Md.: Naval Institute Press, 1957.

Collins, J. Lawton. *War in Peacetime*. Boston: Houghton Mifflin, 1969.

Cooper, Norman V. *A Fighting General: The Biography of Gen. Holland M. "Howlin' Mad" Smith.* Quantico, Va.: Marine Corps Association, 1987.

Cray, Ed. *General of the Army George C. Marshall: Soldier and Statesman.* New York: W. W. Norton, 1990.

Davis, Burke. *Marine! The Life of Lt. Gen. Lewis B. (Chesty) Puller, USMC (Ret.).* Boston: Little, Brown, 1962.

Duncan, David Douglas. *This Is War: A Photo-Narrative of the Korean War.* Boston: Little, Brown, 1951.

Dyer, George C. *The Amphibians Came to Conquer: The Story of Admiral Richmond Kelly Turner.* Vols. 1, 2. Washington, D.C.: Department of the Navy, 1969.

———. *On the Treadmill to Pearl Harbor.* Washington, D.C.: Naval History Division, Navy Dept., 1973.

Falk, Stanley. *Palaus: America's Pacific Offensive.* New York: Ballantine Books, 1974.

Fehrenbach, T. R. *This Kind of War: A Study in Unpreparedness.* New York: Macmillan, 1963.

Feiffer, George. *Tennozan.* New York: Ticknor and Fields, 1992.

Finney, Ben. *Once a Marine, Always a Marine.* New York: Crown, 1977.

Fleming, Charles A., Robin L. Austin, and Charles A. Braley III. *Quantico: Crossroads of the Marine Corps.* Washington, D.C.: History and Museums Division, HQMC, 1978.

Frank, Benis M., and Henry I. Shaw, Jr. *Victory and Occupation.* Vol. 5, *History of U.S. Marine Corps Operations in World War II.* Washington, D.C.: MCHC, 1968.

Garfield, Brian. *The Thousand-Mile War.* Garden City, N. Y.: Doubleday, 1969.

Geer, Andrew. *The New Breed: The Story of the U.S. Marines in Korea.* New York: Harper and Row, 1952.

Goulden, Joseph. *Korea: The Untold Story of the War.* New York: Time Books, 1982.

Gugeler, Russell A., ed. *Combat Actions in Korea.* Washington, D.C.: Combat Forces Press, 1954.

Hallas, James H. *The Devil's Anvil: The Assault on Peleliu.* Westport, Conn.: Praeger, 1994.

Halliday, Jon, and Bruce Cumings. *Korea: The Unknown War.* New York: Pantheon Books, 1988.

Hammel, E. M. *Chosin: Heroic Ordeal of the Korean War.* Navato, Calif.: Presidio Press, 1990.

Hastings, Max. *The Korean War.* New York: Simon and Schuster, 1987.

Heinl, Robert Debs, Jr. *Soldiers of the Sea: The United States Marine Corps, 1775–1962.* Annapolis, Md.: Naval Institute Press, 1962.

———. *Victory at High Tide: The Inchon-Seoul Campaign.* Philadelphia: Lippincott, 1968.

Higgins, Marguerite. *War in Korea: The Report of a Woman Combat Correspondent.* Garden City, N.Y.: Doubleday, 1951.

Hoffman, Jon T. *Once a Legend: "Red Mike" Edson of the Marine Raiders.* Novato, Calif.: Presidio Press, 1994.

Hopkins, William B. *One Bugle, No Drums: The Marines at Chosin Reservoir.* Chapel Hill, N.C.: Algonquin Books, 1986.

Hoyt, Edwin P. *The Pusan Perimeter.* New York: Stein and Day, 1984.

———. *On to the Yalu.* New York: Stein and Day, 1984.

———. *The Bloody Road to Panmunjon.* New York: Stein and Day, 1985.

James, D. Clayton. *The Years of MacArthur: Triumph and Disaster 1945–1964.* Boston: Houghton Mifflin, 1985.

Janowitz, Morris. *The Professional Soldier.* New York: Macmillan, 1971.

Knox, Donald. *The Korean War: An Oral History, from Pusan to Chosin.* New York: Harcourt Brace Jovanovich, 1985.

Krulak, Victor H. *First to Fight: An Inside View of the U.S. Marine Corps.* Annapolis, Md.: Naval Institute Press, 1984.

Langley, Michael. *Inchon Landing: MacArthur's Last Triumph.* New York: Time Books, 1979.

Larrabee, Eric. *Commander in Chief: Franklin Delano Roosevelt, His Lieutenants, and Their War.* New York: Harper and Row, 1987.

Leckie, Robert. *The March to Glory.* Cleveland: World Publishing, 1960.

———. *Conflict: The History of the Korean War 1950–1953.* New York: Putnam, 1962.

———. *Okinawa: The Last Battle of World War II.* New York: Penguin Books, 1995.

Lejeune, John A. *The Reminiscences of a Marine.* Philadelphia: Dorrance, 1930.

MacArthur, Douglas. *Reminiscences.* New York: McGraw-Hill, 1964.

MacDonald, Callum A. *Korea: The War before Vietnam.* New York: Free Press, 1986.

Manchester, William. *MacArthur: American Caesar.* New York: Dell, 1979.

———. *Goodbye Darkness.* New York: Dell, 1980.

Marshall, S. L. A. *The River and the Gauntlet.* New York: William Morrow, 1953.

———. *The Military History of the Korean War.* New York: Franklin Watts, 1963.

McCloskey, Paul N. "Pete," Jr. *The Taking of Hill 610.* Woodside, Calif.: Eaglet Books, 1992.

McCullough, David. *Truman.* New York: Simon and Schuster, 1992.

Meskos, Jim. *Armor in Korea: A Pictorial History.* Carrollton, Tex.: Squadron/Signal Publications, 1984.

Miller, Francis Trevelyn et al. *The Complete History of World War II.* Chicago: Reader's Service Bureau, 1945.

Millett, Allan R. *Semper Fidelis: The History of the United States Marine Corps.* New York: Free Press, 1982.

———. *In Many a Strife: General Gerald C. Thomas and the U.S. Marine Corps, 1917–1956.* Annapolis, Md.: Naval Institute Press, 1993.

Montross, Lynn. *Cavalry of the Sky: The Story of U.S. Marine Combat Helicopters.* New York: Harper and Brothers, 1954.

Montross, Lynn, and Nicholas A. Canzona. *U.S. Marine Operations in Korea 1950–1953.* Vol. 1, *The Pusan Perimeter.* Washington, D.C.: Historical Branch, HQMC, 1954.

———. *U.S. Marine Operations in Korea 1950–1953.* Vol. 2, *The Inchon-Seoul Operation.* Washington, D.C.: Historical Branch, HQMC, 1955.

———. *U.S. Marine Operations in Korea 1950–1953.* Vol. 3, *The Chosin Reservoir Campaign.* Washington, D.C.: Historical Branch, HQMC, 1957.

Montross, Lynn, Hubbard D. Kuokka, and Norman W. Hicks. *U.S. Marine Operations in Korea 1950–1953*. Vol. 4, *The East-Central Front*. Washington, D.C.: Historical Branch, HQMC, 1962.

Morrison, Samuel Eliot. *The Two-Ocean War: A Short History of the United States Navy in the Second World War*. Boston: Atlantic Monthly Press, 1963.

Moskin, J. Robert. *The U.S. Marine Corps Story*. New York: McGraw-Hill, 1977.

Mossman, Billy C. *U.S. Army in the Korean War: Ebb and Flow*. Washington, D.C.: GPO, 1990.

Parker, William D. *A Concise History of the United States Marine Corps, 1775–1969*. Washington, D.C.: HQMC, 1970.

Perret, Geoffrey. *There's a War to Be Won: The United States Army in World War II*. New York: Random House, 1991.

———. *Old Soldiers Never Die: The Life of Douglas MacArthur*. New York: Random House, 1996.

Pogue, Forrest C. *George C. Marshall: Statesman 1945–1959*. New York: Viking Press, 1987.

Potter, E. B. *Nimitz*. Annapolis, Md.: Naval Institute Press, 1976.

———. *Bull Halsey*. Annapolis, Md.: Naval Institute Press, 1985.

———. *Admiral Arleigh Burke*. New York: Random House. 1990.

Rees, David. *Korea: The Limited War*. New York: St. Martin's Press, 1964.

Ridgway, Matthew B. *Soldier: The Memoirs of Matthew B. Ridgway*. Garden City, N.Y.: Doubleday, 1967.

———. *The Korean War: How We Met the Challenge: How All-out Asian War Was Averted: Why MacArthur Was Dismissed: Why Today's War Objectives Must Be Limited*. Garden City, N.Y.: Doubleday, 1967.

Roe, Patrick C. *The Dragon Strikes: China and the Korean War, June–December 1950*. Novata, Calif.: Presidio Press, 2000.

Ross, Bill D. *Peleliu, Tragic Triumph: The Untold Story of the Pacific War's Forgotten Battle*. New York: Random House, 1991.

Sandler, Stanley, ed. *The Korean War: An Encyclopedia*. New York: Garland Publishing, 1995.

Simmons, Edwin H. *The United States Marines: The First Two Hundred Years*. New York: Viking Press, 1974.

Sledge, E. R. *With the Old Breed at Peleliu and Okinawa*. Novato, Calif.: Presidio Press, 1981.

Smith, S. E., ed. *The United States Marine Corps in World War II*. New York: Random House, 1969.

Stanton, Shelby L. *America's Tenth Legion: X Corps in Korea, 1950*. Novato, Calif.: Presidio Press, 1989.

Stokesbury, James L. *A Short History of the Korean War*. New York: William Morrow, 1988.

Summers, Harry G., Jr. *Korean War Almanac*. New York: Facts on File, 1990.

Toland, John. *In Mortal Combat: Korea, 1950–1953*. New York: William Morrow, 1991.

Trotter, William R. *A Frozen Hell: The Russo-Finnish Winter War of 1939–1940*. Chapel Hill, N.C.: Algonquin Books, 1991.

Truman, Harry S. *The Years of Trial and Hope, 1946–1952*. Garden City, N.Y.: Doubleday, 1956.

Tuchman, Barbara W. *Stillwell and the American Experience in China, 1911–1945*. New York: Macmillan, 1971.

USMA Association of Graduates. *1980 Register of Graduates*. West Point, N.Y.: USMA Association of Graduates, 1980.

Vandegrift, A. A., and Robert B. Asprey. *Once a Marine: The Memoirs of General A. A. Vandegrift, United States Marine Corps*. New York: Norton, 1964.

Wheeler, Richard. *A Special Valor*. New York: Harper and Row, 1983.

Williams, Robert H. *The Old Corps: A Portrait of the U.S. Marine Corps between the Wars*. Annapolis, Md.: Naval Institute Press, 1982.

Willock, Roger. *Unaccustomed to Fear: A Biography of the Late General Roy S. Geiger, U.S.M.C.* Princeton, N.J.: privately published, 1968.

Wilson, Jim. *Retreat Hell: We're Just Attacking in Another Direction*. New York: William Morrow, 1988.

INDEX

The Gentle Warrior

was designed and composed by Christine Brooks

in 10/13.5 Minion with display type in Miehle Classic Condensed;

printed on 50# Supple Opaque stock;

Smyth sewn and bound over binder's boards,

and wrapped in dust jackets printed in two colors

by Thomson-Shore, Inc., of Dexter, Michigan;

and published by

The Kent State University Press

KENT, OHIO 44242